Beyond Ideology

D1569442

WITHDRAWN
WVU
LIBRARY

Beyond Ideology

Politics, Principles, and Partisanship in the U.S. Senate

FRANCES E. LEE

THE UNIVERSITY OF CHICAGO PRESS   CHICAGO AND LONDON

DOWNTOWN
JK
1611
.L428
2009
c.2

FRANCES E. LEE is associate professor in the Department of Government and Politics at the University of Maryland. She is coauthor of *Sizing Up the Senate: The Unequal Consequences of Equal Representation*, published by the University of Chicago Press. Her work has also appeared in the *American Political Science Review, American Journal of Political Science, Journal of Politics,* and *Legislative Studies Quarterly.*

The University of Chicago Press, Chicago 60637
The University of Chicago Press, Ltd., London
© 2009 by The University of Chicago
All rights reserved. Published 2009
Printed in the United States of America
18 17 16 15 14 13 12 11 10 09   1 2 3 4 5

ISBN-13: 978-0-226-47074-0 (cloth)
ISBN-13: 978-0-226-47076-4 (paper)
ISBN-10: 0-226-47074-1 (cloth)
ISBN-10: 0-226-47076-8 (paper)

Library of Congress Cataloging-in-Publication Data

Lee, Frances E.
    Beyond ideology : politics, principles, and partisanship in the U.S. Senate / Frances E. Lee.
        p. cm.
    Includes bibliographical references and index.
    ISBN-13: 978-0-226-47074-0 (cloth : alk. paper)
    ISBN-13: 978-0-226-47076-4 (pbk. : alk. paper)
    ISBN-10: 0-226-47074-1 (cloth : alk. paper)
    ISBN-10: 0-226-47076-8 (pbk. : alk. paper)   1. United States. Congress. Senate.
2. Political parties—United States.   3. United States—Politics and government—20th century.   4. United States—Politics and government—21st century.   I. Title.
JK1161.L428 2009
328.73′071—dc22

                                                2009010044

♾ The paper used in this publication meets the minimum requirements of the American National Standard for Information Sciences—Permanence of Paper for Printed Library Materials, ANSI Z39.48-1992.

Contents

Figures

Tables

Acknowledgments

Like many before it, this book got its start while its author was serving as an American Political Science Association Congressional Fellow. There is perhaps nothing like working for a party organization to heighten one's sensitivity to the institutional dimensions of legislative party politics. As part of the fellowship, I worked for the Senate Democratic Policy Committee in 2002–2003. One of the committee's main tasks was to organize events that would bring Senate Democrats together regularly to discuss issues, air disagreements, and develop common strategies. Staffers monitored legislative activity and put together research and events to assist the party's initiatives and criticize the opposition and its approaches. Observing these activities, it became manifestly clear that a legislative party's members do not just "happen" to agree with one another on so many issues, agendas, and strategies. Even in the highly partisan 108th Congress, much of the party's consensus could only be uncovered through internal give-and-take. Consensus was also actively created through party leadership and the willing collaboration of party members. Legislative parties are more than the sum of their individual members. They are institutions.

This project benefited from much institutional support of its own. The University of Maryland, College Park provided a wonderful scholarly home. Faculty and graduate students commented on early and late drafts of chapters, offering useful substantive and methodological advice all throughout the development of this book. I owe thanks to the Department Chair Mark Lichbach and to all of my colleagues in the American politics field, especially Geoff Layman, Paul Herrnson, Ric Uslaner, Irwin Morris, Jim Gimpel, Mike Hanmer, Karen Kaufmann, and Wayne McIntosh. The University of Maryland's American Politics Workshop provided a great venue for discussing research in progress. Maryland's Undergraduate

Research Assistantship Program sent excellent help my way, including Lisa Kenney, Sadia Sorathia, Devin Lynch, and Olivia Brice. Kerem Ozan Kalkan provided valuable research for chapters 5 and 7. Finally, I benefited from a semester's leave funded by a Graduate Research Board grant from the College of Behavioral and Social Sciences.

I also received much assistance from outside of my home institution. For helpful advice along the way, I thank Sarah Binder, Diana Evans, Larry Evans, Linda Fowler, Wendy Schiller, Barbara Sinclair, and Steve Smith. I am also grateful to Jamie Carson, Jason Roberts, Kevin Roust, and Glen Krutz, who served as discussants when parts of this project were presented at conferences. Michael Bailey, Bruce Cain, Larry Janezich, Robb McDaniel, Eric Schickler, Jeff Stonecash, Sean Theriault, Rob Van Houweling, and Joe White also offered useful feedback. David Mayhew read a critical early draft of chapter 3, and his comments simultaneously provided needed encouragement and sparked rethinking on my part. Discussions with Richard Bensel and John Hibbing were enormously helpful. The project benefited in numerous ways from the participants of research seminars at Case Western Reserve University, Duke University, University of Minnesota, Georgetown University, the College of William and Mary, and the Centennial Center at the American Political Science Association.

I owe special thanks to Dave Rohde and Bruce Oppenheimer. Dave Rohde invited me to present this book manuscript to his annual Political Institutions and Public Choice Book Seminar at Duke University. The critical commentary that I received from Dave and from the lively and perceptive participants in his seminar was invaluable. Just the invitation to the seminar alone was tremendous motivation to complete the book on time and to produce the strongest first draft possible. To Bruce Oppenheimer I owe my first introduction to scholarly work on Congress, and his friendship and insights continue to benefit my work in innumerable ways today.

My understanding of Congress was indelibly shaped by conversations and experiences I had while serving as an APSA Congressional Fellow. I thank 2002–2003 DPC staffers Clare Amoruso, Celine Senseney, Tim Gaffaney, Mike Mozden, Brian Hickey, Doug Connolly, and Ted Zegers, along with DPC staff director Chuck Cooper, who gave me the opportunity to work for the committee. The DPC's Record Votes series was a superb resource for studying the Senate's roll-call vote record. I am also grateful for the many insights gained while working in the Office of Congressman

Jim Cooper, from the congressman personally, from his then-Legislative Director Anne Kim, and from my other co-workers. The director of the fellowship program Jeff Biggs enriched the experience throughout.

Working with the University of Chicago Press is a pleasure. I thank my editor John Tryneski for his commitment to the project and for the highly constructive review process he supervised. Jean Eckenfels provided expert and elegant copy-editing. I also appreciate the assistance of others at the Press, including Rodney Powell, Mary Gehl, Dustin Kilgore, and Megan Marz.

Although most of what follows has not previously appeared in print, parts of two chapters have appeared in journals. The groundwork for chapter 4 was first laid in "Dividers, Not Uniters: Presidential Leadership and Senate Partisanship, 1981–2004," *Journal of Politics* 70 (October 2008): 914–28. Some material in chapter 7 appears in "Agreeing to Disagree: Agenda Control and Senate Partisanship, 1981–2004," *Legislative Studies Quarterly* 33 (May 2008): 199–222. The journals' anonymous reviewers and the editorial guidance I received from John Geer and Larry Evans improved both the articles themselves and the subsequent development of the book.

I am grateful to my parents, Philip and Beverly Utter, from whom I undoubtedly inherited a strong interest in politics. They have contributed to my work in more ways than I can detail, including in one of the most practical ways possible: helping take care of my baby daughter Beverly while I finished writing this manuscript.

Finally, I simply cannot say adequate thanks to my husband Emery. Not only was he impossibly tolerant of my long hours working on this project, but he read every word of every draft. He encouraged me when I needed encouragement and never seemed to be bored by our long conversations about the book when I could think of little else. Considering how much of his time was taken up with this project, I am sure he must be even more glad of its completion than I am. But he would never let me know that.

CHAPTER ONE

Ties That Bind

Untangling the Roots of
Congressional Partisanship

Throughout its deliberations, a convention to revise the Pennsylvania State Constitution

> was split into two fixed and violent parties. . . . In all questions, however unimportant in themselves, or unconnected with each other, the same names stand invariably contrasted on the opposite columns. Every unbiased observer may infer . . . that, unfortunately passion, not reason, must have presided over their decisions. When men exercise their reason coolly and freely on a variety of distinct questions, they invariably fall into different opinions on some of them. When they are governed by a passion, their opinions, if they are so to be called, will be the same.

James Madison is famous, at least in American government courses, for his distrust of "faction," a term he used interchangeably with "party." Often overlooked, however, is his insightful analysis of partisan blocs in *Federalist* 50 (Hamilton, Jay, and Madison 1987, 317). In that essay, Madison argues that, were individual legislators to reason through each public policy issue, they would "invariably" reach different conclusions "on some of them." But, even in the 1780s, the experience of legislatures proved to be very different from what one would expect from the exercise of legislators' individual reason. Instead of variable and shifting alignments of legislators "on a variety of distinct questions," Madison observes two blocs of legislators standing opposed to one another across the broad spectrum of issues, time after time. For Madison, this consistent bloc voting reveals that legislators simply do not reason issues through on their own.

Like James Madison in *Federalist* 50, the American public tends to view the pervasive party conflict in Congress as "bickering" motivated by partisan passions or self-interest. Studies have shown that Americans perceive congressional partisanship as excessive and as evidence that legislators do not have the public interest at heart (Hibbing and Theiss-Morse 1995, 2002). From this perspective, continual partisan clashes across so many separate issues serve to confirm that parties reflexively oppose one another and that members of Congress fail to think for themselves.

On this point, political scientists tend to be much more willing to assume good faith on the part of legislators. From a reading of the political science literature, one would quickly conclude that the reason Democrats and Republicans in Congress vote differently across a wide variety of issues is that they hold different ideological beliefs about the role or purpose of government. Where Madison saw "fixed and violent parties" "governed by passion" instead of reason, and the general public sees needless bickering, contemporary political science sees principled, even philosophical, disagreement.

In its most rigorous form, legislative scholars' dominant theoretical perspective begins by positing that all legislators possess an ideal point on an abstract ideological spectrum ranging from liberal to conservative that constrains voting decisions on all matters before Congress. If members' ideological preferences and the policy issues before Congress can both be lined up on a single dimension, then stable, patterned, and—assuming members tend to sort themselves into parties by ideology—partisan voting coalitions in Congress would indeed emerge. Scholars generally agree that members' ideological preferences are the principal cause of partisan conflict, regardless of whether they embrace a party government model of legislative decisionmaking (Aldrich 1995; Cox and McCubbins 1993, 2005; Rohde 1991) or a pure legislative majoritarianism (Brady and Volden 1998; Krehbiel 1993, 1998).

The central argument of this book is that ideological disagreement alone does not begin to account for the extent of party conflict in Congress. Matters of ideological controversy are a potent source of partisan discord in the contemporary Congress, and Republican and Democratic legislators are undoubtedly farther apart in ideological terms than they were 30 or 40 years ago (Binder 2003; Brownstein 2007; McCarty, Poole, and Rosenthal 2006; Rohde 1991; Sinclair 2006; Theriault 2008). Nevertheless, there is far more party conflict in the Congress than one would expect based on the ideological content of the congressional agenda or the policy differences between liberals and conservatives.

To routinely attribute disagreement between congressional Republicans and Democrats to individual members' ideological differences is to overlook how the parties' competition for elected office and chamber control systematically shapes members' behavior in office. Party conflict also stems from the competitive struggle for office and influence, not only from members' policy preferences. Failure to take adequate account of ongoing electoral and power struggles results in theories of congressional politics without the politics.

Congressional parties hold together and battle with one another because of powerful competing *political interests*, not just because of members' *ideals* or *ideological preferences.* Party members experience what David Truman (1959) called "shared risk." Members' electoral and institutional interests are bound up with the fate of their parties. Control of the institution enables a political party to further its members' political goals of winning office and wielding power, as well as its ideological goals. Majority party members have a common interest in maintaining that control. Members of the minority party have a collective interest in becoming the majority and taking control.

This book argues that fellow partisans' shared risk has wide-ranging effects on congressional party politics. It leads members of one party to support efforts to discredit the opposition party on the grounds of its incompetence and lack of integrity, not simply to oppose its ideological policy agenda. It persuades members to rally around the initiatives of their own party's president, and, as a mirror image, the other party to resist initiatives championed by an opposing party's president. It prompts members to routinely back up their own party leadership's efforts to exert control over the floor agenda. And it encourages members and leaders to steer the congressional agenda toward issues that allow them to differentiate themselves from their partisan opposition and thus to make the case that voters should prefer one party over the other. Members' diverging political interests drive the parties apart on many issues that bear no clear or direct relationship to the principled policy disagreements between liberals and conservatives.

Tracing the sources of party conflict speaks to the very purposes political parties serve in a democratic system. If party conflict in Congress were only rooted in members' disagreements over policy, then partisan debate would simply represent the range of public policy preferences that exist within the country's elected leadership. It would do no more than give voice to officeholders' legitimate, policy-based disagreements over matters of public concern. If, however, party conflict also stems from legislators' competition over power and office, then parties do more than reflect the underlying policy disagreements that exist in American government and society. Parties also systematically institutionalize, exploit, and deepen those divisions. Indeed, partisan political interests can even create conflict where it would not have otherwise existed. Evidence presented in this book suggests that legislative partisans engage in reflexive partisanship, in which they oppose proposals because it is the opposing party's president that advances them.

A clear implication of this analysis is that the public's well-documented skepticism about political parties—a skepticism greatly at odds with political scientists' general attitude—is well founded. At the same time that political parties help make government more coherent and understandable to the broad public, they also have some negative consequences. In seeking to advance their collective interests of winning elections and wielding power, legislative partisans stir up controversy. They impeach one another's motives and accuse one another of incompetence and corruption, not always on strong evidence. They exploit the floor agenda for public relations, touting their successes, embarrassing their opponents, and generally propagandizing for their own party's benefit. They actively seek out policy disagreements that can be politically useful in distinguishing themselves from their partisan opponents. All of these sources of partisan conflict would continue to exist regardless of members' different ideological orientations. Even if there were ideological consensus in the Congress, political parties would continue to score points in their fights over power and office. In all these important respects, the American public is hardly misguided in thinking that "partisan bickering" goes on in Congress.

Not All Issues Are Ideological

In order to gain analytical traction on the role of ideology and partisan interests in structuring conflict in Congress, this study begins from the simple recognition that many of the issues considered in Congress do not

speak in any direct way to liberalism or conservatism and cannot meaningfully be situated on an ideological spectrum.

At some level, scholars have long known that not all issues are ideological. Examining important federal laws enacted between 1946 and 1991,
Erikson, MacKuen, and Stimson (2002, 329–31) found that only 124 out of
200 laws could be classified as either "moving policy in a conservative or a
liberal direction." In other words, the ideological content of *fully 38 percent of important laws* passed during that era could not be characterized
even in the most general terms possible. Among these neither-liberal-nor-
conservative laws were many significant policy departures, including the
1956 Federal Highway Act (authorizing the interstate highway system),
the 1958 creation of the National Aeronautics and Space Administration,
the 1973 structuring of health maintenance organizations (HMOs), the
1976 copyright law revision, and bailouts of the Chrysler Corporation
(1979), failed savings and loans (1989), and the airlines after the September 11 attacks (2001). Reviewing these classification decisions, Mayhew
(2006, 245) rejects any inference that something was wrong with the study
and concludes that these laws were "plausibly rated 'neutral'" or "off-
cleavage" with respect to ideology.

Similarly, on the many occasions when Congress makes decisions about
how to allocate a given amount of federal funds across states or congressional districts, scholars have acknowledged that it is not possible to say
that one distribution scheme moves policy in a more "liberal" or "conservative" direction than another. Cox and McCubbins (2005, 46) observe
that distributive policy cannot be "represented on spatial or left-right
policy dimensions. . . . [When] Congress must decide how to divide the
federal budget pie among members' districts . . . *there simply is no median legislator.*" The extensive scholarly literature on distributive politics
consequently makes no use of spatial theory (see, for example, Baron and
Ferejohn 1989; Lee 2000; Stein and Bickers 1995; Weingast 1979).

Politicians themselves regularly distinguish between policy debates
that involve ideological questions and those that do not. As Sen. Charles
Schumer (D-N.Y.) observed during a 2003 appropriations debate, "This
is not an ideological issue. No one disputes whether Government should
do this."[1] Schumer's point is that an issue must involve some disagreement
over the role or scope of government before it can relate to members' different ideological orientations. Drawing the same distinction, Sen. Barry
Goldwater (R-Ariz.) famously proclaimed, "I have little interest in streamlining government or making it more efficient, for I mean to reduce its

size" (1960, 23). No one—liberal or conservative—maintains in principle that government should be inefficient, duplicative, or excessively complex. Reforms designed simply to generate efficiencies in existing government operations do not speak to the fundamental differences between liberals and conservatives over the extent and responsibilities of government. Streamlining government is thus a consensus, nonideological policy goal, one that Goldwater regarded as peripheral to his central (ideological) purposes.

Distinctions between ideological and nonideological issues figured explicitly in a debate during the 2008 race for the Democratic presidential nomination.[2] Asked by a debate moderator why *National Journal* magazine had rated him the Senate's "most liberal member" for 2007 (Friel 2008),[3] then-Sen. Barack Obama (D-Ill.) observed that there were only two roll-call votes included in the ratings on which he and his then-rival Sen. Hillary Clinton (D-N.Y.) had voted differently.[4] Looking to the specific issues raised by these votes, Obama contended that neither involved a matter that spoke to members' liberalism or conservatism. One disagreement occurred on Obama's support for the creation of an independent office of public integrity to monitor Senate ethics investigations.[5] "I don't think that's a liberal position," Obama argued, "I think there are a lot of Republicans and a lot of Independents who would like to make sure that ethics investigations are not conducted by the people who are potentially being investigated." The other difference concerned a provision in a proposed guest worker program that would allow workers to come to the United States for two years, return for a year, and then come back for another two years. Both Clinton and Obama supported the establishment of a guest worker program in the context of comprehensive immigration reform (Witt 2008).[6] The particular manner of administering the guest worker program at question in the amendment, Obama said, "meant essentially that you were going to have illegal immigrants for a year, because they wouldn't go back, and I thought it was bad policy."[7] For policy debates where liberalism and conservatism do not present clear alternatives to one another, Obama remarked, "the categories don't make sense." Various proposals for congressional ethics reform have long been championed by both liberals and conservatives. Proposed guest worker programs are debated among both liberals and conservatives. Neither of these issues clearly differentiates liberalism from conservatism in American politics.

When policy questions do not relate to basic values distinguishing liberals from conservatives, then individual members' ideological preferences alone cannot structure their voting decisions. Nonideological issues likely constitute a substantial proportion of the matters before Congress. In 1969, Matthews and Stimson (1975, 33) interviewed a random sample of members of Congress to ask "how often bills had 'sufficient ideological flavor' that voting decisions could be made 'largely on the basis of ideology.'" Only 5 percent said that they were "almost always" able to base their voting decisions largely on ideology; 10 percent said that they were "never" able to make decisions in this way; and 48 percent of members said that they were "seldom" able to do so. Consider that these members were interviewed in the midst of a historic era of liberal activism—an era that produced the Open Housing Act (1968), the Housing and Urban Development Act (1968), highly progressive new tax legislation (1969), the creation of the Occupational Safety and Health Administration (1970), and the Clean Air Act (1970). Given that context, it is rather remarkable that most members of Congress said that ideology could not serve as an adequate voting guide on most issues.

Aside from their work on distributive politics, however, scholars have devoted little effort to study, empirically or conceptually, issues that do not locate on the spectrum from liberal to conservative. The scholarly literature on legislative party politics typically fails to distinguish in any way between partisan conflict and ideological polarization; the one is typically equated with the other. If members' diverging ideological preferences are the source of all partisan conflict, however, one would expect to find partisan behavior on ideological issues and nonpartisan behavior on nonideological issues. If partisanship has roots outside of members' ideological differences, however, partisan conflict will not be confined to issues that involve left-right disputes.

Common Interests as Partisan "Glue"

It is tempting to think that parties are simply "collections of people with similar patterns of constraint over issues" (Poole 1988). But parties are "more than mere coalitions of like-minded individuals" (Aldrich 1995, 23). Legislative parties are *institutions* with members who have shared interests in winning elections and in wielding power.

In his influential book on congressional committees, Richard Fenno (1973) posited three goals that members of Congress seek to achieve: reelection, good public policy, and internal influence in the Congress. Although

Fenno conceived these as individual goals, members' ability to achieve them depends in part on their capacity to cooperate effectively as partisans. Members can better advance each of these goals when their party collectively enjoys a favorable public image and when it is able to control the floor agenda.

Many vote decisions have consequences for their parties' electoral and power interests, even when the issues before the Congress do not speak to the ideological differences between liberals and conservatives. In such situations, members' political interests can give a partisan structure to legislative voting behavior, even when individual members' policy goals alone would not divide them along party lines. Party conflict can thus arise even when it does not have any direct source in members' ideological preferences.

Electoral interests and public image

Members of Congress have an electoral interest in how the public perceives the two parties as collective entities. Members do not win or lose elections solely on the basis of their own personal qualities and records. They recognize that a substantial and perhaps growing proportion of the support they need to win elections derives from their association with one of the major political parties (Jacobson 2009, 135–44). They thus want to associate their party with popular policy outcomes and effective government.

Even though most politicians would probably prefer to be judged solely on individual performance—a matter they can personally control—they recognize that the image of their party as a whole affects their electoral prospects. Following his 2006 election loss, former Sen. Lincoln Chafee (R-R.I.) acknowledged this unavoidable linkage, "I give the voters credit: They made the connection between electing even popular Republicans at the cost of leaving the Senate in the hands of a leadership they had learned to mistrust" (quoted in MacKay 2008). Despite their efforts to distinguish themselves as individuals, fellow partisans in Congress are nevertheless "groups of politicians who are allied under certain symbols and who are responsible, willy-nilly, for the past performances associated with the symbols" (MacRae 1958, 211). This linked electoral fate encourages fellow partisans to cooperate on issues that range far beyond the disputes between liberals and conservatives.

To build a positive party image, partisans must collaborate to deliver on a popular policy agenda (Cox and McCubbins 1993, 110–35; Matthews and Stimson 1975, 95–97). As one anonymous congressman explained to political scientist Randall Ripley (1967, 144), "We need a party record—and principles—as well as an individual record. The decline of the party image between 1962 and 1964 cost me 6 percent at the polls." Along the same lines, Rep. Tom Davis (R-Va.) lamented his party's poor prospects in the 2008 congressional elections: "The House Republican brand is so bad right now that if it were a dog food, they'd take it off the shelf" (quoted in Kane 2008).

In a two-party system improving a party's brand name is not just a matter of working well with one's fellow partisans on an attractive policy agenda. In electoral terms it is often just as valuable to undercut the collective reputation of the opposing party. Members have a political interest in tarnishing the opposing party's image. They thus do not confine their opposition to their principled objections to the opposing party's policy proposals. Instead, they exploit opportunities to embarrass its members and deride its initiatives. They demand investigations into the other party's policy failures, seek the production and release of embarrassing studies and reports, scrutinize its officials and nominees for conflicts of interest, seize upon any evidence of incompetence, and denounce its officials' ethical lapses, real and imagined. Along these lines, opposition to "waste, fraud and abuse" and to "pork barrel spending" tends to emanate primarily from the party not responsible for congressional appropriations (Turner 1951, 56–60). For example, "President Bush has never shown much distaste for Congressional pork," observed *New York Times* journalist David D. Kirkpatrick (2008). "In the last seven years [of Republican control of Congress] he has signed spending bills containing about 55,000 earmarks. . . . But in his last year in office, with his party out of power on Capitol Hill . . . he threatened to veto future spending bills unless Congress cut in half the number of earmarks."

Party politics is not only about ideological differences on policy matters; instead, "accusations by one group against the other of dishonesty, corruption, or favoritism constitute a continuing dimension of conflict" (MacRae 1958, 211). This dimension generally results in voting behavior *indistinguishable* from that on ideological disputes (i.e., in votes structured largely or entirely along party lines), but this behavioral similarity has its roots in party politics, and the outcomes of these conflicts have no direct effect one way or another on the ideological content of American public policy. The grim logic of two-party competition is that a party can potentially gain as much electoral mileage from damaging its opposition's reputation as from building a positive record of policy achievement of its own.

As the leader of his party, no one plays a more important role in shaping a party's public image than the president of the United States. A presidential pronouncement on any issue raises the partisan stakes. Members of Congress suddenly have a political investment in the disposition of this issue, in addition to their individual policy preferences. Because of its increased salience, presidential success on an issue is likely to enhance his party's reputation. Presidential achievements create beneficial electoral spillovers for his whole party, giving his fellow partisans in Congress a political interest in the president winning on presidential agenda items, separate from whatever ideological preferences they might have on those issues.

At the same time, members of the opposing party have an electoral stake in the president losing, giving them reason to block the president and prevent his party from gaining credit-claiming opportunities on issues, even if they have no ideological objections to the president's proposals. "It might be argued that either party's support for the executive depends less upon ideology than upon the question of which party's leader occupies the White House," observed Turner (1951, 105); "Democrats, in other words, will support executive power as long as a Democrat is in office, but will revert to the assertion of legislative supremacy when the president is a Republican." "The partisan composition of Congress," write Howell and Pevehouse (2007, 96), "has historically been the decisive factor in determining whether lawmakers will oppose or acquiesce in presidential calls for war." Reflecting on Republicans' and Democrats' different attitudes toward President Clinton's intervention in Bosnia and President Bush's intervention in Iraq, commentator Al Felzenberg said, "We have reached a situation that, were the partisan composition of the White House and Congress reversed, spokesmen for both parties would change positions on a dime" (quoted in Cannon 2006).

Power interests and party conflict

In addition to a common investment in their party brand, party members are also drawn together against their partisan opponents by their interest in wielding political power. Indeed, many democratic theorists have defined political parties primarily in terms of their collective power motive (Downs 1957; Schattschneider 1942; Schumpeter 1942). As Schumpeter (1942, 283) put it, "A party is not a group . . . who intend to promote public welfare 'upon some principle upon which they are all agreed.' . . . A party is a group whose members propose to act in concert in the competitive struggle for political power." Pulling no punches, Schattschneider (1942, 37) wrote: "It is ridiculous to assume that men cannot collaborate to get power unless they are actuated by the same impulses. Possession of the vast resources of a modern government, its authority, its organization, administrative establishment, and so on, will provide something for nearly everyone willing to join hands in the political enterprise."

A substantial share of Senate roll-call votes occurs not on direct policy questions (such as whether to pass a bill or alter its language) but on procedural matters determining which issues will be considered when. Control of the agenda involves far more than influence over the ideological direction of public policy. Procedural votes also always raise questions about the *power* to control the flow of business on the Senate floor. The power stakes alone can spark partisan conflict, separate from the policy differences dividing liberals from conservatives. Within the congressional context, one might modify Schattschneider's language to read, "control of the issues that appear on the congressional agenda provides something for nearly all partisans to join hands in the political enterprise."

It is not merely that agenda control affects public policy. At stake in addition is a party's ability to exploit the floor to convey a political message to voters and other audiences, communicate its priorities, advance its arguments, level its criticisms, and tout its successes. The majority party attempts to monopolize the agenda for its message, while the minority party contests the majority's control and tries to change the subject to its advantage (Evans 2001; Sinclair 2006, 255–307). Minority party members continually try to force the majority to take positions on difficult or controversial issues. In many cases, minority members fully recognize that the amendments they offer will not affect policy outcomes, but they want to force majority party members to go on record on matters that may prove embarrassing or contentious. In response, the majority will often engage in bloc voting to table troublesome amendments and dodge thorny issues.

Control of the agenda can affect not only the ideological content of legislation, but its distributive content. Parties cooperate on the basis of patronage broadly conceived, not just on the issues on which partisans are ideologically proximate. Members seek to direct governmental benefits to groups and interests important to their party coalitions. A party able to control the floor agenda is also better able to secure policy benefits for the constituencies that its members rely upon. Party conflict on procedural matters can thus result from the simple fact that minority party members have not had (to their minds) sufficient input on legislation. Through disciplined support of its agenda prerogatives, majority party members can disproportionately direct policy concessions to its supporters and deny minority party legislators the opportunity to redirect benefits to their key constituencies.

Votes involving procedural questions elicit far more party conflict than one would expect based on the content of the underlying issues at stake. In fact, procedural votes are highly partisan, even when they occur on types of issues that are not at all divisive. Analysis presented in this book reveals that procedural votes on issues not involving ideological questions are just as intensely partisan as substantive votes on some of the *most* ideologically controversial issues in American politics.

Taken together, partisans' shared political interests nurture bonds of trust and reciprocity among themselves and sow mistrust and antagonism with members of the opposing party. Even before a member has a full understanding of the policy content of a legislative proposal, the mere fact that it is sponsored by a member of one party is likely to create a barrier to obtaining support from the other party's members.

Along the same lines, partisans' electoral and power interests are likely to foster patterns of communication that will further exacerbate partisan conflict. If members need additional information to make a voting decision, they do not turn to any member of the relevant committee of jurisdiction. They are far more likely to ask a member of the committee who is also a member of their party (Kingdon 1981, 72–106). That fellow partisan can argue for a particular position on legislation without any reference to any values or preferences dividing liberals from conservatives. Nonideological arguments may turn on explicitly *political* reasons to assist one's party—for example, that a particular vote is important to the leadership, helpful to constituents, popular with key groups in the party's coalition or with the electorate at large. Nonideological policy arguments can also simply catalogue problems with the opposing party's proposals, focusing on flawed assumptions, poor policy design, or inefficiency. Unless a member affirmatively seeks out views from an opposition partisan, she may never actually hear another perspective on the political or policy issues involved. Biases and roadblocks in communication are thus likely to intensify conflict between the parties beyond what would exist on the basis of the different ideological preferences of individuals alone.

Overcoming Obstacles to Collective Action

Common interests, of course, are not enough to ensure that individuals will organize effectively to advance those interests. Under many conditions, as Mancur Olson (1965, 2) contends, "rational self-interested individuals will not act to achieve their common or group interests." Scholars have fruitfully applied the collective action problem to legislative parties (Cox and McCubbins 1993, 2005; Mayhew 1974; Smith 2007), particularly to account for periods of party disunity.

Although legislative parties unquestionably face challenges of coordination and organization, collective action problems have been exaggerated in the study of congressional party politics. The logic of collective action was developed primarily to explain why large groups fail to cooperate in pursuit of their collective interests. But, as Olson elaborates at length, there are important differences between large and small groups. Unlike large groups, "small groups . . . may very well be able to provide themselves with a collective good simply because of the attraction of the collective good to the individual members" (1965, 36). By any standard, the parties in Congress are small groups. The hurdles to organization are not nearly so high for legislative parties as for those attempting to organize on behalf of diffuse societal interests.[8]

First, to put the matter in Olson's terms, legislative parties are not so large that individual members' failure to contribute will have no effect on the achievement of the collective good. Recognizing this, members may go along with their parties, simply because they personally value the collective goal and recognize that their contribution can make a difference to its achievement. Legislative parties do not have so many members and potential members that—as in the case of a citizen considering whether or not to contribute to an organization on behalf of a broad social interest—an individual's contribution could not conceivably affect the result one way or another. Furthermore, the face-to-face setting of the legislature enables social pressure to be leveraged effectively. Members of Congress know one another personally, and their votes are known to one another. Senate parties are small enough to allow their members to meet around a common lunch table, as they do weekly at their policy luncheons when Congress is in session. Free-riding in legislative parties is not in the least anonymous. Members who refuse to participate in the achievement of their party's common electoral and power interests will be subject to individualized persuasion. For small groups, Olson's logic of collective

action is "indeterminate," meaning that organization may or may not occur (Marsh 1976).[9]

Second, there are many "selective incentives" (Olson 1965, 51) that encourage legislative partisans to contribute to their party's collective goods.
Members who go along with their parties find it easier to achieve many
of their individual goals. Obtaining desirable committee assignments or
other leadership roles is often dependent on being of assistance to the
party. Ambitious members will calculate the likely effect of their votes on
their career advancement, motivating them to cooperate with their parties even in the absence of ideological reasons to do so. Even members
who do not have ambitions to climb the institution's internal hierarchy
recognize that support from party leaders can help them achieve their personal objectives. "When you do things for the . . . leadership it is like putting money in the bank," observed one congressman (Ripley 1967, 154).
"You build up a reservoir of good feeling and friendship." Working with
the party affords legislators private (excludable) goods, in addition to any
effect that their participation has on the attainment of collective (nonex-
cludable) party goals.

Third, the financial costs of organization are not borne by party members alone. "Often forgotten is the fact that certain collective party efforts can be provided without costing the rank-and-file party member
anything" (Smith 2007, 30). In the case of the congressional parties, the
"costs of communication among group members, the costs of any bargaining among them, and the costs of creating, staffing, and maintaining any
formal group organization" (Olson 1965, 47) are all significantly defrayed
at taxpayer expense. Party leadership staff, activities, and office expenses
are funded by annual appropriations. These subsidies go a long way toward solving any collective action problems stemming from the need to
maintain a formal organizational structure.

Figure 1.1 displays the total appropriations for the offices of Senate majority and minority leaders, majority and minority whips, and the policy
committees from FY 1981–2005. These amounts have been adjusted for
inflation and are expressed in 2004 dollars. Clearly, members have prioritized funding their party leaderships in recent years. Funds appropriated
for Senate party leadership offices increased by 69 percent in constant
dollars between 1981 and 2004. The increases for leadership offices substantially outpaced those for legislative branch appropriations generally.
Overall legislative branch appropriations in 2005 were only up by 33 percent over 1981 levels, with much of the boost dedicated to additional se-

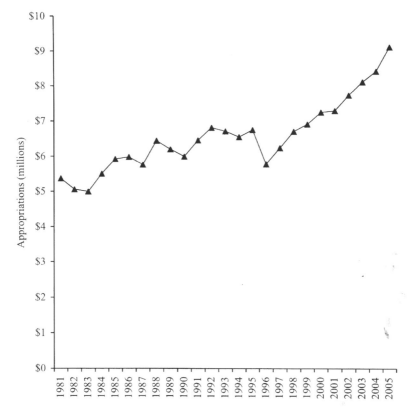

FIGURE 1.1. Institutional party strength: funds for leadership offices.
Source: Funds for leadership organs are from annual legislative branch appropriations legislation and include funds for the offices of majority and minority leaders, the majority and minority whips, and the policy committees. They have been adjusted for inflation and are displayed in constant 2004 dollars.

curity following the attacks of September 11, 2001 (Dwyer 2005). Budgets for leadership offices have grown at more than twice the rate of total legislative branch appropriations. Although not the subject of this book, increases for House party leaders have mirrored those in the Senate (Smith 2007, 31).

Figure 1.2 shows the number of staff allocated for Senate personal, committee, and leadership offices annually between 1981 and 2001.[10] Staff levels for Senate leadership offices were up fully 108 percent over the period. By contrast, staffing for Senate committees was down by 22 percent, and staffing for Senate personal offices only increased by 1 percent. Only

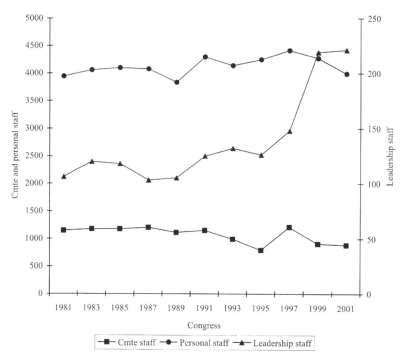

FIGURE 1.2. Senate staffing levels: personal offices, committees, and leadership offices.
Source: Ornstein, Mann, and Malbin 2002.

Senate leadership staffs were substantially augmented. In this sense, senators have opted to strengthen party institutions relative to other centers of legislative power (individual member offices and committees).

Fourth, and perhaps most important, legislators often bear no costs at all for working with their parties. Olson's collective action problem is based on an economic logic in which contributing to the attainment of a collective good always comes at a cost in terms of time and/or money. This assumption does not accurately translate to the context of legislative parties. It is not necessarily a costly endeavor for legislators to contribute to their party's collective interests. Members are going to cast votes anyway. They have no alternative, aside from not voting, which presents its own difficulties. Once a legislator is going to vote at all, voting with the party need not be any more costly than voting against the party. Legislators often aren't doing anything "extra" by going along with their parties. Voting with one's party in Congress is not analogous to volunteering time or writing a check to underwrite a collective effort to achieve a public good.

On rare occasions, party leaders may ask legislators to take tough votes that might endanger their electoral prospects. But there is no reason to assume that furthering collective party goals is always or even usually costly for legislators. Acting to further their party's collective electoral and power goals often *benefits* members. Legislators can reap political profits from supporting presidents of their own party, attacking opposition party presidents, defending their own party's reputation for competence and integrity, impeaching the other party's reputation, or cooperating in agenda control efforts to promote the party's message. All of these activities are probably popular with their most important constituents, their party's supporters. It may help insulate them from primary challenge. It can help them rise in the ranks of their party's power structure.

Collective action, after all, is not an optional activity for senators. Unlike a firm, which experiences profits and losses as an individual unit, a legislator can *only* achieve legislative goals in collaboration with other legislators. Similarly, a legislator can only gain institutional power by working with others. Even a legislator's electoral interests are affected by the perception of other officeholders in her party. Because a legislator's job inherently requires many kinds of collective action, legislators—unlike firms—have no choice but to find some way to cooperate with allies. Working with one's party is hardly an inefficient way for most legislators to locate the support they need to achieve their goals. Economic analogies thus have limited usefulness in theorizing about legislative politics.

For legislative parties, the logic of collective action may often be precisely opposite that laid out by Olson. For most legislators most of the time, it may be beneficial to work with their parties, while only occasionally being costly. If this is the case, legislators will not require an affirmative reason to cooperate with their party in pursuit of its collective goals; instead, they need a specific reason *to defect.* And, indeed, an earlier scholarly literature on members' voting decisions characterizes members' tendency to vote with their parties in precisely these terms: as a standing predisposition (Kingdon 1981; Matthews and Stimson 1975; Ripley 1967, 139–59). The typical member of Congress "feel[s] duty bound to ascertain the views of the party leaders and [to] go along in the absence of contrary inclinations" (Matthews and Stimson 1975, 95). Murphy (1974, 176) writes of a norm of partisanship on the House Public Works committee: "'One thing you notice right away,' said a newcomer [member of Congress], 'is that you are supposed to vote with your party.' 'Unless you are really thick,' added another, 'you pick things like that up right away. It's no problem.' . . . 'A good reason,' advised a ranking Republican member, is required to be let off the party hook."

The historical record certainly suggests a high degree of successful collective action on the part of congressional parties. Indeed, American political parties themselves first began to organize in legislative settings (Aldrich 1995). Even during periods of relatively low partisan conflict, the parties still managed to organize the Congress, elect leaders, and distribute committee assignments. Despite variation in the strength of party organizations over time, legislative parties have almost always been able to overcome obstacles to collective action in pursuit of their shared political interests.

Outline of the Argument

The central question of this book is, Why should fellow partisans in Congress agree across so many diverse issues while simultaneously disagreeing with members of the opposing party? To return to the quotation from Madison that began this chapter, the answer is not simply that individual members' preferences on so many different public policy issues align along party lines. Not all partisan structure in congressional roll-call voting can be traced back to individual legislators' ideological inclinations. Although political ideologies have wide-ranging and important effects on legislative decision-making and position-taking, the extent and pervasiveness of party conflict in Congress can only be fully understood in the context of legislative partisans' collective electoral and power goals.

Parties are institutions with members who have common political interests in winning elections and wielding power, not just coalitions of individuals with similar ideological preferences. Furthermore, the two parties' communal interests are fundamentally at odds with one another, and they can bring the two parties into conflict even when their members' ideological differences do not. Collective action problems do not prevent partisans from pursuing these shared interests. Parties' collective interests can thus structure legislative behavior across an array of issues that extends beyond ideology.

In this sense, this book provides a largely voluntaristic account of party politics. The importance of party does not derive from the (limited) ability of leaders to discipline rank-and-file members.[11] It rests, fundamentally, on partisans' widespread and willing cooperation in pursuit of collective goals and on the inherent zero-sum conflicts between the two parties' political interests as they seek to win elections and wield political power.

The broad public is not entirely wrong in thinking that party conflict in Congress has roots in members' team play, rather than in each individual member's individual opinions about policy questions. In this sense, this project seeks to reintroduce "partisan bickering" back into scholarly understandings of parties.

To untangle the roots of partisan behavior, this study develops and employs an original dataset to classify roll-call votes on the basis of the ideological content of the issue at stake. The findings reveal that disagreement on ideologically controversial issues can only account for a portion of the partisanship observed in congressional voting. Ideological issues significantly increase the likelihood of partisan conflict in Congress, but an enormous amount of partisan conflict in Congress occurs on issues that are not identifiably ideological.

Beyond ideology, this study identifies four additional factors that systematically generate party conflict: (1) presidential leadership, (2) "good government" causes in which one party attacks the integrity and competence of its partisan opposition, (3) conflicts over which party will control the legislative agenda, and (4) manipulation of the legislative agenda toward party cleavage issues.

The focus of the study is on patterns in partisan voting across different types of issues, not on individual legislators' voting decisions. The goal is not to explain when and why individual members vote with their parties. Instead, the question is on the role of ideology and collective partisan interests in structuring aggregate patterns in congressional party politics. When and where do partisan voting patterns appear? How much party conflict occurs on issues that can be broadly understood as liberal-vs.-conservative? How do the parties respond to presidential leadership, to attacks on their competence and trustworthiness, and during contests over agenda control? How does the issue content of the legislative agenda over time affect the level of overall party conflict?

Although the book gives some sustained attention to the subject, the primary purpose of the book is not to account for the rise of party conflict since the 1980s. Instead, the book centers on the consistently high level of party conflict and the extent to which it manifests itself along recognizable left-right lines. Party conflict may wax and wane, but throughout U.S. history it is always the most significant line of cleavage in Congress. In every era the congressional parties line up on opposite sides of an enormous number of issues. Despite the great scholarly interest in understanding variation in party strength over time, intense partisan conflict has been the

norm for U.S. congressional politics. Over the broad sweep of congressional history, the relatively low levels of partisanship of the 1960s and 1970s
are the anomaly, not the rule (Brady and Han 2004).

Focusing on changes in partisanship over time—as political scientists tend to do—obscures the more fundamental fact that a high level of
partisanship is a constant fact of legislative life. The primary goal of this
book is to shed light on how and why party can simultaneously structure
conflict across so many diverse issues. The causes of increased partisanship in the contemporary Congress have been the focus of a number of
recent books by scholars and journalists, including Sean Theriault's *Party
Polarization in Congress* (2008), Nolan McCarty, Keith Poole, and Howard Rosenthal's *Polarized America: The Dance of Ideology and Unequal
Riches* (2006), Barbara Sinclair's *Party Wars: Polarization and the Politics of National Policy Making* (2006), Juliet Eilperin's *Fight Club Politics:
How Partisanship Is Poisoning the House of Representatives* (2006), and
Ronald Brownstein's *The Second Civil War: How Extreme Partisanship
Has Paralyzed Washington and Polarized America* (2007). Rather than
concentrating on increases in conflict, this book analyzes how party can
organize conflict on matters that extend far beyond ideological disagreements between liberals and conservatives. Although further research
would be necessary to assess how well this theory applies in other eras,
the argument advanced here—that parties in Congress cohere internally
and battle with one another because of the power and electoral stakes
involved, not only because they disagree over policy—is not in principle
confined to the present.

This study employs both quantitative and qualitative methods. Quantitatively, I use measures of party cohesion and conflict in roll-call voting,
the issue content of the presidential agenda, changes in the strength of
party institutions and constituency contexts as well as a new classification
scheme for the issue content of roll-call votes. Qualitatively, I document
the history of ideology as a concept. In addition, extensive use is made of
the *Congressional Record*, both in terms of coding the quantitative data
and in interpreting particular legislative debates. The time range examined, 1981 to 2004, affords every permutation of divided and unified party
control.[12]

The theories about the role of collective partisan interests in organizing
party politics in Congress are examined in the context of the U.S. Senate.
In part, this choice is motivated by the simple fact that the U.S. Senate is
understudied. One of the central themes of Smith's (2007, 7, 213–14) as-

sessment of the state of the scholarly literature on the role of parties in Congress is simply, "The Senate is not well understood." But the Senate also offers a tougher test case for any theory that collective interests structure legislative party politics. Senators are more independent than House members. Enjoying longer terms and a chamber with more permissive rules, individual senators are freer to adjust their behavior in accordance with their own preferences and calculations of self-interest. The Senate operates more on personal relationships, often highly informal ones, than on the relationships institutionalized in parties or elsewhere (Baker 2001, 80–96; Truman 1959, 95–96). All these factors would lead one to expect that the Senate sets a higher bar for confirming the theory than the U.S. House.

Organization of the Book

Chapter 2 explores how ideology came to be viewed as the central source of party conflict in Congress. It tracks the evolution of ideology as an analytical concept, drawing on both a comprehensive review of the literature going back to the earliest work on parties in political science as well as on journalistic coverage of Congress. The analysis reveals that the concept's current meaning is of relatively recent vintage. It first came into currency in U.S. political journalism to describe intraparty conflicts, such as between progressive and conservative Republicans or between Southern and Northern Democrats. The concept was subsequently picked up by political scientists. Methodological and theoretical developments within academia during the 1950s and the 1980s then led scholars to make increasingly extensive use of ideology to analyze congressional politics. The result is a contemporary focus on ideology that obscures the collective political interests that spark conflict between Democrats and Republicans.

Chapter 3 begins to disentangle the extent to which party conflict can be attributed to the dynamics of competitive team play rather than to ideological disagreement. Employing conventional understandings of what it means to be liberal and conservative in contemporary American politics, a dataset is created to cull out all votes in Congress that bear any discernible relationship to the issue positions that differentiate liberals from conservatives. If ideology is all that holds partisans together, one would expect to find relatively little partisanship on issues that raise none of these issues. The analysis reveals that disagreement on conventional left-right issues characterizes only a little more than half of all the party votes observed in congressional voting. Well over a third of the party votes that took place during the period studied occurred on issues that could not be classified as involving any of the conventional distinctions between liberals and conservatives. Furthermore, the dramatic increase in party conflict over the 25 years of the study results from both ideological polarization and improved party teamwork. In addition to having diverged from one another on the liberal-conservative dimension, Senate parties have become more distinctive teams as they do battle across a wide range of issues that cannot be meaningfully situated on a liberal-conservative continuum.

Chapter 4 argues that presidential leadership is a vital wellspring of partisan conflict, separate from members' individual ideological preferences. Given the president's unique status as national party leader, members of Congress know that how they handle a president's priorities affects his party's collective reputation. This knowledge gives the president's fellow partisans political incentives to support the president and the opposition party political motives to resist his leadership, thus making presidential leadership inherently party polarizing. Findings indicate that a president mentioning an issue in the State of the Union Address generally widens the distance between the parties. Party conflict is higher on presidential agenda items compared to baselines on the same types of issues when they are not part of a president's agenda. The effect is evident across most areas of national policy, both in domestic and foreign affairs.

Chapter 5 examines how senators strategically deploy "good government" causes to enhance their own party's reputation and to undercut their opposition's. Good-government measures—such as policies to streamline government, fight corruption, probe government failures, collect and report information, encourage fiscal responsibility, and guarantee electoral integrity—are not matters of ideological disagreement in American politics. However, congressional partisans exploit these issues using the resources at their disposal—including agenda-setting, floor debate, and roll-call votes—to "maximize their identification with positive values and their opponents with negative ones" (Stokes 1992, 146). As a result, some of the most highly partisan conflicts in Congress occur over precisely these issues. Indeed, no other type of issue examined in this study was as likely to result in a unanimous party vote in the Senate, with 100 percent of Republicans on one side and 100 percent of Democrats on the other.

Chapter 6 examines the partisan politics of floor procedure, another important arena of partisan contestation. As with presidential agenda items and good government causes, the parties' images are very much at stake in decisions about the content of the floor agenda. The majority party wants to focus debate on its party "message," while the minority would like to change the subject to other issues. Furthermore, the outcome of procedural disputes determines who will wield legislative power. Power is itself a political commodity, separate from its effects on policy outcomes, and partisans wrangle over power taken alone as well as over policy. Analysis shows that members' policy preferences alone cannot account for the extremely high levels of partisan conflict on procedural matters. Instead, the evidence strongly suggests that partisans act as teams on procedural matters, teams in pursuit of common electoral and power interests, not simply as ideological coalitions. Procedural votes are far more controversial along partisan lines than one would expect based on issue content. Indeed, procedural votes are highly partisan, *regardless* of underlying issue content. Time-series analysis reveals that the heightened levels of partisan conflict in the contemporary Senate are to a great extent the result of improved teamsmanship on procedural matters.

Chapter 7 examines variation in the presence of ideological issues on the Senate agenda. It argues that the strengthening of the "parties as teams" discussed in previous chapters has helped to focus the legislative agenda on the ideological questions that most reliably differentiate the parties from one another. A substantial portion of the rise in Senate party conflict during the study period can be explained by changes in the content of the Senate agenda. The types of ideological issues that were most divisive along partisan lines in earlier periods became progressively more prominent on the congressional agenda. Meanwhile, those issues that tended to divide the parties internally in earlier periods constituted a smaller share of the agenda. In short, the content of the Senate agenda was altered in ways that promoted higher levels of partisan voting.

CHAPTER TWO

Before "Ideology"

A Conceptual History

"**M**y loyalty to the Republican Party—indeed, my love for the Republican Party—has played no small part in this decision," said Rep. Tom DeLay (Tex.). "Having served under Republican and Democrat control in the House, I know first hand how important it is for Republicans to maintain their national majority."[1] In saying farewell to the House of Representatives, the former majority leader used terms contemporary political scientists rarely use to describe the relationship between members of Congress and their political parties. "Love" is not a term that one often encounters in political science. Even "loyalty" has greatly fallen from scholarly favor. Contemporary legislative scholars do not typically interpret individual legislators' behavior as motivated to protect or advance the collective interests of their party organizations, as in DeLay's stated goal of maintaining a national majority.[2] Instead, legislators' decisions are most frequently ascribed to individual policy preferences. Today's "prototypic congressional study relies on . . . indicators of a legislator's ideology" (Burden 2007, 9). Members are thought to make voting decisions by evaluating competing policy proposals in terms of their individual policy preferences, defined in degrees of liberalism or conservatism. Legislators are assumed to measure policy alternatives against their own ideological values or tastes and to support the policies closest to those preferences.

As a scholarly concept for understanding the U.S. Congress, ideology is of relatively recent vintage. American politics had traditionally been characterized as nonideological (Hartz 1955; Hofstadter 1948). Whether or not this characterization is correct — Gerring (1998b) strongly disputes the Hartzian thesis — it is certainly true that scholars did not describe congressional politics using ideological concepts. Indeed, "ideology" did not figure in early studies of Congress at all. Important works such as Woodrow Wilson's *Congressional Government* (originally published in 1885) and George Haynes's *Senate of the United States* (1938) made no use of ideology or the related concepts of liberalism and conservatism. Indeed, the term "ideology" was not employed in any major scholarly article on Congress prior to the 1940s.[3]

Rather than seeing a dimension of conflict ranging "liberalism" against "conservatism," nineteenth- and early twentieth-century scholars, politicians, and political journalists tended to speak of "party principles." The Democratic party stood for "Democratic principles," and the Republican party stood for "Republican principles." Full-text searches in ProQuest Historical Newspapers database of the *New York Times* (1857-current file) locate hundreds of articles on Congress prior to the 1930s referring to "party principles," "Republican principles" or "Democratic principles." This language was common in early reporting on Congress from the 1860s through the 1930s. It has become unusual in contemporary reporting, with only 7 *New York Times* articles on Congress between 2000 and 2007 making such references.

The "party principles" terminology is suggestive. The clear implication is that the political parties were viewed as bundling various interests and policy commitments together. The language implies that there is not necessarily any abstract "ism" or underlying ideological dimension dictating how the parties bundle issue positions together. In the process of building electoral majorities, parties aggregate interests, develop policy proposals, prioritize legislative goals, and construct narratives and arguments in support of a party platform.

In this conceptualization, political conflict is not ordered by a preexisting dimension of individual preferences, but by the collective or the coalition — sometimes even by the love of a political party. "I am one of those men who believe that little that is great or good or permanent for a free people can be accomplished without the instrumentality of party," said Rep. George Hoar (R-Mass.) in 1899, "And I have believed religiously, and from my soul, for half a century, in the great doctrines and principles of the Republican Party."[4] Or as Democratic Sen. David Hill (N.Y.) rebuked his fellow partisans during an 1894 debate over the income tax, "You foist

upon the party a principle of taxation never sanctioned by the Democratic
National Convention. You do not seem to realize that you have no jurisdiction to add to or change the principles of our party."[5] Scholars during
this era did not speak of "ideology" or "liberalism versus conservatism."
Instead, they would refer to "party platforms" (Altman 1936, 1104), "party
pledges" (Binkley 1949, 74), "the party line" (Schattschneider 1942, 192),
or "loyal[ty] to the party program" (Herrington 1933, 420). Such language
does not presuppose that legislative conflict stems from a continuum of
individual ideological preferences that exists outside of party politics.

The purpose of this chapter is to track the evolution of ideology as an
analytical concept in the study of Congress. As political science has developed as a discipline, the concept of ideology has gone from occasional,
unsystematic use in the literature on Congress to the center of contemporary legislative scholarship. When and why did it become the dominant
concept in theorizing about legislative behavior? How has the concept
evolved over time? My analysis reveals that ideological explanations first
came into currency in U.S. political journalism to explain intraparty conflicts, such as those between progressive and conservative Republicans or
between Southern and Northern Democrats. The concepts were picked
up by congressional scholars shortly afterwards. Dramatic growth in political scientists' use of ideology to analyze congressional politics was then
fueled by methodological and theoretical developments within academia
during the 1950s and the 1980s. The result is a contemporary focus on
ideology that obscures other forces dividing Democrats from Republicans
in Congress.

Origins

"Liberalism," "conservatism," and "ideology" are obviously not terms of
art confined to political science. These terms—and the sense in which
empirical political scientists employ them—were used by writers outside
of political science before they became widespread in legislative scholarship. "Ideology" as understood by scholars of American politics refers to
systems of ideas relating to politics or society. Although "ideology" is a
broad term that can encompass a variety of different meanings (Sartori
1969), political scientists have "converged on several elements of a core
definition of ideology" (Knight 2006, 619). Gerring (1998a, 980) defines
ideology as a "set of idea-elements that are bound together, that belong

to one another in a nonrandom fashion." In Converse's (1964, 207) definition, the concept refers to "a configuration of ideas and attitudes in which the elements are bound together by some form of constraint or functional interdependence." Taking stock of all uses of the term in the *American Political Science Review*, Knight (2006, 625) concludes that "the core definition of ideology as a *coherent and relatively stable set of beliefs or values* has remained constant in political science over time." In short, "ideology" denotes interrelated political beliefs, values, and policy positions.

"Ideology" did not take on this empirical, nonnormative definition until the twentieth century. Although the word *ideologie* has its origin with the *philosophes* of the late eighteenth century, it initially referred to efforts to study the origin and development of ideas with the goal of stripping away prejudice in favor of scientifically verifiable understandings: "Early 'ideologues' attempted to develop a 'science of ideology' devoted to unmasking bias and maximizing objectivity" (Minar 1961, 318). In *The German Ideology* (1998, originally published in 1846) Marx and Engels inverted this original notion. Instead of viewing ideology as a science aimed at removing obstacles to objective analysis, they defined ideology as inherently biased, as the system of ideas used to justify the interests of the ruling class. This understanding of the concept is best summarized in the statement that "the ruling ideas are nothing more than the ideal expression of the dominant material relationships" (Marx and Engels 1998, 67).

Contemporary uses of "ideology" in the study of American politics are distinct from these eighteenth- and nineteenth-century understandings in that empirical scholars do not view the study of ideology as an effort to unmask biased ideas in favor of an objective perspective. Nor do they assume that ideologies are necessarily rooted in the interests of a dominant economic class. In the *Oxford English Dictionary* (2d ed.) the first example of "ideology" used in the nonnormative sense of a "systematic scheme of ideas relating to politics or society" is from a 1909 British magazine, referencing the "ideology behind the German proposals . . . as worked out in the Conservative programme." Searches in the *New York Times* Historical database do not turn up any news reports on Congress making reference to "ideological" differences among members prior to 1939.[6]

The first instance of a *New York Times* reporter employing "ideology" to describe politics in Congress was in July 1939, before any major scholarly article on Congress had yet made use of the term.[7] In an article about debates over the effects of the Fair Labor Standards Act of 1938, Delbert Clark, manager of the newspaper's Washington bureau, wrote:

> We are thus in the midst of an ideological battle. On the one hand, we are told
> that the one sure cure for the depression is for the Federal Government to re-
> turn to its classic police powers—or at least to the powers it had in 1929 and "let
> business alone." . . . On the other hand, there are the New Dealers, who have
> evolved the theory that with our changing economy private business never again
> will be able to bring prosperity to America.[8]

Clark's understanding of ideology is consistent with the way the term
would later be used by political scientists. Significantly, the earliest use
of the concept was to describe congressional conflicts that did not divide
strictly on party lines, a conflict that could not be described in the existing
language of "Republican principles" versus "Democratic principles." So
it appears that "ideology" was introduced to describe a coalitional pattern in which a substantial number of one party allied with members of
the opposing party. After President Roosevelt's attempted purge of party
conservatives in 1938, this "ideological battle" was waged both within the
Democratic party and between the parties of that era. But it was only
because the battle internally divided one of the party coalitions that the
new term was needed.

Although not making reference to ideology per se, newspapers were
using the term "conservative" to denote the programmatic policy preferences of certain politicians prior to the 1930s. In 1903, long before any
political science journal article had used the term to describe congressional politics, the *New York Times* took note of House Speaker Joseph
Cannon's efforts to stack the Labor Committee with conservatives:

> The Labor Committee is reorganized. Only four of the old members are re-
> tained. . . . Peculiar interest attaches to this committee, in the view of Mr. Can-
> non's effort to make it up conservatively and yet to represent all forms of labor.
> The labor agitation of last year has given him more anxiety about the construc-
> tion of this committee than any other.[9]

As another example, the *New York Times* in 1910 published the names of
senators as a "list of the forty-five Republican conservatives who have un-
dertaken to stand together to establish a firm control of the Senate proceedings and put through what remains of the Administration's programme."[10]
In these cases, journalists are also employing ideology as a nonnormative,
empirical concept to describe politicians who exhibit a particular type of
"constraint" in the positions they take across a range of issues.

As in U.S. political journalism, early scholarly uses of ideological concepts were deployed to describe disputes that divided one of the major parties internally. In the first appearance of "conservative" in a major journal article on Congress, James Miller Leake (1917) describes an intraparty conflict as the "friction between the conservative and progressive wings of the Republican party" (p. 252).[11] In 1922, Lindsay Rogers assesses President Harding's promise to "inaugurate party government," finding that the party fractured when "a powerful revolt by members representing the agricultural sections of the county [developed] against the more conservative leadership of the party" (pp. 41–42). Even as late as 1958, in one of the earliest scholarly efforts to systematically study ideological voting behavior in Congress, political scientist Charles D. Farris specifically excluded all party votes from his analysis, arguing that "when the parties disagree sharply on a question, they are, after all, acting in a way that parties, by definition are 'supposed' to act. If the major parties are regarded as fundamental political institutions, then the finding that they sharply differ from one another is ordinarily enough to set at rest further inquiry into the reason for their disagreement . . . whether [it] is a matter of 'principle' (ideology) or mere 'power' (patronage, spoils, pelf)" (Farris 1958, 310).

In sum, "ideology" as a concept for understanding Congress was originally used to explain what party could not: conflict within parties or the formation of cross-party coalitions. So many different factors could bring parties into conflict with one another—principle, power, patronage, spoils, pelf—that party votes were originally thought to need no further explanation at all.

Tracking "Ideology" over Time

When did ideology become central to scholarly understanding of congressional politics? Table 2.1 tracks the use of ideology and related concepts in the literature on Congress from 1900 to 2005. For each decade over the twentieth century, the table displays the number and percentage of major journal articles on the U.S. Congress employing any variant of the words "ideology," "liberal," or "conservative."[12] More than 80 percent of the articles published on Congress (131 out of 159) between 1990 and 2005 made reference to legislators' ideologies. Based on a similar content analysis, Knight (2006) finds that about 44 percent of all recent political science

TABLE 2.1 **"Ideology" as an analytical concept in the study of Congress**

Years	Percent of articles on Congress referencing "ideology" (n)		Percent of articles on Congress* referencing "ideology," "liberal(s)," or "conservative(s)" (n)		Total articles on Congress*
2000–2005	80	(32)	91	(37)	40
1990–1999	64	(76)	78	(94)	119
1980–1989	43	(47)	66	(71)	110
1970–1979	39	(29)	71	(51)	76
1960–1969	50	(26)	61	(36)	52
1950–1959	27	(5)	33	(11)	18
1940–1949	2	(1)	9	(15)	42
1930–1939	0	(0)	42	(11)	26
1920–1929	0	(0)	31	(4)	13
1910–1919	0	(0)	16	(1)	6
1900–1909	0	(0)	0	(0)	4

Source: Compiled by the author from Boolean searches in the JSTOR database. Search terms were written so as to capture any variant of the word "ideology," "conservative," or "liberal."
*Includes *American Political Science Review, Journal of Politics, American Journal of Political Science* (and its predecessor, *Midwest Journal of Political Science*), and *Political Science Quarterly*.
Articles about Congress were identified as those with "House," "Senate," or "Congress" in the title, excluding articles about any legislature other than the U.S. Congress.

articles make use of the concept of ideology. If the incidence of the term in journal articles is a good indicator, congressional scholarship is almost twice as reliant on ideological concepts as the broader discipline.

At the turn of the century, by contrast, ideological concepts almost never appeared in congressional scholarship, not even as a single reference to "conservatives" or "liberals" in Congress. Before 1920, only one out of 10 articles on Congress had used any ideological concept to refer to legislators (Leake 1917, 252). Between 1900 and 2000, ideology became increasingly prevalent in the congressional literature. Even after the "behavioral turn" in legislative studies in the late 1950s, increases in the use of the concept did not level off. In the 1950s, about one third of articles discussed ideology in some form; in the 1960s, 1970s and 1980s around two-thirds of articles employed the concept. Since 2000, more than nine in ten articles on Congress made reference to legislators' ideologies. Growth in the application of these concepts has not halted, though it is approaching the 100 percent ceiling.

As the concept of "ideology" has become more prominent in the congressional literature, its meaning and uses have evolved. Early articles referred to liberals and conservatives as distinct groups, but ideology was not clearly conceived as a personal attribute of individual legislators. Although the language does not always draw definitive distinctions, "ideology" is at first employed to describe groups or coalitions of legislators. One was denoted as a "conservative" because of membership in a particular faction, not so much because of one's individual beliefs. Thus, early legislative scholars would refer to a "conservative faction" of legislators (Altman 1936, 1102) or to New England as "solidly conservative" (Roach 1925, 525) or to "the conservative element in the Senate Appropriations Committee" (Herring 1935, 992). It is only in later scholarship that ideology became explicitly conceived as a matter of individual members' personal preferences, values, or beliefs as opposed to group memberships.

With the shift of focus to individual legislators, the conceptualization of ideology became more abstract. Scholarly articles became more likely to refer to ideology as a general phenomenon, rather than to specific liberal or conservative groups, legislators, or political controversies. Figure 2.1 displays by decade the number of journal articles on Congress referring to "ideology" broadly and the number of journal articles that refer only to "liberals" or "conservatives." Prior to the 1950s, scholars generally spoke only of particular liberal or conservative coalitions or legislators. Since

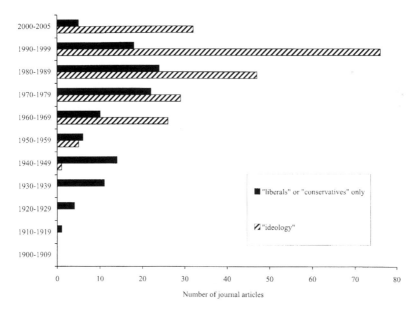

FIGURE 2.1. Use of ideological concepts in major journal articles on Congress.
Source: Word Compiled by the author from Boolean searches in the JSTOR database.

the 1960s, more abstract conceptualizations have become the norm in the literature, with the number of articles discussing "ideology" far outpacing the number of articles that merely mention liberals or conservatives.

The evolution of "ideology" in the congressional literature can be sketched out as follows. "Conservative" and "liberal" originated to denote particular groups or factions and then by a process of abstraction came to stand for the principles associated with those groups. Eventually, these concepts were used to describe individual legislators' policy orientations, without any acknowledged role for groups or factions in constructing and bundling together the combinations of issues that are thought of as "liberal" and "conservative."

Explaining the Trends: External Influences

Has scholarly reliance on the concept of ideology been driven by factors internal to the academic field or by influences from the broader political environment? To what extent do these shifts reflect changing realities in congressional politics or influences from the broader political discourse outside of academia?

In the context of congressional politics, the increasing use of ideology to account for legislative behavior is surprising in light of the dramatic decline of the twentieth century's only long-standing voting alliance that crossed party lines, the conservative coalition. As discussed above, ideology was first perceived as an influence on legislative politics when it led significant numbers of legislators to cross party lines. When partisans voted together, there was nothing to explain; that was just what legislative parties did. But when Southern Democrats began to make common cause with Republicans on a variety of causes in the 1930s—principally on issues relating to labor, social welfare, and race—ideology offered a way to account for these patterns. The concept of ideology explained what party could not—why "conservative" Southern Democrats would vote with "conservative" Republicans against "liberal" Northern Democrats. The coalition was a prominent factor in congressional politics, emerging on around 20 percent of roll-call votes in Congress between 1957 and 1979. The coalition was highly successful, prevailing on almost all the roll-call votes on which it coalesced between 1939 and 1956 and on 60 percent of votes during the 1970s (Brady and Bullock 1980). By the end of the Reagan presidency, this voting pattern had virtually disappeared (Ornstein,

TABLE 2.2 **"Ideology" as an analytical concept in reporting on Congress**

Years	Percent of news articles on Congress referring to "ideology" (n)		Percent of news articles on Congress referring to "liberal(s)," "conservative(s)," or "ideology" (n)		Number of *New York Times* articles on Congress
2000–2003	5	(87)	22	(429)	1890
1990–1999	4	(184)	23	(1232)	5286
1980–1989	2	(185)	19	(1440)	7545
1970–1979	1	(110)	17	(1386)	7973
1960–1969	1	(66)	14	(1358)	9962
1950–1959	1	(34)	9	(583)	6422
1940–1949	1	(43)	6	(368)	6268
1930–1939	0	(10)	9	(1200)	13585
1920–1929	0	(0)	5	(480)	9259
1910–1919	0	(0)	4	(290)	6586
1900–1909	0	(0)	4	(188)	5152

Source: Compiled by the author from the results of Boolean searches in the ProQuest Historical Newspapers database of the *New York Times*. Articles about Congress were identified as those with "House," "Senate," or "Congress" in the title, with the dateline "Washington." Articles using ideological concepts were identified as those containing any variant of the word "ideology," "conservative," or "liberal."

Mann, and Malbin 1996, 200), and no recurring cross-party ideological alliance has been noted since. To the extent that ideology drives voting patterns today, it is difficult to disentangle it from the other reasons Republicans vote differently from Democrats. Nevertheless, the concept has become increasingly dominant in the literature on Congress.

Political journalism represents a second possible explanation for the rising use of ideological concepts to describe congressional politics. After all, the concepts originated outside of academia. If journalists became more likely to discuss congressional politics in terms of ideology, then scholars may simply be reflecting broader changes in the conventional wisdom.

One way of gauging the effect of external influences on congressional scholarship is to examine the usage of ideological concepts in political journalism. Table 2.2 displays the number and percentage of *New York Times* articles on Congress referring to "ideology" and to "liberals" and "conservatives."[13] It is clear from these data that ideology has become a more prominent analytical concept in reporting on Congress, as well as in scholarship. Use of ideological concepts has more than doubled in journalistic reports on Congress since the 1930s, from 9 percent to 22 percent of news reports. Part of this increase probably reflects the rise of interpretive journalism (Patterson 1994). Nevertheless, over the entire time journalists became more and more likely to use ideological concepts in reporting on Congress.

The shift toward "ideology" in political journalism differs from the scholarly use of the concepts in one notable respect. News articles are far more likely to discuss groups of "liberals" and "conservatives" in Congress than to refer to the more abstract "ideology."[14] By contrast, as shown in figure 2.1, the majority of scholarly articles on congressional politics since the 1960s go beyond identifying liberals and conservatives to discuss the effects of "ideology" more generally. It may be that journalists assume that "ideology" is a theoretical concept inaccessible to many newspaper readers. Or it may be that journalists prefer to describe phenomena that can be observed directly. "As a latent set of values that organize personal political attitudes," ideology "defies direct observation" (Burden, Caldeira, and Groseclose 2000, 237). Legislators and coalitions who describe themselves as "liberal" and "conservative" can be observed doing things, but "ideology" as a legislative motivation can only be inferred or assumed.

Can the rise in legislative scholars' use of ideological concepts be attributed to the influence of political journalism? Figure 2.2 displays the percentage of *New York Times* articles on Congress that make use of ideological concepts, as well as the comparable percentage in scholarly journal articles on Congress. Even given the lower baseline use by journalists, it is possible that increasing use of ideological concepts in newspaper reports predated broader use of the concepts in scholarly analyses of Congress. A simple regression analysis, however, shows that the increased prevalence of ideological concepts in congressional journalism does not systematically precede greater use among scholars.[15] The causal arrow does not appear to move in the opposite direction, either; there is no evidence that journalists follow in the footsteps of scholars.[16] Both trend lines have risen, but decade-to-decade changes are not directly correlated with one another.[17] Changes in political journalism cannot explain political scientists' increased reliance on the concept.

External influences do not appear to drive the explosive growth of "ideology" in congressional scholarship over time. Scholars did not become more interested in ideology because cross-party ideological alliances became more common; to the contrary, this type of coalition has declined almost to the point of nonexistence. As measured by content analysis of *New York Times* articles on Congress, the intense scholarly focus on ideology also does not follow in the wake of larger trends in U.S. political

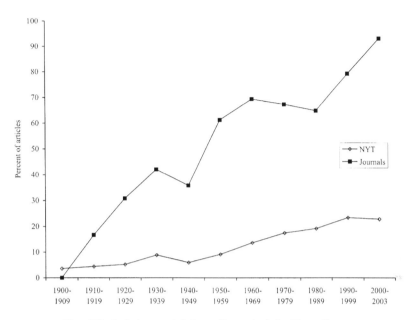

FIGURE 2.2. Use of ideological concepts in journalism and scholarship on Congress.
Source: Compiled by the author from Boolean searches in the JSTOR database and in the
ProQuest Historical Newspapers database of the *New York Times.* Includes *American Political Science Review, Journal of Politics, American Journal of Political Science* (and its predecessor, *Midwest Journal of Political Science*), and *Political Science Quarterly.*

discourse. It is unlikely that the changes in congressional scholarship were
primarily driven by factors outside academia.

Explaining the Trends: Internal Influences

Even in political science, academic inquiry has a life independent of
broader trends in politics and society. Is the increased interest in ideology
a result of scholars' changing substantive interests? Or, alternatively, is the
shift a result of methodological or theoretical developments within social
science itself?

Scholars' growing focus on ideology cannot be explained by any rising
interest in congressional parties and partisanship. Although Roberts and
Smith (2003, 305) are correct in observing that "no feature in congressional politics has received more notice than the increase in partisanship,"
scholars were equally interested in the decline of partisanship that pre-

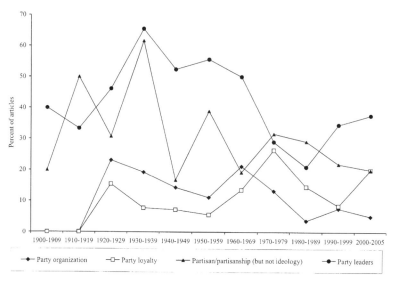

FIGURE 2.3. Scholarly interest in congressional parties.
Source: Compiled by the author from Boolean searches in the JSTOR database.
Articles about Congress were identified as those with "House," "Senate," or "Congress" in the title. Articles dealing with party loyalty were identified with full text searches for "party w/2 loyalty." Articles discussing party organization were identified with full text searches for "party w/3 organization or partisan organization." Articles on party leaders were identified with full text searches for "party leader* or majority leader* or minority leader* or speaker." Articles on partisanship were identified with searches for "partisan* NOT ideology*."

ceded the recent high levels of party voting (Brady, Cooper, and Hurley 1979; Cohen and Nice 1983; Collie 1988; Cox and McCubbins 1991; Hurley and Wilson 1989; Patterson and Caldeira 1988). A long tradition in American political science views parties as central to the operation of democratic government (Schattschneider 1942; Sundquist 1988), and so the degree and extent of party conflict has always been of interest to American political scientists. The first major scholarly article on this subject, A. Lawrence Lowell's "The Influence of Party upon Legislation in England and America," appeared in 1902 and is still cited occasionally, more than 100 years later.

Figure 2.3 displays the results of a content analysis of major journal articles on Congress, looking for terms related to parties. Searches were designed to track the incidence of articles dealing with party leaders, party organizations, party loyalty, and partisanship.[18] Unlike the growth in the use of ideological concepts shown in figure 2.1, no stark trends are evident here. Interest in topics related to congressional parties waxes and wanes from decade to decade, with trend lines chasing data points up and down. But, if anything, discussion of legislative parties comprises a smaller proportion of contemporary congressional scholarship than in earlier eras. Interest in party leaders has plummeted since the 1930s and 1940s. Interest in party organizations trended downward from the 1960s to the first decade of the twentieth century. Interest in party loyalty remained relatively flat over time, despite substantial increases in the observed levels of party loyalty in congressional voting over the same period. Since the 1970s, fewer articles have discussed partisanship without also discussing ideology. Scholarly concern with ideology cannot be explained by any increased substantive interest in understanding congressional parties.

It appears more likely that methodological and theoretical developments internal to social science have fueled the wider use of ideological concepts among scholars. These developments enriched the concepts intellectually and gave rise to debates that have engaged increasing numbers of scholars since the late 1940s. The focus of political science on ideology undoubtedly has important roots in these internal, scholarly concerns and controversies.

Psychometrics

The first social scientists to develop systematic measures of congressional ideology were psychologists. During the early years of the twentieth century, the rapidly developing field of psychometrics had accustomed psychologists to thinking of intelligence, personality, and moral attitudes as individual characteristics that could be quantitatively measured. From there, it was not a great leap to envision ideology as an individual orientation that could be measured similarly. The author of one of the earliest such articles noted that he was simply transferring "factorial methods, which were developed primarily in connection with the analysis of mental abilities, to the analysis of opinions" (Harris 1948, 591). Beginning in the late 1940s, a spate of articles advancing various methodologies for using roll-call votes to measure congressional ideology appeared in such outlets as the *Journal of Applied Psychology* (Brimhall and Otis 1948), *Educational and Psychological Measurement* (Harris 1948), and the *Journal of Abnormal and Social Psychology* (Gage and Shimberg 1949). These early articles blazed the trail for later political scientists by demonstrating the utility of correlation matrices, scale analysis, and factor analysis to uncover ideological constraint in roll-call votes.

   In the earliest of these articles, Brimhall and Otis (1948, 1) took what was then a novel approach: they employed an advocacy organization's roll-call vote scorecard to measure members' liberalism and conservatism. They turned to the first liberalism scorecard available, the *New Republic* magazine's ratings of congressional "progressivism." In 1944, four years before the Americans for Democratic Action first began compiling its widely used annual scorecard of political liberalism, the editors of the *New Republic* selected a set of roll-call votes in the House and Senate to indicate each individual member's programmatic liberalism across the issues on the congressional policy agenda.[19] Brimhall and Otis calculated a simple percentage indicating the proportion of the time each member had voted in the liberal direction (as specified by the *New Republic*) on each of these issues. Their major finding was that members were generally consistent in their voting from year to year, in that they received similar ratings on the *New Republic*'s scorecard across the four years in the study.

   These earliest articles already contain the seeds of debates that still occupy legislative scholarship. Writing of members' ideological "consistency over time," Brimhall and Otis foreshadow the later controversies over whether members of Congress "die in their ideological boots" (Jenkins 2000; Nokken 2000; Poole 1998). As the first scholarly study utilizing an advocacy organization's scorecard to measure members' liberalism and conservatism, Brimhall and Otis can also be seen as instigators of the extensive disputes over the merits and appropriateness of interest group scores in social scientific work (Burden, Caldeira, and Groseclose 2000; Fowler 1982; Hill, Hanna, and Shafqat 1997; Jackson and Kingdon 1992; Krehbiel 1994; Snyder 1992).[20]

   A second article represents the first entry in what would later develop into a long-standing scholarly controversy over the dimensionality of roll-call voting behavior. After analyzing a set of "significant" roll-call votes identified by a 1947 League of Women Voters pamphlet, Harris (1948) concludes that there were three dimensions underlying senators' roll-call voting behavior in the 80th Congress: views on the role of government in regulating business, on foreign relations, and on a third "unexplained" factor. The question of dimensionality aroused considerable controversy in the congressional scholarship of the 1970s and 1980s (Clausen 1973; MacRae 1970; Sinclair 1982). Although the idea that congressional votes are determined by a single ideological dimension does not command universal consensus (Heckman and Snyder 1997; Katznelson and Lapinski 2006; Wilcox and Clausen 1991), most contemporary researchers, as Wilcox and Clausen (1991, 393) observe, "have accepted the view that a single liberal-conservative dimension accounts for much of congressional roll-call voting" (Poole 1981; Poole and Rosenthal 1997; Schneider 1979).

A third psychological study can be seen as the forerunner of the "party" versus "preferences" debate. In a study of Senate roll-call voting of the 83d and 84th congresses (1953–56), Dempsey (1962, 161) asks, "Are liberalism-conservatism and party loyalty isolable as generalized variables, and do they exhibit sufficient reliability to be considered enduring personal characteristics of individual senators?" In other words, Dempsey envisions both "ideology" and "party loyalty" as two separate personal traits that vary among individual senators, and he argues that spurious estimates of ideology's influence will result if variation in loyalty is not taken into account. To disentangle the two traits, Dempsey analyzes party votes separately from votes not breaking along party lines, on the assumption that party pressure does not operate on votes that do not divide the parties from one another, similar to the technique used by Snyder and Groseclose (2000). After comparing senators' behavior on party and nonparty votes, Dempsey (1962, 168) isolates two groups of senators: those who show marked shifts toward conformity with their party on party votes (a majority of senators in both parties) and those "doctrinaire extremists whose party loyalty is in all respects negligible." This question of the relative importance of members' party loyalty and personal ideology is by no means settled. The "party vs. preferences" controversy alone has driven much of the increase in scholarly attention to congressional ideology between 1990 and 2005 (Aldrich and Rohde 2000; Ansolabehere, Snyder, and Stewart 2001a; Binder, Lawrence, and Maltzman 1999; Cooper and Young 2002; Cox and Poole 2002; Herron 1999; Krehbiel 1993, 2000; McCarty, Poole, and Rosenthal 2001; Nokken 2000; Schickler 2000; Sinclair 2002; Snyder and Groseclose 2000).

Psychometrics has had an indelible influence on the conceptual development of "ideology." The idea that political ideology is a personal trait of individuals that can be rigorously quantified emerged out of psychologists' efforts to study other personal traits that cannot be measured directly, especially intelligence. In particular, the development of factor analysis is important, in that it accustomed social scientists to thinking in terms of a small number of unobserved, hypothetical factors or dimensions explaining a great deal of variation in observed data. Without these methodological developments and the controversies associated with them, it is unlikely that "ideology" would have become as central to congressional scholarship.

Spatial voting theory

Spatial voting theory represents a second set of internal scholarly developments that greatly contributed to ideology's importance in the study of Congress. If ideology is understood as an individual-level value or taste, especially one that—drawing on advances in psychology—can be measured quantitatively, it becomes straightforward to make use of microeconomic concepts of utility, preference relations, and indifference curves, among others. The concept of an ideological spectrum ranging from extreme left to extreme right also allowed policy alternatives to be situated relative to one another on a common metric, a "choice dimension." These conceptual developments made it possible to theorize about policy choices in the same way that economists theorize about the relative valuation of goods, or—more abstractly—about choices among any set of alternatives that can be rank ordered.

Two seminal works greatly extended the uses to which "ideology" could be put in legislative studies: *The Theory of Committees and Elections* (Black 1958) and *An Economic Theory of Democracy* (Downs 1957). Since the publication of these works, political scientists' thinking about ideology has become progressively more influenced by economics than by psychology (Enelow and Hinich 1984).

William Riker (1990, 178) hailed Black's median voter theorem as "certainly the greatest step forward in political theory in this century." Assuming (1) the existence of a common metric on which policy alternatives in committee deliberation could be ranged, (2) that each committee member's preference over alternatives was single-peaked (meaning that the farther an alternative lies from the member's most preferred outcome, the less preferred it is), and (3) that decisions would be made by majority vote, Black (1948) demonstrated that the median member's preferred alternative would be adopted.

The idea that a distribution of individual preferences along an ordered continuum would enable equilibrium outcomes in a legislature lies at the center of Krehbiel's (1998) pivotal politics theory (see also Brady and Volden 1998) and of most formal models of the separation of powers (Cameron 2000; Kiewiet and McCubbins 1991). Building upon median voter theory, scholars have developed principal-agent theories of interactions between congressional committees and the floor (Krehbiel 1991; Maltzman 1997) and between legislatures and bureaucracies (Calvert, McCubbins, and Weingast 1989; Huber and Shipan 2000). Median voter theory has also prompted extensive debate about the role of legis-lative parties. Aldrich and Rohde (2000; Rohde 1991) advance a theory of conditional party government in which cohesive, homogenous parties can enact nonmedian outcomes on agenda items. Cox and McCubbins (1993, 2005) argue that the majority party cartelizes the legislative agenda, usurps the institution's legislative power, and systematically pulls policy outcomes away from the median legislator.

Combining the single-peaked preferences assumption with earlier the-orizing about the spatial location of firms (Hotelling 1929), Downs (1957, 117) derived his famous proposition that party platforms in a two-party system will converge toward the median voter until "the two parties be-come nearly identical . . . and practically all voters are indifferent between them." Downsian theory launched a variety of research agendas explor-ing the relationship between constituent preferences and legislative be-havior (Cameron, Cover, and Segal 1990; Clinton 2006; Miller and Stokes 1963; Shapiro et al. 1990; Wright 1978), including how candidates posi-tion themselves ideologically during campaigns (Ansolabehere, Snyder, and Stewart 2001b; Fowler 2005) and in office (Canes-Wrone, Brady, and Cogan 2002; Erikson 1990), how proximity to elections affects legislators' ideological positioning (Bernstein, Wright, and Berkman 1988; Thomas 1985), and whether legislators "shirk" their constituents' expectations in favor of their own personal ideological preferences (Kalt and Zupan 1984, 1990; Uslaner 1999; Van Houweling 2003).

As the concept evolved to enable scholars to apply economic theory to legislative politics, "ideology" became more central. Economic theorizing gave rise to intellectual disputes and research agendas that have inspired scores of models and empirical studies. It has become easy to take for granted the assumptions that undergird such theories, but "ideology" has not always been understood as a matter of individual-level preferences along an abstract dimension. In addition, "ideology" has not always im-plied a common metric along which all or most public policies could theo-retically be ranged. These relatively recent conceptual developments are undoubtedly a more important cause of congressional scholars' focus on ideology than influences from the broader political environment.

NOMINATE

Out of psychology emerged the view of "ideology" as a more-or-less fixed attribute of individuals that can be quantified and measured. Out of economics emerged the view that legislative decisions can be conceived as existing in a choice space within which legislators calculate relative utility based on their own ideological preferences and the spatial locations of policy alternatives. These two conceptual parents have given birth to increasingly sophisticated statistical techniques for analyzing patterns in roll-call votes. Most important of these is NOMINATE, the scaling algorithm developed by Keith Poole and Howard Rosenthal (Poole and Rosenthal 1997). The variety of scores produced by this methodology have "become a staple of most modern studies of decision making in Congress" (Roberts 2007, 342), although alternative methodologies are gaining currency (Clinton, Jackman, and Rivers 2004). NOMINATE and subsequent approaches assume that all legislators can be thought of as having an "ideal point" or "level of conservatism that [they] would like to see in any issue that is voted on" (Poole and Rosenthal 1997, 12) and that they will always vote for the policy alternative closest to it within the choice space. The ideal points of members and the estimated spatial locations of legislative alternatives derived from these methods only make sense within the understandings of ideology that emerged out of previous developments in psychology and economics.

The widespread acceptance of these methods rests heavily on their ability to describe accurately large amounts of data. In most eras, patterns in roll-call voting exhibit markedly low dimensionality, a finding consistent with the inference that a dominant left-right dimension accounts for most political conflict (Poole and Rosenthal 1997). Members' ideal points on the first dimension derived by NOMINATE accurately account for their votes across a wide range of issues and, in most cases, their voting behavior over an entire career in Congress. The validity of these scores is further reinforced by their high correlation with other measures of members' liberalism and conservatism. Interest group scorecards such as those produced by the Americans for Democratic Action and the U.S. Chamber of Commerce are based on only small numbers of votes targeted on issues of concern to the organization, while NOMINATE scores are generated out of all nonunanimous votes without respect to issue content. Nevertheless, all such ratings of members are remarkably consistent (Burden, Caldeira, and Groseclose 2000; McCarty, Poole, and Rosenthal 2006). Such findings have greatly bolstered the construct validity of NOMINATE and related scores, persuading scholars to think in terms of spatial voting theory.

Despite the almost universal acceptance of NOMINATE, there are grounds for skepticism. The capacity of individual preferences alone to structure conflict in Congress is doubtful. This is especially true in light of the existence of congressional parties, another plausible explanation for the structure of conflict in Congress. Indeed, if most political conflict in Congress stems from legislators' preferences on a left-right dimension—a largely fixed, personal value orientation—then why does the methodology fail to function when there are not two major parties? Poole and Rosenthal (1997, 30) themselves state that the "spatial model breaks down in two periods." Unsurprisingly, these are the two periods in U.S. history when the state of the congressional parties departed from the two-party norm: (1) the Era of Good Feelings, from 1815 to 1825, when "the United States had, in effect, a one-party government" (31); and (2) in the early 1850s, "when the conflict over slavery led to the collapse of the Whig party" (31). It seems implausible that individual preferences matter less when there aren't two parties to structure conflict—arguably they should matter more. A similar lack of low dimensional structure is evident in the roll-call voting patterns in legislatures without two-party systems, such as Nebraska's non-partisan legislature (Welch and Carlson 1973; Wright and Schaffner 2002), and the Confederate House of Representatives (Jenkins 1999, 2000).

Heckman and Snyder (1997, S168–69) undermine the proposition that members' votes are organized according to an underlying continuum of in-dividual preferences by showing that a model using only dummy variables for Southern Democrats, Northern Democrats, and Republicans performs as well as ideal points in correctly classifying members' votes: "These two observed attributes predict voting about as well as, and sometimes better than, a model formulated in terms of unobserved attributes. 'Ideology' in [the Poole and Rosenthal] model turns out to be just party and regional loyalty" (S184). The low dimensional voting behavior identified by ideal point estimation techniques may be largely a function of the ability of fellow partisans to form stable coalitions in support of a bundle of policy positions (as modified by the effect of North-South constituency differ-ences) rather than a consequence of a preexisting underlying ideological continuum on which every individual legislator has an "ideal point."

Studies of party-switchers also raise questions about whether roll call votes reflect "preferences" more than "party loyalty." The few members of Congress who switch their party affiliations exhibit very substantial shifts in their voting behavior once they take on the new label (McCarty, Poole, and Rosenthal 2001; Nokken 2000).

Although the dominant patterns in roll-call voting are highly regu-lar and relatively simple in structure, the causes of this regularity and structure remain fundamentally ambiguous: Faced with this ambiguity, Truman (1959, 279) concluded, "the actions of [members of Congress] are not to be accounted for by any simple ascription of motive or intent, and this injunction applies with special force when these actions are manifest primarily in the form of a series of record votes." Despite the massive literature on roll-call voting in Congress that has been published since, Truman's warning is still worth heeding.

After "Ideology"

This chapter has tracked the evolution of ideology as a concept for understanding, describing, and theorizing about legislative politics. Ideological concepts are a relatively recent innovation. "Ideology," in fact, was not used by either scholars or journalists to describe congressional politics prior to the 1930s. The earliest uses of ideological concepts in congressional scholarship followed their use by journalists covering Congress to explain conflicts that divided the parties internally.

Before the New Deal, scholars did not conceive of parties as vehicles for an ideological dimension of conflict that existed outside of party politics, the sense in which the relationship between party and ideology is so often understood today. Instead, parties were viewed as fundamental political institutions that bundled policy commitments together and developed principled justifications for these bundled commitments. In this sense, earlier understandings were closer to that articulated by Gerring (1998b). Indeed, Gerring's own title *Party Ideologies in America* explicitly envisions parties as key actors in the development of ideologies as they change over time: "It is important to state the obvious: party ideologies were formulated, disseminated, and executed by party leaders. They did not rise spontaneously" (Gerring 1998b, 272). In this regard, Gerring's understanding of "party ideology" is far closer to the earlier scholarly concepts of "party principles" than to the ideological continuum envisioned by so many contemporary congressional scholars and theorists.

As ideological concepts evolved in political science, they were deeply influenced by developments in behavioral science and economic theory. Under the influence of behavioral psychology, "ideology" came to be seen as a largely fixed personal attribute existing outside of and separate from politics. Under the influence of economics, ideology came to be seen as a metric that can rank order policy choices and structure legislative utility functions. At this stage, such concepts are so widespread and dominant in the study of legislative politics that they constitute a Kuhnian paradigm (Kuhn 1996).

Within this paradigm, characterizations of legislative politics tend to operate at very high levels of abstraction. The assumptions of spatial voting, combined with the findings of great regularity in voting patterns, have led to greatly simplified accounts of congressional politics. The first efforts to scale roll-call votes identified many issue distinctions that affected members' decisions. For example, in his analysis of the 81st Congress, Duncan MacRae (1954, 192) isolated two sets of considerations that shaped Republican reactions to the "Fair Deal": beliefs on the role of government in promoting social welfare and positions on labor and management issues. Farris's (1958, 334) analysis of roll-call voting in the 79th Congress drew distinctions among "liberal pacifists, liberal internationalists, conservative internationalists, conservative jingoes, and conservative isolationists." The single, global left-right continuum postulated in contemporary theories and models obliterates all such subtleties.

Political scientists even reinterpret the much more nuanced scholarship of the past in today's bare-bones terms. Truman (1959), for example, is often cited for the proposition that legislative leaders will reflect the median ideological position among a legislative party's members (Heberlig, Hetherington, and Larson 2006; McGann, Koetzle, and Grofman 2002). But Truman's "leader as middleman" thesis is actually more complex than the claim that a leader will tend to mirror the median member of the party. For Truman, the legislative leader not only reflects a moderate position within his party, he is also "engaged in repeated, even continuous, efforts at restructuring, reconstituting the group" (p. 115). The leader's lack of exclusive affiliation with any particular faction within the party enables her to remain "above the fray" and to maintain open lines of communication with the entire party membership. This position allows the leader to build common ground where it does not initially exist—literally "restructuring" and "reconstituting" the party itself—and to adjust the bundle of commitments that characterize the party at any given time. This kind of constructive and creative leadership cannot be accommodated within theories that conceive of congressional politics as reducible to fixed individual preferences, exogenous to legislative politics. Conceptualizations have become so abstract that some scholars have even stopped referring to liberalism and conservatism, preferring the more generic term "preferences."

The dominance of ideology in the study of congressional politics has led to diminishing scholarly interest in patterns of communication among members, cue-taking, caucus deliberation, and party consensus-building. If discussion and negotiation are necessary for parties to bundle issue positions into a platform or agenda, to coordinate stances among their members, or to develop a "party line" that most party members can support, the dominant paradigm largely assumes them away. None of these activities are necessary if "what goes with what" (Converse 1964, 212) is already predetermined by an underlying ideological dimension that exists outside of politics. Put more generally, the methodological individualism inherent in contemporary conceptions of ideology systematically deemphasizes the role of internal deliberation and coalition-building in holding parties together. If legislators have incentives to adopt party-consensus positions as their own, or to weigh their own preferences against the interests of their parties, or to adjust their proposals or positions in anticipation of the reactions of fellow partisans, then the "preferences" revealed in legislative behavior are neither purely individual phenomena nor exogenous to legislative politics and policymaking. In short, the understanding of ideology as "members' fixed preferences along a dimension" obscures the kind of collective considerations that led Tom DeLay to retire from Congress long before he personally lost interest in waging ideological combat.

The chapter that follows will investigate the extent to which we can understand party conflict in the contemporary Congress as ideological in nature. Rather than conceiving of ideology as an underlying dimension that structures members' behavior across all votes, I set out a definition of ideology that puts some boundaries around the concept. Even as broadly relevant as "left" and "right" appear to be in contemporary political debates, they simply do not apply to every type of issue that Congress considers. If we still find a substantial amount of party conflict even on matters that bear no clear relationship to the disputes between liberalism and conservatism, then we need to consider more carefully how parties can engender political conflict, separate from the tendency of party labels to signal the ideological preferences of individual members. In doing so, we will return to earlier understandings of parties as central mediating institutions, capable of bundling issue commitments and policy priorities, rather than merely reflecting policy disagreements along a preexisting continuum of individual preferences.

CHAPTER THREE

Sources of Party Conflict

Ideological Disagreement and Teamsmanship

"Ideology" refers to systems of beliefs, values, and preferences about politics and public policy. As such, it is distinct from a politician's political interests in cooperating with fellow partisans to climb the career ladder in the legislature, wield power, foster a favorable collective party reputation, or maintain good social standing among party colleagues. The distinction is not a fine one, and politicians themselves are capable of drawing it. Speaking to Mike Allen of the *Washington Post*, former Majority Leader Tom DeLay describes two resources a congressional leader can call upon to enlist support from party members: "You understand the dynamics of a tough vote. You may not have every vote in hand as you walk on the floor during the vote. But you understand how things work around here. . . . When you appeal to their sense of principle, it's hard for them to deny you. And there are others that just understand the dynamics of teamwork, sticking together, working with each other, that you appeal to."[1] In other words, some members will work with their party because of agreement on general policy principles and others will do so because they understand the value of team play—or, in the words of Speaker Sam Rayburn, they understand how to "go along to get along." As discussed in chapter 1, likemindedness—ideological simpatico—is not the only reason members of Congress will support their fellow partisans on a controversial issue. If members of Congress are to cultivate a favorable reputation as a party or reap extra benefits for their constituents from majority status, they must work together as teams.

The unanswered question is just how much of the partisan conflict in Congress can be attributed to the dynamics of competitive team play and how much to ideological disagreement. Because party votes can occur for reasons that go beyond ideology, it is necessary to inquire into the nature of the issues that give rise to party votes. Answering this question can also shed some new light on the higher levels of party conflict in the contemporary Congress. How much of the increase in party conflict in Congress between the presidencies of Jimmy Carter and George W. Bush can be attributed to the parties moving farther apart from one another on the ideological spectrum and how much resulted simply from partisans working together more effectively as teams?

To answer these questions, I have constructed an original dataset classifying roll-call votes on their ideological content. As discussed in chapter 1, this project begins from the observation that many of the issues considered in Congress do not speak to liberalism and conservatism and cannot be situated on an ideological spectrum (Matthews and Stimson 1975, 32–37). Ideology alone simply cannot structure congressional voting on those issues. If ideological commonality on policy issues is all that holds parties together, one would expect to find little partisanship on such issues. However, if members' political *interests* create party conflict separate from their ideological *preferences*, party voting will occur even in the absence of ideological controversy.

The analysis reveals that ideological disagreement explains only a portion of the partisanship observed in congressional voting. As expected, votes on ideological issues are far more likely to break along party lines than votes on nonideological issues. But much partisan conflict occurs on issues that are not identifiably ideological. The analysis reveals that disagreement on conventional left-right issues characterizes only a little more than half of the party votes observed in congressional voting. A great deal of partisan conflict occurs on roll-call votes where it is not possible to specify whether voting "yea" or "nay" is the more liberal or more conservative position in policy terms.

The increase in party conflict over the past 25 years results from both ideological polarization and improved party teamwork. Party conflict has become sharper on ideological issues, with members of the two parties voting more cohesively with their fellow partisans against their party opposition. But party conflict has also increased across the board, across all types of roll-call votes, regardless of issue content. In addition to having diverged from one another on the liberal-conservative dimension, Senate parties have become more distinctive teams as they do battle over policies that cannot be situated on a liberal-conservative continuum.

The Necessity of Defining Terms

If ideology is to offer useful explanations of political behavior, the concept must be defined so that it is falsifiable in empirical terms. It is necessary, as Sartori (1969, 399) observes, "to declare what ideology is not. . . . if no such opposition is justified, then the notion of ideology loses much of its interest and has little explanatory value." If ideology is not defined, it becomes merely a tautological catch-all for behavior that is not explained in some other way. A member voting "yea" is thought to do so because it maximizes her utility in policy terms, but without any assessment of the policy content of the legislative proposal, we are only left with the circular logic that the legislation must have maximized the member's ideological preferences relative to the alternative because she voted "yea" and not "nay."

With respect to votes in Congress, a researcher must be able to specify, before observing voting patterns, which is the more conservative or the more liberal position on the issues. If that is not possible, then "ideology" means nothing more than patterned behavior in congressional voting, and "if the term ideology were not employed, no loss of conceptual content would follow" (Sartori 1969, 400).

Ideology is a complex and multifaceted concept. To make matters even more complicated, ideologies change over time. Gerring (1998b, 17), for example, documents how the central ideological conflict between left and right during the 1896–1948 era focused on issues involving redistribution of wealth, often framed as "the people versus the interests." After 1948, however, the "left versus right" cleavage expanded beyond economic issues to include a host of "postmaterialist" concerns (18), including the rights of women and racial and ethnic minorities. Before equal opportunity and civil rights became part of what is understood as liberalism or progressivism, opposition to the rights of minorities actually coexisted with strong preferences for redistributive economic programs, a pattern historian C. Vann Woodward (1951) termed "progressivism for whites only." Many of the strongest early supporters of the New Deal in Congress were also some of the most strident segregationists.[2]

In another remarkable example of how ideological conflicts shift over time, Poole and Rosenthal (1997, 112) show that even an issue as central to distinguishing liberals from conservatives today as the minimum wage was not mapped onto the left-right continuum in Congress prior to World War II. According to their analysis, members of the "right" party during the prewar period did not oppose the minimum wage to any greater extent than members of the "left" party. It was not until after World War II that votes on the minimum wage could be predicted with any degree of accuracy using their measure of members' liberalism and conservatism.[3]

As discussed in chapter 2, the difficulty in devising operational definitions of ideology has not prevented the concept from becoming central to political science and the study of legislative politics. But the most widely used methodologies for measuring ideology cannot answer the questions being posed here. The typical methodologies—including the principal components analysis used by *National Journal* to create its ideology scores and the NOMINATE algorithm developed by Poole and Rosenthal—cannot distinguish ideological likemindedness from team play. No methodology that looks only at the patterns in vote outcomes can isolate what is meant by the concept of "ideology" and differentiate it from team play.

The reason vote patterns are inadequate as an indicator of ideology is that votes can exhibit a partisan pattern even when the issue at stake has no identifiable ideological content. In the 107th Congress, for example, Sen. Jon Kyl (R-Ariz.) offered an amendment to the Veterans' Affairs–Housing and Urban Development Appropriations bill that would change the formula used to distribute federal grants for constructing wastewater treatment facilities. As a long-standing intergovernmental grant program, Kyl argued, the existing distribution was out of date; he proposed instead that the grants be distributed on the basis of the Environmental Protection Agency's quadrennial wastewater infrastructure needs survey, a method that would redirect funds to growing states like Arizona.[4] In the course of debate, Kyl presented data (never disputed) showing that 27 states and the District of Columbia would all receive more funds as a result of the formula change he was proposing. No one claims that liberals and conservatives in the United States have different positions on how a fixed sum of money for infrastructure grants should be distributed among the states. Nor do ideological principles dictate whether one believes that wastewater treatment grants should be allocated on the basis of the EPA's most recent needs survey, on 1970s census data, or any other criterion. Nevertheless, a party line vote occurred on the amendment, with 73 percent of Senate Democrats voting to table Kyl's proposal and 56 percent of Republicans voting against the tabling motion.[5] In short, the parties disagreed on the matter, even though the adoption or rejection of the amendment would have had no effect on the ideological direction of American public policy. If we look only at vote patterns, we have no idea how often Republicans and Democrats come into conflict over matters that simply cannot be explained using any conventional definition of liberal-conservative differences.

Votes can even exhibit a partisan pattern in which most Democrats take a policy position directly opposed to what one might expect of a liberal or left-leaning party and most Republicans favor a policy that is precisely the reverse of what would be expected of a conservative or right-leaning party. This is an inconvenient fact for methodologies that assign ideological direction to votes based on voting patterns alone, as it sometimes leads to "counterintuitive" results, to say the least. For example, Republicans in the 1890s supported a variety of programs that would unquestionably be viewed as liberal measures today, including federal aid to education, high tariffs, and federal enforcement of voting rights for African Americans, while Democrats generally opposed these programs (Bensel 2004). Within the widely used NOMINATE methodology Republicans are interpreted as the right-leaning party and Democrats the left-leaning party. As a consequence, a nineteenth-century member who supports these "big government" programs receives more conservative NOMINATE scores, and a member who opposes them, more liberal scores.

Antilynching bills in the 1920s have a similarly counterintuitive effect on members' NOMINATE scores (Poole and Rosenthal 1997, 110). The pattern of votes on civil rights bills during this period generally followed party lines, with Democrats largely opposed to making lynching a federal crime and Republicans generally supportive of antilynching legislation. Because the "left" party opposed civil rights legislation and the "right" party supported it, any member who voted in favor of civil rights scores as having taken a *conservative* position on that issue and any member who voted against civil rights scores as having taken a *liberal* position. Although Poole and Rosenthal's first dimension is usually interpreted as involving economic issues and the second dimension as involving racial issues, civil rights issues actually track in and out of the first dimension. At times, voting patterns on civil rights legislation map onto the main line of cleavage between the two parties; at other times such proposals divide the parties on sectional lines and are picked up by the second dimension (Poole and Rosenthal 1997, 109–11). When Republicans were more in favor of civil rights than Democrats (as in the 1920s), a position in favor of civil rights received conservative scores. When the issue divided the parties internally, civil rights issues mapped onto the second dimension. Once Democrats were more in favor of civil rights than Republicans (as in the contemporary era), a position in favor of civil rights receives liberal scores. The issue content of the first dimension is entirely dependent on how the two parties behave.

The *National Journal*'s liberal-conservative ratings from 2003 offer a contemporary example of the problem of equating partisan voting patterns with liberal-conservative ideology: the vote on the expansion of Medicare to cover prescription drugs. This program authorized the federal government to assume responsibility for subsidizing the cost of insurance for prescription drugs for seniors. Prior to this program's adoption, seniors had to pay the full cost of all outpatient prescription drugs unless they had private insurance or qualified for Medicaid. Regardless of how extensively the new program relied on private insurance companies to administer the benefits, it strains credulity to argue that the creation of this program moved national health policy in a conservative direction relative to the status quo. Even so, members divided along party lines on the measure, with most Republicans voting in favor and most Democrats against. Because Republicans are assumed to be the conservative party, the *National Journal* methodology automatically classifies members who voted in favor of the new prescription drug benefit as taking the "conservative" position. The few hard-line conservative Republicans in the Congress who stood against their own party leaders and their own party's president because of their stated "limited government" principles actually found that their opposition to a new government entitlement program resulted in scores that made them appear more *liberal*. Movement conservatives such as Rep. Jim DeMint (R-S.C.), Rep. Steve Chabot (R-Ohio), Sen. Trent Lott (R-Miss.), and Sen. Don Nickles (R-Okla.) all received more liberal scores in that Congress as a direct result of their refusal to support a dramatic expansion of a major Great Society program (Cohen 2004). Meanwhile, Democrats voting in favor of expanding Medicare to cover prescription drugs received more conservative scores. Democrats who voted to reject this new social insurance program are classed as taking the "left" position.

Any vote that tends to divide the two parties from one another, *regardless of the reason*, will be treated by such methodologies as measuring members' ideology. Any issue on which members of the two parties take opposing stands, whether or not it has any ideological content, will map on the first dimension in NOMINATE. The principal components analysis used by *National Journal* will identify any vote with a partisan pattern as reflecting "general ideology," rather than "regional or special interest concerns" (National Journal Staff 2007).

Equating party votes with ideological votes is not warranted if, as argued in chapter 1, partisan conflict can have *any other source* besides members' differing preferences on public policy. Just as the incidence of party voting alone offers no evidence that parties actually exercised any influence on members' votes (Krehbiel 1993), one cannot conclude that simply because Republicans vote together on an issue while voting against Democrats (or vice versa) that different ideological preferences were the cause of the disagreement. Neither assumption is warranted.

Statistical manipulations of raw voting data cannot address this fundamental problem of interpretation. A legislature in which two machine parties led by opposing bosses did nothing other than wrangle over the spoils of patronage could be analyzed using principal components analysis or scaling methodologies. Voting in an entirely patronage-driven legislature would be largely unidimensional in structure, but the cause of that structure could only be party team cooperation and not ideology, because the battles in the legislature were *not about ideology.* Ideological positions of members and parties cannot be discerned without paying attention to the substantive issues at stake.

Scaling analyses of congressional voting are thus inherently ambiguous. The methodologies can describe patterns in congressional votes, but they cannot determine the causes of those patterns. Poole and Rosenthal (1997, 46) recognize the difficulty and stipulate that first dimension NOMINATE scores "can be thought of as ranging from strong loyalty to one party . . . to weak loyalty to either party and to strong loyalty to the second opposing party." The NOMINATE methodology establishes that voting in Congress is largely unidimensional in structure, but it cannot reveal how much of this structure is caused by partisan teamsmanship and how much is the result of the distribution of members' ideological preferences. It only provides a map of a congressional voting structure that is simultaneously and in unknown proportions organized by ideology and party, by individual policy preferences and organized team play. Political scientists have been using NOMINATE as a measure of ideology without taking into account these weaknesses for a long time now.

Defining Ideological Conflict

Rather than employing scaling techniques, this study takes an approach more akin to that used in contemporary studies of public opinion. To measure voter ideology, public opinion scholars do not look for patterns across all survey items on which respondents are polled. They instead use survey items that measure what is meant by "ideology." Similarly, to assess the effect of ideology on congressional party politics, this study specifies the issues that divide liberals from conservatives in American politics and classifies roll-call votes by whether or not they involve any of these issues. In other words, votes are classified based on criteria specified in advance of the observed voting behavior. An issue does not become "ideological" simply because Republicans and Democrats vote differently from one another in handling it. If ideology is a social science concept, it must be possible to define it separate from the behavior one hopes to explain with it. It is not simply a synonym for "partisan."

Developing an operational definition of ideology for purposes of studying congressional politics is not as difficult as it may initially appear. There are conventional scholarly understandings of liberalism and conservatism as the terms are applied to American politics. In the public opinion literature, there is widespread consensus on what types of survey items are appropriate measures of voters' ideological orientations. One widely used measure is a set of items included in the National Election Study (NES) asking respondents about (1) the role of government in improving the social and economic position of blacks and other minorities, (2) whether or not the government should provide health insurance, (3) if the government should spend more to provide more services or spend less to provide fewer services, (4) whether the government should guarantee a job to everyone who wants to work, (5) if women should have an equal role in running business, industry, and government, and (6) when abortion should be allowed. When results from earlier versions of the NES are used, scholars sometimes use items surveying views on the Vietnam War, busing for desegregation, or marijuana legalization (Jennings 1992; Stimson 1975). There does not appear to be any controversy in the public opinion literature about the validity of such items as indicators of ideology, and they are utilized with little comment in a wide array of studies (Abramowitz and Saunders 1998, 2008; Brewer 2005; Layman and Carsey 2002).

Along the same lines, most introductory textbooks of American government offer reasonably concise discussions of the ideological issues that differentiate liberals from conservatives in American politics. These definitions exhibit as much consistency across texts as do most other concepts in political science. Fiorina, Peterson, and Voss (2005, 111, 113) provide one of the more comprehensive definitions:

American liberalism supports an active government in the economic sphere but permits a high degree of autonomy when citizens make moral choices. Liberals endorse using political institutions to address widespread social inequalities, such as those associated with race or gender, but not to promote other forms of good behavior. They prefer more international cooperation to solve world problems . . .

Conservatism, meanwhile, endorses less government regulation of economic matters but favors public policies that will shape the nation's culture in a moral direction rather than an amoral one. . . . [Conservatives] endorse a strong military and an independent foreign policy focused on national security concerns.

Patterson (2008, 178) offers a more succinct, but generally consistent definition: "Liberals are those who say that government should do more to solve the country's problems and who say that government ought not to support traditional values at the expense of less conventional ones. . . . Conservatives are those who think government should be sparing in its programs and who feel government should use its power to uphold traditional values." In their discussions of ideology, Wilson and DiIulio (2006, 169–71) and Janda, Berry, and Goldman (2008, 23–27) offer a similar discussion, distinguishing between social and economic issues in order to illustrate that views on social and economic issues can be paired in different ways, resulting in liberalism, conservatism, libertarianism, and populism-communitarianism. Although there is some variation in definitions, there is remarkably broad scholarly agreement on the specific policy disagreements that differentiate liberalism and conservatism in the United States.

Early scholarship on congressional politics took an approach similar to that used in public opinion research. Scholars used conventional understandings of the differences between liberals and conservatives to identify roll-call votes that could serve as valid indicators of members' ideological orientations. In the first political science article attempting to quantify ideological positioning in Congress, Huntington (1950) examined congressional voting behavior on a subset of votes that had been selected as representative of programmatic liberalism by the *New Republic*.[6] MacRae (1952) selected and analyzed votes dealing with government's role in redistribution. Clausen's (1967, 1023) study of the dimensions of legislative conflict was confined to "legislation concerned with socio-economic, regulatory, and fiscal policy, [which] are policy issues commonly thought of in terms of a single liberal-conservative dimension." Shapiro's (1968, 494) analysis of roll-call voting in the House of Representatives begins by identifying votes "dealing with the expansion of the federal role." It is only relatively recently that most legislative scholars have abandoned efforts to disaggregate roll-call votes based on their a priori relationship to definitions of liberalism and conservatism.

Across both general interest textbooks and professional scholarship, there is wide agreement on the specific issue positions that differentiate contemporary liberalism and conservatism. Where does this consensus come from? What is its intellectual or empirical foundation? How do we know that this is what liberalism and conservatism "really" mean? An early scholar struggling with these questions, Charles Farris (1958, 334–35) concluded his study asking, "Are the selected issues the 'right' ones—the only issues that 'should' be used" to define ideology? His answer: "A political scientist interested in 'ideology' has three alternative research strategies: (1) He can engage in verbalism about the meaning of the term. (2) He can postpone behavioral research on 'ideology' until most members of the profession agree on what the word means. (3) He can propose, and, while he remains committed to them, he can consistently apply operational criteria for defining 'ideology.'" Like Farris, this study takes the third approach—advancing definitions of the terms and then applying them to the data—while noting the widespread consensus in the profession on the meaning of the terms. An empirical study of the role of "liberalism" and "conservatism" in structuring conflict in Congress does not need to begin from first principles of political philosophy to derive definitions of liberalism and conservatism. All that is necessary is that the concepts be defined clearly and applied systematically.

What "Ideology" Excludes

As discussed in chapter 1, Congress considers many matters unrelated to the policy disagreements that distinguish liberalism from conservatism. Some of these are routine and noncontroversial. Many appropriations bills are passed without any debate about overall spending levels (as an ideological question of government's share of the economy) or any ideologically controversial policy riders. Nevertheless, issues can be both highly controversial and partisan in Congress even when they do not have implications for the ideological direction of American public policy. Debates over good-government causes, institutional powers and procedures, and government programs that are neither regulatory nor redistributive are three broad categories of issues that cannot be understood using the concepts of "left" and "right."

First, liberals and conservatives do not hold different substantive views on the range of issues typically thought of as good-government causes. Liberals and conservatives all support integrity, efficiency, and competent management in government. No one favors government corruption. As will be explored in detail in chapter 5, there is often substantial controversy between Republicans and Democrats in Congress over lobbying registration rules, voting technology and election recount rules, anti–voter-fraud measures, congressional ethics, limits on gifts to members and their staffs, conflict-of-interest regulations, and campaign-disclosure requirements. But it is not appropriate to refer to the different positions members take in such disputes as ideological.

Similarly, there is no ideological disagreement over waste, fraud, and abuse. No one is in favor of these things, although there is a lot of disagreement about what counts as waste, fraud, or abuse, and about how to eliminate them. Controversy over the Superconducting Supercollider or the Tennessee Tombigbee Waterway takes the form of a dispute about cost-benefit analysis and relative efficiencies, not over the proper role of government. Support for building a bridge to nowhere—actually connecting Ketchikan, Alaska, to an airport on Gravina Island—does not make Sen. Ted Stevens (R-Alaska) "liberal" nor opponents of the bridge "conservative."[7] Liberals and conservatives all agree that government programs should be effective, efficient, well administered, and well designed.

In the same good-government vein, liberalism and conservatism provide no guidance on the proper role of government in investigating government performance, collecting data, and disclosing information. Members of Congress nevertheless frequently disagree along party lines over which investigations to conduct, which studies to fund, which independent commissions to create, which reports to release and to whom. During the 109th Congress, for example, the two parties strongly disagreed about whether an independent commission was necessary to investigate the government's emergency response to Hurricane Katrina. Liberalism and conservatism say nothing about the proper role of government in undertaking this or other studies of governmental performance, but control of this information had obvious consequences for the parties' electoral fortunes. On the subject of investigating the government's response to Katrina, the parties divided perfectly along party lines, with all Republicans voting against a commission and all Democrats in favor.[8]

Second, there are no consistent, identifiably liberal or conservative positions on the proper roles and procedures for the different institutions of
American government. How broad is the president's power to reorganize
the executive branch or to take military or other executive action without congressional approval? What are the appropriate rules governing
majority and minority rights in congressional debate? What does "advise
and consent" mean with respect to Senate approval of federal judges and
high administrative appointments? The positions the parties take on these
questions generally depend on majority or minority status, or control of
the presidency, rather than on abstract principle. Even federalism issues
are similarly ambiguous. Conservatism in the United States has historically been associated with a narrow view of federal power, but when state
control undermines conservative policy goals (e.g., state courts' more ex-
pansive treatment of tort liability, states' permissive medical marijuana or
right to die policies, and states' more relaxed welfare eligibility standards)
conservatives will generally support federal control instead. The same pattern obviously describes liberals' relationship to federalism. Liberals are
perfectly prepared to invoke states' rights arguments themselves to support California's stricter environmental laws, states' medical marijuana
and right to die statutes and to oppose expanded federal jurisdiction over
product-liability class actions, among other issues. Liberals and conservatives typically invoke such arguments opportunistically. Generally speaking, liberalism and conservatism do not offer clear guidance on questions
of institutional design, even though these issues are perennially controversial in American politics.

Third, many federal domestic programs are neither regulatory nor designed to redress economic inequalities among groups or classes in American society, and therefore liberalism and conservatism do not have clear,
differentiated positions on them. The list of such programs is potentially
endless. But one might begin by pointing to large-scale science projects,
medical research and development, space exploration, infrastructure
for transportation in all of its modes (trucking, rail, air, maritime), flood
control, irrigation, homeland security, military salaries, base construction and staffing, disaster relief, crop insurance, small business loans,
and veterans' benefits. In the nineteenth century there was intense ideological dispute over the proper role of the federal government with respect to internal improvements, but liberals and conservatives do not
disagree in principle on such matters today. Some libertarian strands
of conservatism may reject government's role in the provision of most

public goods, but no one would posit this view as characteristic of mainstream American conservatism as practiced in the U.S. Congress. Liberals and conservatives do not embrace different views on whether these programs fall within government's proper authority and role, and voting on such issues generally cannot be structured by members' ideological preferences.

Liberals and conservatives may dispute the amount of funds to devote to nonregulatory, nonredistributive programs, but Congress does far more than decide on the amount of funding for such programs. Funding disputes may touch on ideological differences in American politics, with conservatives favoring lower levels of spending and liberals supporting or tolerating higher levels. But there are many issues of policy design separate from overall funding levels. Should NASA pursue a manned mission to Mars, or should it focus on robotic probes and spacecraft? Should the Veterans' Affairs Department reorganize to serve the needs of service personnel suffering from post-traumatic stress disorder? Should tax legislation raising a given amount of revenue include tax loss carry-backs that allow current losses to be credited against income reported in earlier years, or should it include credits to encourage investment in research and development? Generally speaking, once a given level of federal funding for a program is established, liberalism and conservatism cannot guide members' decisions on how dollars should be divided. A recurring controversy, for example, has focused on whether homeland security grants should be distributed on the basis of a fixed formula or on assessments of the risk of terrorist attacks in particular areas.[9] Conflicts over such matters may be lengthy and intractable in Congress, but they cannot be described as ideological in any meaningful sense.

In sum, important policy controversies fall outside the clusters of ideas associated with liberalism and conservatism. What structure should we expect to find on issues that ideology does not organize? If policy preferences alone drive congressional voting, then on nonideological issues each member votes simply on the basis of his or her own individual assessment of the policy merits of the matter. If members make policy decisions based on their own individual judgment, it is highly improbable that a majority of the members of one party would just coincidentally wind up voting on one side and a majority of the other party on the other side, time and again. If we nevertheless find party members lined up on opposite sides even on nonideological issues, then partisanship has roots outside members' differing policy preferences on the ideological continuum.

A Note on Time-Boundedness

This study does not claim that the terms of ideological conflict are fixed, nor that the ideological issues identified here will still be valid for American politics one hundred years from now. Even over the course of the United States' relatively short history, the terms of ideological conflict have evolved in dramatic ways. Indeed, prior to the emergence of populism and progressivism toward the end of the nineteenth century, it makes little sense to attempt to describe the conflicts between the two major parties in the United States using the terminology of "left" versus "right."

Gerring's (1998b) analysis of the ideological sources of party conflict over more than 150 years of American history richly illustrates the complex and creative combinations of policies and values that the major parties have bundled together over their long histories. Between 1828 and 1896, the Democratic party continually intermingled positions that would today be characterized as both "left" and "right," though it is probably anachronistic to use either concept to describe mid-nineteenth-century party politics in the United States. The Democrats touted themselves as the party of white supremacy, limited government, and free trade. At the same time, it was also an agrarian party opposed to modern capitalism, banking, and credit that frequently indulged in harsh "diatribes against speculation, mammon, gambling, and other figurative allusions to marketplace activity" (Gerring 1998b, 174). During the same era, the Whig and Republican parties also combined policy commitments that, using today's understandings of the terms, would be described as simultaneously "liberal" and "conservative." Bearing a strong Yankee protestant influence, the Whig and Republican parties were socially conservative, emphasizing "order [and] inveighing against the dangers of unrestrained individualism" (Gerring 1998b, 57). But they also favored high tariffs, national banking institutions, and government-funded infrastructure projects ("internal improvements") and envisioned a large role for government in the national economy: "For National Republicans . . . it was axiomatic that the art of government involved successful intervention into the marketplace" (Gerring 1998b, 66).

Even though mid-nineteenth-century Republicans and Democrats combined issue positions—party principles—that would be described as both "left" and "right" if politicians adopted them today, they were not "centrist" parties whose members overlapped in their voting behavior. Even before party conflict can be legitimately described using left-right terminology, the parties were approximately just as "polarized" as they are in the contemporary Congress.[10] After the presidential candidacy of William Jennings Bryan in 1896, party conflict in the United States begins to be organized along more recognizable left-right lines, with Democrats explicitly embracing government regulation and redistribution in ways that had "hitherto only [been found] outside the mainstream of American party politics" (Gerring 1998b, 189). But this shift had little effect on the extent of partisanship in Congress. Party conflict in Congress was nearly as intense in the period before the populist takeover of the national Democratic party as it was afterward.

The value of distinguishing the congressional politics of issues that can be described using contemporary ideological concepts from issues that cannot—as this study seeks to do—lies not in determining which issues are "ideological" in any essentialist or ontological sense. Its value is analytical. How useful are conventional understandings of ideology for explaining congressional party politics? How much conflict between today's Republicans and Democrats is directly rooted in the different beliefs and values characteristic of individual liberals and conservatives? To what extent can the rise in party conflict over the last quarter century be attributed to *ideological* polarization, a widening disagreement on the proper role of government?

Coding Ideological Content

This project employs conventional understandings of what it means to be liberal and conservative in contemporary American politics. The goal is to cull out all votes in Congress that bear a discernible relationship to the issue positions that differentiate liberals from conservatives. For purposes of this study, "ideological issues" are identified as disputed understandings of the proper role and purpose of government with respect to:

- *Economic issues* include all votes involving government programs to redress social and economic inequalities, regulations of private economic activity for public purposes, government's share of the economy, and the distribution of the tax burden. Because so many votes fall into this category, it is divided into four subcategories for more refined analysis.
- *Social issues* include all votes that set values of individual equality or freedom in opposition to the traditional moral and social order, including abortion, school prayer, affirmative action, drugs, and crime.

- *Hawk vs. dove issues* take in all votes involving the use of force and the alloca-
  tion of resources to military defense.
- *Multilateralism vs. unilateralism issues* encompass votes involving international
  treaties (such as the chemical weapons ban, nuclear test ban, land mine ban,
  arms reduction agreements) and international institutions (such as the UN,
  IMF, World Bank, and the International Criminal Court).

This is a less elaborate classification scheme than others in use (Baumgartner and Jones 1993; Clausen 1973; Katznelson and Lapinski 2006), but it
has the advantage of mirroring analytical concepts widely used by journalists and political scientists (Miller and Schofield 2003; Sundquist 1983,
376–411).

Data collection begins from the premise, "if members are to use ideology as a decision shortcut, *bills* must have ideological content" (Matthews
and Stimson 1975, 34). Votes involving any of the issues listed above are
classed as having "ideological content." These include all votes dealing
with the distribution of the tax burden, regulations of private economic
activity for public purposes, government's share of the economy (budgets,
across-the-board spending cuts, tax increases or reductions), social programs to redress inequalities, social issues (abortion, school prayer, affirmative action, crime, etc.), the amount of resources devoted to the U.S.
military, the use of military force, and support for international treaties
and multilateral institutions. The key coding criteria are whether the vote
falls into any of these broad categories of issues and whether it is possible
to specify which position ("yea" or "nay") is the more liberal or the more
conservative. Table 3.1 provides brief definitions of each category, along
with examples of policy issues that fall into each.

Most roll call votes can be classified on the basis of legislative language
alone. Far more votes are taken on amendments than on passage of legislation, and amendments are usually narrowly drafted and thus simple to
place in the appropriate category. When legislative language did not clearly
involve any of the ideological categories, I turned to the debate in the *Congressional Record* to see if senators raised any issue in discussing the vote
that would allow me to classify it in one of the ideological categories.[11]

For votes on passage of legislation or amendments in the nature of a
substitute, which often involve complex packages of policies, the debate
in the *Congressional Record* was consulted to ascertain if senators discussed an issue in a way that could be classified in one of the ideological
categories. If any aspect of the proposed legislation sparked debate raising

I. Economic issues ($n = 2232$): This category captures four different types of issues that separate liberals from conservatives on economic policy.

   A. Government's share of the economy ($n = 505$). Conservatives support measures to limit government's share of the economy; liberals oppose them.
- Across-the-board cuts in or caps on domestic spending
- Procedural mechanisms (points of order, supermajority requirements, budget caps) to inhibit revenue and spending increases
- Revenue reductions in budget resolutions (before specific tax cuts are reported from the Finance Committee)
- Line item veto
- Social Security and Medicare lockbox, and measures to restrain the growth in entitlement spending
- Federal jobs programs to reduce unemployment
- Privatization initiatives (contracting out government workers, services, programs)

   B. Regulation of private economic activity for public purposes ($n = 904$). Conservatives oppose new regulations on private business activity and seek to roll back or limit existing regulations; liberals support new and existing regulations.
- Labor protections and regulations (prevailing wage, minimum wage, overtime, workplace safety, striker replacement, union political activity)
- Antidiscrimination and equal-access legislation for the disabled
- Antitrust laws
- Environmental regulation
- Consumer protections (product safety, consumer privacy)
- Property rights enforcement
- Cost-benefit requirements for new regulations
- Regulatory relief
- Restrictions on campaign contributions
- Firearm safety locks and background checks before sales
- Restrictions on class-action lawsuits

   C. Distribution of the tax burden ($n = 261$). Conservatives favor a less progressive tax policy, liberals favor a more progressive tax policy.
- Personal income taxes (including marginal tax rates, capital gains taxation, deductions for health insurance)
- Limits on tax cuts or deductions for top brackets
- Tax preferred savings accounts
- Flat tax proposals
- Estate taxes

   D. Redistributive social programs ($n = 512$). Liberals support programs designed to reduce social and economic inequality and seek to increase funding for them; conservatives do not.
- Food stamps
- Head Start
- Child care development block grants
- State children's health insurance
- Temporary Assistance to Needy Families
- Medicaid
- Earned Income Tax Credit
- Unemployment benefits (and extensions)
- Community Development Block Grants
- Job training programs
- Prison literacy and rehabilitation programs, Legal Aid
- Title I education funding

   E. More than one economic policy category ($n = 50$). These are votes that involve more than one of the economic categories above. Votes on final passage of the budget resolution typically fall in this category.

Table 3.1 *(continued)*

II. Social issues ($n = 672$): This category includes all votes that set values of individual equality or freedom in opposition to the traditional moral and social order.
   - School vouchers and tax-exempt accounts to fund religious and private education
   - Punishments for crime, including the death penalty, mandatory minimums, and nonrestoration of voting rights for felons
   - Affirmative action
   - Limits on abortion rights and access
   - School prayer
   - Making receipt of government benefits depend upon good behavior (not doing drugs, attending school, having no more kids while on welfare, etc.)
   - Homosexual rights
   - Needle exchange programs
   - School desegregation and consent decrees
   - Hate crimes laws
III. Hawk vs. dove ($n = 368$): Conservatives favor devoting more resources to military defense than liberals and are more likely to favor the use of force.
   - Strategic Missile Defense (SDI), MX Missile
   - Covert military aid (anticommunism)
   - Nuclear test moratoriums
   - Nuclear weapon research and development
   - Across-the-board increases or cuts in defense spending
   - Authorizations of the use of force
IV. Multilateralism vs. unilateralism ($n = 113$): Liberals are more willing to support international treaties and institutions than conservatives.
   - Support for international institutions (UN, IMF, World Bank, international criminal court)
   - International arms control treaties (chemical weapons ban, nuclear test ban, land mine ban, arms reduction agreements)

one of the ideological issues identified in the dataset, then the vote on the package was coded in the relevant category. In this sense, the classification scheme is weighted toward identifying an appropriate ideological category; if there is a case to be made that the involvement of any ideological issue could have influenced senators' voting decisions, then the vote is classified as such. This means that the categories are defined expansively; a vote does not need to be narrowly targeted on an ideological controversy in order to be classed in the categories defined in this dataset.

For nominations, appropriations, and trade agreements it was not possible to classify votes on the basis of legislative language alone. For these, the debate in the *Congressional Record* was examined to determine if a senator made an argument relating to any of the ideological issues specified above. If during a debate on a nomination a senator expressed concern about the nominee's views on economic, social, or military policy, then the nomination was coded into the appropriate category.[12] When the debate revealed that an appropriations bill was controversial because of overall spending levels, it was coded as involving an ideological issue.[13] When a trade agreement or trade legislation was objected to because of its effect on environmental and labor protections in the United States, the vote was coded in the economic policy category.[14]

Procedural and parliamentary votes were coded based on the underlying policy issue at stake. If the underlying issue fell into one of the specified categories, then these votes were coded as having ideological content. For example, a motion to waive the Budget Act to permit consideration of a permanent repeal of the estate tax was coded as an *economic issue* (in the "distribution of the tax burden" category). A motion to table an amendment restricting government funding for abortions in the District of Columbia was classed as a *social issue*.

A little more than 40 percent of all roll-call votes taken from 1981 through 2004 can be categorized as having "ideological content" using this scheme.[15] Economic issues are by far the most common type ($n = 2,232$), with regulatory issues dominating the economic policy agenda ($n = 904$). Social issues came up about one-third as often as economic issues ($n = 672$). Issues tapping the hawk vs. dove cleavage ($n = 368$) and multilateralism vs. unilateralism disputes ($n = 113$) constitute only a small proportion of the roll-call agenda.

The Ideological Content of Partisanship

How much partisanship in congressional voting behavior can be attributed to conflict over the ideological issues identified in this study? As an initial rough cut at the question, figure 3.1 displays separately the issue composition of all roll-call votes on which senators did and did not divide along party lines.[16] As can be seen here, a much larger proportion of party votes than of nonparty votes had identifiable ideological content: only 23 percent of the votes that failed to divide on party lines involved issues in any of the ideological categories while fully 56 percent of all party votes involved ideological issues.[17]

Nevertheless, it is striking that party votes *regularly* take place on issues that cannot be described using conventional understandings of left-right conflict: 44 percent of all the party votes that occurred over the period involved issues that could not be classified in any of the ideological categories identified in the dataset. Conflict between Republicans and Democrats

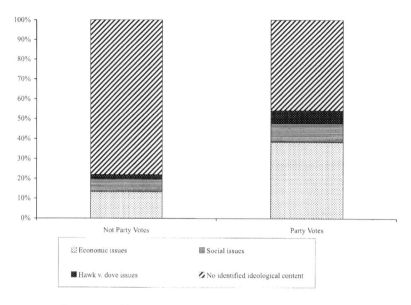

FIGURE 3.1. Issue composition of party votes and nonparty votes in the Senate, 97th–108th Congress.

goes far beyond their disagreements on government redistribution, regulation, government's share of the economy, progressive taxation, social issues (abortion, gay rights, etc.), and military policy. Votes involving none of these issues regularly break along party lines. There is far more congressional party conflict than can be comprehended within conventional understandings of political ideology in American politics.

The proportion of party conflict that can be attributed to ideological differences between liberals and conservatives does not vary wildly from Congress to Congress over the period. For each Congress from 1981 to 2004, figure 3.2 displays the proportion of all party conflict that occurred on the ideological issues identified in this study and the proportion that took place on issues falling into none of the ideological categories.[18] Around half of conflict between Republicans and Democrats can be explained by conventional understandings of the different policy preferences of conservatives and liberals in contemporary American politics. But left-right issues do not account for more than 60 percent of the party conflict that occurred in any Congress in the study. Republicans and Democrats disagree about far more than liberals and conservatives do.

One should not minimize the importance of ideological conflict. Nearly all types of ideological issues are associated with dramatically increased partisanship. Table 3.2 displays the percentage of Senate roll-call votes within each issue type on which at least a majority of Republicans disagreed with at least a majority of Democrats. Across the whole time period, 53 percent of Senate roll calls were party votes. By comparison, 72 percent of all votes involving any of the ideological issues resulted in a party division. Votes dealing with any of the economic policy issues broke along party lines 76 percent of the time. Votes on social issues resulted in party divisions 60 percent of the time. Partisanship is so highly pronounced on economic policy, and economic issues arise so frequently on the Senate agenda, that disagreement over the government's role in the economy clearly figures as the most important ideological issue differentiating the parties.

All but one of the ideological issues identified in the study was a highly potent source of party conflict. When the Senate considered votes on the distribution of the tax burden or government's share of the economy, a party vote occurred more than 80 percent of the time on average. More than 70 percent of all votes involving regulations of private economic activity and redistributive social programs also divided along party lines. The hawk vs. dove cleavage ($n=368$) was also highly partisan: 78 percent of

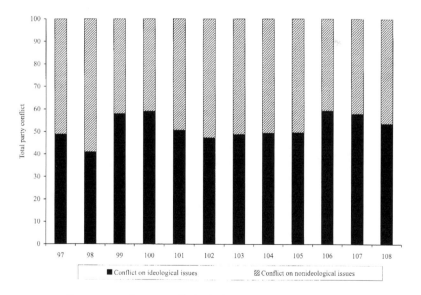

FIGURE 3.2. Issue content of party conflict in the Senate, by Congress.

TABLE 3.2 **Ideological content and partisanship in Senate roll-call votes, 97th–108th Congress**

	Did the Senate divide on party lines?		
Did the vote present an ideological issue?	Yes (%)	No (%)	n
Any economic policy issue	75.7	24.3	2232
Government's share of the economy	81.4	18.4	505
Regulation of private economic activity	71.7	28.3	904
Distribution of the tax burden	82.0	18.0	261
Redistributive social programs	72.5	27.5	512
More than one economic policy category	92.0	8.0	50
Social issue	60.4	39.6	672
Hawk vs. dove issue	78.5	21.5	368
Multilateralism vs. unilateralism	48.7	51.3	113
More than one category of ideological issue	64.7	35.3	34
No identifiable ideological content	39.4	60.6	5000
Any ideological content	72.0	28.0	3420
Average	52.7	47.9	8597

Note: The difference of means are statistically significant ($p < .001$) for every category of vote except for multilateralism vs. unilateralism. Votes on multilateralism vs. unilateralism issues are not more partisan than the typical matter considered in the Senate.

votes on these issues divided at least a majority of Republicans from at least a majority of Democrats. The least polarizing ideological issue was foreign policy multilateralism vs. unilateralism ($n = 113$), which sparked a party division less than half of the time (49 percent), a lower level of partisanship than on the average matter considered in the Senate.[19]

Despite the importance of ideology for congressional partisanship, the data reveal that there is far more voting along party lines than would be predicted on the basis of the ideological content of the congressional agenda alone. Even when issues had no identifiable ideological content, roll-call votes still divided along party lines 39 percent of the time. Clearly, party voting is at best an inexact proxy for the ideological content of votes.

Party Polarization or Improved Teamsmanship?

The dramatic increase in partisan conflict represents one of the most striking developments in Congress over the past 25 years. Figure 3.3 displays a measure of this rising partisanship, the average party difference score for all Senate votes each Congress from 1981 to 2004. The increases shown here are striking: senators in the 107th Congress were fully 63 percent more divided along party lines than senators in the 97th Congress. Marked increases in Senate partisanship began in the 102d Congress and climbed steadily over the next three Congresses. Party conflict leveled off at slightly lower levels in the 105th and 107th Congresses, but jumped back to near its 1995–1996 peak in the 108th Congress.

Journalists and commentators typically describe this growing party differentiation in ideological terms. Columnist Robert J. Samuelson (2004) encapsulates the conventional wisdom: "Democrats are more liberal, Republicans are more conservative, and 'moderates' are scarcer." "Where each party used to have an ideological mixture, each is now more clearly defined in opposition to the other," writes David S. Broder (2007), "The result is a Republican Party that is far more universally (and stridently) conservative; and a Democratic Party whose center of gravity has moved equally far to the left." The conventional wisdom extends beyond the op-ed pages, with journalists appraising the results of retirements and electoral defeats as "Republicans shifting more to the right and Democrats more to the left" (Dewar and Pianin 2004). There is some disagreement on whether polarization has meant both parties diverging from one another or if one party is primarily responsible for the shift. "American politics has become more polarized because Republicans have shifted to the right, and Democrats haven't followed them," argues Paul Krugman (2002), "The right is on the offensive; the left—occupying the position formerly known as the center—wants to hold the line." In an earlier era, Charles Krauthammer

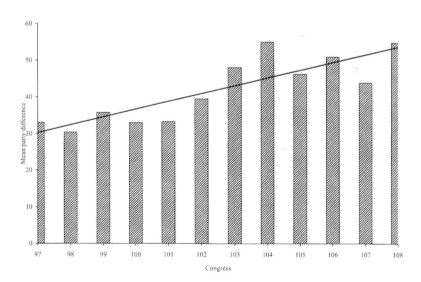

FIGURE 3.3. Party conflict in the Senate, by Congress.

(1988) opined, "The real Democratic story this year is that centrists need not apply. At the presidential level, the McGovernization of the Democratic party is complete." Regardless of who is to "blame," there is little disagreement that the two parties in the United States have become more ideologically polarized in recent decades.

Aggregate roll-call data do not, however, speak for themselves. Higher levels of partisan disagreement in congressional roll-call voting behavior do not necessarily indicate ideological polarization. The parties may simply be working together more effectively as teams, without respect to issue content. If the parties become more successful at negotiating deals among fellow partisans and then holding those agreements together through bloc voting (as will be discussed in chap. 6) then partisanship would go up across the board, regardless of whether issues have anything to do with matters that differentiate liberals from conservatives in American politics. Without disaggregating votes by subject matter, it is not possible to interpret shifts in aggregate voting behavior.

Are the parties farther apart on traditional left-right issues? Are they more differentiated on nonideological issues? Or have gaps between the parties widened across the board? Table 3.3 displays the results of a simple analysis in which the levels of party differentiation in different categories of roll-call votes are regressed on year. Results show that the parties are more different from one another in every category of vote, regardless of issue content. Year takes a positive, statistically significant coefficient in every regression model. Even on issues that bear no relationship to conventional distinctions between liberals and conservatives, Senate Republicans and Democrats became notably more distinct from one another in their voting behavior between 1981 and 2004.

There is certainly evidence of significant ideological polarization. Indeed, intensifying partisanship was considerably more pronounced on ideological than on nonideological issues. The coefficient on year in the model of party conflict on ideological issues is nearly three times as large as in the model for nonideological issues. The increases in party polarization were most striking on tax, regulatory, and social issues. Multilateralism vs. unilateralism issues also became a greater source of party conflict, particularly during the tenures of Presidents Bill Clinton and George W. Bush.

The parties ran away from one another on ideological issues faster than on other types of issues, but rising partisanship was not confined to the usual left-right disputes. Around two-thirds of the increased partisanship can be explained by party polarization on ideological issues, but just over

TABLE 3.3 **Trends in party differentiation in the Senate, 97th–108th Congress**

Issue content	Time trend (s.e.)
Types of vote	
No identifiable ideological content	.61*** (.06)
Any ideological issue	1.79*** (.07)
Economic issues	1.67*** (.08)
Government's share of the economy	1.66*** (.15)
Regulations	1.78*** (.15)
Distribution of the tax burden	1.89*** (.22)
Redistributive programs	1.41*** (.17)
Social issues	2.06*** (.14)
Hawk vs. dove issues	1.33*** (.20)
Multilateralism vs. unilateralism	2.47*** (.45)

*p < .05; **p < .01; ***p < .001, two-tailed tests.

one-third of the rise occurred on issues that fell into none of this study's broad ideological categories. There is more to the story of contemporary congressional partisanship than an ideological sorting out of the two major parties. The parties have also become better coordinated as institutionalized teams. The balance of this book will seek to provide more insight into party coordination and conflict on nonideological issues.

Conclusion

In order to understand congressional party politics, there is no escape from interpretation. Roll-call data cannot interpret themselves; voting patterns are inherently ambiguous. To understand congressional party politics, it is necessary to pay attention to the substantive issues at stake. If "liberalism" means something other than "generally supporting the Democratic party" and "conservatism" means something other than "generally supporting the Republican party," then ideological concepts must be defined separately from party members' observed voting behavior.

To reduce all partisan voting patterns to differing "ideology" or "policy preferences" is to assume away all of the *political* reasons that prompt members of Congress to work with and through their parties. If members stand to gain *anything* from cooperating with fellow partisans—for example, advancement in the leadership, goodwill and reciprocity from fellow partisans, greater power over national policy, an enhanced collective party reputation—then it is necessary to consider members' *interests*, not just their ideologies, as a potential source of party conflict. Members' political interests will be in play on both ideological and nonideological issues. But the effects of political considerations become more distinguishable from members' policy preferences on issues that do not involve left-right disputes. When Congress considers issues that do not relate to the policy differences between liberals and conservatives, the ideological differences between Republicans and Democrats cannot be the direct cause of party conflict. In such cases, party conflict must have other sources.

By employing conventional definitions of liberalism and conservatism, this study disaggregates roll-call votes depending on whether they involve matters of ideological dispute in American politics. Doing so yields findings that are of both substantive and theoretical importance for understanding congressional partisanship.

First, I find there is far more party structure in roll-call voting than one would expect if all party conflict originated in individual members' ideological inclinations and shared ideology were the only source of "party glue." As a baseline for comparison, it is possible to calculate the probability of a party vote occurring purely by accident. If an issue does not speak to matters that can be situated on the left-right ideological continuum—such that the greater average liberalism of Democrats and the greater average conservatism of Republicans can create partisan structure in voting—then voting purely on the basis of individual policy preferences would require each member to make an assessment of the policy merits. Is manned space flight a good use of NASA funds? Would a reorganized VA meet veterans' needs better? Assuming that the probability of each member voting yea is .65 (which is the mean percentage of members voting yea across all votes in the dataset), the probability of a party vote occurring randomly in a Senate with 50 Republicans and 50 Democrats is less than .01.[20] In other words, fewer than one out of 100 votes on nonideological issues should break along party lines simply by chance.

The fact that 39 percent of votes on nonideological issues still divide along party lines means that there is a tremendous amount of nonrandom

behavior in Senate voting that breaks according to members' party affiliation. To understand this behavior, it is necessary to go beyond ideology,
to consider how parties can cut deals internally to structure behavior on
any kind of issue and to account for how the two parties' diverging political interests can drive their members apart. Partisan cue-taking, caucus
activity, agenda-setting, intraparty negotiation, deal-making, coordination, and leadership all become highly relevant. Collective decisionmaking cannot be reduced to individual members' fixed and preexisting policy
preferences.

Second, this disaggregation provides a new perspective on the increased
levels of partisanship in recent years. The findings show that greater party
conflict is more than party polarization on an ideological continuum; it is
also the result of stronger, more effective partisan coordination across the
board. There was notable party polarization on the left-right continuum
between 1981 and 2004, but contemporary Republicans and Democrats
simply come into conflict with one another over all types of issues to a
greater extent than they did in the past. The parties diverged more on everything, not simply on matters that differentiate liberals from conservatives. Recognition of these trends has lead journalist Ronald Brownstein
(2007, 14–15) to lament that partisans in the contemporary Congress do
not disagree only on matters of ideological principle, but simply "reflexively vote against any initiative that originates with the other [party]."

The central purpose of the remaining chapters of this book is to investigate why the parties take opposing positions on so many matters uncon-
nected to conventional understandings of liberalism and conservatism.
So far, the analysis provided here only shows that ideological differences
cannot account for nearly all the conflict that occurs between Republicans
and Democrats in Congress. As an effort to identify the sources of partisan
strife that go beyond ideology, the following three chapters will examine a
series of important political motives. These political motives are likely to
lead congressional parties to oppose one another separate from the different ideological preferences of party members: (1) presidential leadership;
(2) concern for party reputations on good-government matters; and
(3) procedural and parliamentary conflict. Chapter 4 focuses on one of the
most important but understudied sources of congressional party coordination and conflict, partisan team play on presidential agenda items.

Dividers, Not Uniters

*Presidential Leadership and
Legislative Partisanship*

Political actors often refer to "political motives" for supporting or opposing presidents. Presidential advisor Karl Rove, for example, complained that Democrats opposed some of President George W. Bush's initiatives not out of sincere policy disagreement but because they wanted to deny him a political success or because they did not want to buck their party leaders: "This was a great idea, and Democrats opposed it. And why? Because they didn't want to give this president a victory. I had Democrats tell me, face to face, 'We'd love to work with you on Social Security, but our leadership won't let me,' or, 'I'd love to work with you on Social Security, but my leaders are afraid of giving the president a political victory.'"[1] Kingdon (1981, 181) quotes an anonymous congressman who likewise resents party opponents who have regularly voted against his party's president for "political motives"; at the same time, he acknowledges his own inclination to return the favor when his party does not control the presidency: "When my guys are in the White House, the vote is close, and they need my vote, then I'll go along. But when theirs are there, and they've always voted against my guys out of political motives, then why should I go along with them?" Similarly, an anonymous senator quoted by Matthews (1960, 140) concedes that he has political motives himself in that he is likely to vote for his own president's proposals when his support is needed: "I believe that if the Republican party is going to stay in power it must support the President. As a result, I sometimes 'hold my nose'—as the saying goes—and go along with the Administration, though I might personally prefer to vote the other way."

As a first step to go beyond ideology in accounting for party conflict in Congress, this chapter argues that presidential leadership generates important political incentives that are likely to increase cohesion within both major parties and to exacerbate conflict between them. As elected officials, members of Congress evaluate administration initiatives with an eye not only to the merits of the proposals but also toward their own political interests. They recognize that in handling an administration's agenda, they are doing more than making decisions on public policy; they are taking actions that affect the collective reputation of the national parties. Whether presidents are able to pass their agenda items, maintain support within their own party, and garner bipartisan assent to their policy proposals all affect perceptions of their leadership and, by extension, the national reputation of their parties. More than the shape of national policy is at stake when Congress considers the president's agenda. Party reputations, which are vital to members' ability to win elections and to gain (or maintain) party control of national governing institutions, are also on the line.

In short, members' dual considerations of politics and policy are likely to make the congressional politics of the presidential agenda distinctive. A "president is a leader of his party, no matter how strong or weak his powers might otherwise be" (Aldrich and Rohde 2000, 67). Given the president's unique status as national party leader, members of Congress know that the way they handle a president's priorities will affect his party's collective reputation. Presidential successes create credit-claiming opportunities for the president's party, and thus a president's fellow partisans "recognize that they have an interest in making him look good" (Sundquist 1981, 423). The reverse of Sundquist's point also applies: in a two-party system a party can benefit by resisting, criticizing, and otherwise making the opposing party's president look bad. Members of the opposing party also have a political interest in denying the president and his party credit-claiming opportunities. These divergent political interests are likely to exert a contrary pull on the two parties' behavior as Congress considers presidential proposals.

Put differently, presidents are the "lightening rod of national politics" (Skowronek 1993, 20). As such, presidential leadership serves to demarcate and deepen lines of cleavage between the parties in Congress. If this argument is accurate, presidents will stimulate and intensify partisan controversy on the issues they champion.

To test whether presidential involvement makes issues more party polarizing than they would otherwise be, it is necessary to control for issue content. Some types of issues obviously are inherently more controversial in policy terms. Using two different classification schemes,[2] this chapter assesses whether roll-call votes within different categories of issues become systematically more polarized along party lines when presidents champion them as part of their legislative agenda compared with the level of party division that occurs on these categories of issues when they are considered in Congress without being part of a president's legislative agenda. Controlling for both issue content and other factors likely to affect the amount of partisan division on roll-call votes, the analysis yields three principal findings.

First, presidential leadership tends to result in wider gaps between the two parties in Congress, controlling for issue type. Party conflict is higher on presidential agenda items than one would expect compared with baselines on the same types of issues when they are not part of a president's agenda. The effect is evident across most areas of national policy, in both domestic and foreign affairs. Votes on generally uncontroversial types of issues are more likely to split down party lines when presidential politics comes into play. In addition, even the most divisive ideological issues in party politics become more polarized than they usually are when presidents take a leadership role on them.

Second, the effects of presidential leadership are generally symmetrical within the two parties. Controlling for issue content, presidential leadership is associated with higher levels of cohesion in both parties. In other words, the partisan clashes on presidential agenda items are not merely the result of members of the president's party enhancing their support for their president; it is also the result of strengthened partisan resistance among the president's opposition. Presidential leadership affects the behavior of both parties, not just the president's own party.

Third, the prominence of presidential agenda items on the congressional agenda can partly account for the growth in overall partisan conflict in Senate roll-call voting between 1981 and 2004. Increases over time in the proportion of the congressional roll-call agenda dedicated to presidential agenda items have contributed to the striking levels of partisanship in the contemporary Senate.

Presidents and Party Brand Names

Between 1993 and 2001, the two parties reversed their positions on the merits of federally sponsored testing in local public schools. In 1993, President Clinton proposed Goals 2000, an education initiative providing for voluntary testing for students in elementary and secondary schools. In doing so, Clinton was supported by Democrats in Congress and opposed by Republicans, who protested the importance of leaving education and testing up to local school districts.[3] In 2001, President Bush proposed an even more ambitious educational assessment program providing for mandatory tests for all students in grades three through eight throughout the United States. In that endeavor, Bush was supported by Republicans and opposed by Democrats, who raised their own concerns about local control and unfunded mandates.[4] If members voted their policy preferences alone, wholesale partisan flip-flops of this nature would be very difficult to explain.

Along similar lines, a party's willingness to support an increase in the debt limit seems to be driven by whether that party controls the presidency. During the Reagan years, Democrats consistently opposed raising the public debt limit, while Republicans supported it.[5] During the Clinton presidency, Republicans regularly opposed raising the public debt limit, while Democrats supported it.[6] Under President George W. Bush, Republicans supported raising the debt limit, while Democrats repeatedly resisted it.[7] In light of these reversals, it would be naive to interpret these party-line votes as sincere expressions of members' views on the appropriate level of publicly held debt in the United States.

Instead, this chapter proposes that we consider how strategic responses to presidential leadership shape legislative party politics. Members of Congress have an electoral interest in the collective image of their parties, and they seek to enhance this image by cooperating with fellow partisans and party leaders to deliver on a popular policy agenda (Cox and McCubbins 1993, 110–35, and 2005; Evans 2001; Matthews and Stimson 1975, 95–97). But "far more than individual members of Congress . . . [presidents] have a particular responsibility for . . . preserving the recognizable meaning of the party label" (Whittington and Carpenter 2003, 500). No member of Congress is as important as the president in defining the collective images of the parties. The president is the most influential agenda-setter in national politics (Baumgartner and Jones 1993). When presidents prioritize an issue, they can set the legislative agenda "single handedly" (Kingdon 1995, 23). Presidents are capable of "creating attention where none exists" (Edwards and Wood 1999, 342), outstripping all members of Congress in their ability to garner media attention.

Responding to presidential leadership is one of senators' most important strategies for affecting party reputations and partisan "brand names." When a president takes a position on an issue, it creates a benchmark for measuring his and his party's effectiveness. Members of the president's party enhance their own party's collective reputation for strong, effective, coherent action by supporting their president's agenda. If members of the president's party take these political incentives into account, they will be predisposed toward support of the president, separate from the policy preferences they may have on presidential agenda issues.

At the same time, members of the opposition party often stand to gain in political terms by withholding support from the president's agenda. This logic holds regardless of the opposing party's majority or minority status. If a party wants to undermine the case for a president's reelection or his party's continuance in government, its members must find grounds on which to oppose the president's initiatives. A party needs to distinguish itself from an opposing president's policies. As Sundquist (1988, 630) observed, "If the president sends a proposal to Capitol Hill or takes a foreign policy stand, the opposition . . . simply must reject it. Otherwise they are saying the president is a wise and prudent leader. That would only strengthen him and his party for the next election, and how can [they] . . . do that, when their whole object is to defeat him when the time arrives?" Even if the opposing party is unable to legislate in accord with its own preferences, it may be able to score political victories by associating a president of the other party with political failures.

In short, when presidents stake their reputation for leadership on an issue, they are likely to alter the politics of its congressional consideration. If this logic holds true, contrary political incentives will pull the parties farther apart on the issues presidents prioritize.

Partisan Cues and Heuristics

Members' *political motives* are not the only reason that presidential leadership is likely to induce partisan responses in Congress. Members' *policy views* themselves are also likely to be shaped by their positive or negative attitudes toward the president, attitudes that are partly a function of their own party identification. A substantial body of research has shown that congressional roll-call voting is affected by patterns of cue-taking (Kingdon 1981; Matthews and Stimson 1975). Members make use of relevant cues for help in many voting decisions. That a legislative proposal is favored by a president of a particular party affords an important cue for members of both parties. When Matthews and Stimson (1975, 94) asked members of Congress whose position they would like to know in a hypothetical voting situation where they could know nothing else, 40 percent identified the president.

Presidential cues, however, will be interpreted differently by members of the two parties in Congress. The literature on public opinion has established the importance of "source cues," meaning that Americans' opinions on policy issues are structured by their attitudes toward the political figures who support or oppose those policies: "Heuristic processing of source cues activates a dynamic in which the individual extends opinion about a source to the policies or issues associated with that source.... with the effect's magnitude dependent on the strength of that approval or disapproval" (Mondak 1993, 171). Much research has shown that partisanship filters receptivity to political messages (Edwards 2003, 218–38; Zaller 1992). As elected officials owing their political careers to one of the two parties, members of Congress undoubtedly identify more strongly with their political parties and have stronger affective responses toward presidents than virtually anyone in the mass public.

Even though members of Congress are far more informed about issues than the mass public, the large number of roll-call votes in every Congress means that they, like respondents on public opinion polls, are frequently asked to make judgments on issues about which they are not well informed. A president's position can serve as a decision-making heuristic. Those members who generally approve of the president are likely to give his policies the benefit of the doubt and those members who generally disapprove of the president will be less inclined to support his policies. For example, House Minority Whip Roy Blunt (R-Mo.) said, "I always had misgivings [about No Child Left Behind].... But I did vote for it on the basis that maybe [President Bush] was right and this was his big domestic initiative and let's give him a chance" (quoted in Baker 2007). Members with less positive views toward President Bush would be more likely to allow their misgivings to prevail and to assume that the president was probably wrong in proposing this initiative. This type of partisan heuristic has the potential to create political contention even on issues that might otherwise have been perceived as uncontroversial.

Data and Coding

In analyzing how presidential leadership affects party polarization, it is necessary to control for the varying levels of preexisting partisan disagreement

on different types of political issues. To do so, I employ two different classification schemes. First, the Policy Agendas Project classifies roll-call votes
based on government function (e.g., agriculture, health, defense, community development, etc.). This classification scheme is exhaustive and mutu-
ally exclusive, and it was designed to "guarantee temporal consistency for
topic categories" (Baumgartner, Jones, and Wilkerson 2002, 33). Second,
I employ the ideological issue dataset discussed in chapter 3 to isolate the
votes that tap ideological divisions on matters of economic, social, and military policy.

Presidential agenda items are identified by whether the roll-call vote
involves a policy issue on which the president took a position in the State
of the Union address immediately preceding the vote. This is a somewhat
broader definition than that frequently used in the scholarly literature:
congressional votes on which the president issued a public position. This
broader definition is appropriate, however, given that this study focuses
on the effect of presidential leadership on congressional partisanship, not
on Congress's policy response to specific presidential requests. Raising a
policy issue in the State of the Union address indicates that the president
is asserting leadership on that issue. Even if the president does not endorse a specific position on particular roll-call votes, presidential standing
is nevertheless affected when Congress disposes of issues that the president has chosen to associate himself with. In any case, there are significant
difficulties with the narrower measure: presidents have long "gamed" the
use of these public statements of position on congressional votes to improve their claims to successful leadership (Rudalevige 2005, 429–30). The
broader definition used here is not affected by this kind of gamesmanship.
If a president makes an issue a priority by requesting action on it in the
State of the Union address, any votes on that topic are treated as involving
a presidential agenda item.

For example, Americorps was one of President Clinton's signature initiatives, a program central to his "New Covenant" vision. He mentioned
the program in nearly every one of his State of the Union addresses, even
inviting Americorps volunteers to sit with the First Lady during his 1995
address. Nevertheless, the administration did not issue a formal position
statement on any votes in the dataset involving Americorps funding, not
even when the Republican majority proposed severe cuts.[8] If I had employed the formal public position measure, I would not have identified as
presidential agenda items any of the Americorps votes after the program's
initial adoption.

To code the presidential agenda status of roll-call votes, every State of the Union address during the period was read line-by-line, highlighting each of the President's action requests (either to pass an initiative or to refrain from passing an initiative). Highlighted items were then transferred to a list that served as a reference point for coding roll-call votes. Each roll-call vote that occurred until the next State of the Union address was measured against the topics on this list. Roll-call votes were coded as involving a presidential agenda item when they dealt with an issue on which the president had requested a course of action from Congress. Appendix A provides a detailed example of the coding process.

Presidential Leadership and Party Conflict

Compared with the House, the Senate offers a better test of the hypothesis that presidential leadership exacerbates partisanship. House floor votes are manipulated by the majority party leadership to a much greater extent than those in the Senate. A wider range of issues can be considered on the Senate floor, providing a more complete picture of members' behavior on issues that are not part of the majority's agenda. In addition, senators face reelection only one-third as often as House members, meaning that many votes on presidential initiatives occur at considerable remove from the next occasion when senators will have to go before the voters to seek reelection. Thus, senators may be less sensitive to the electoral stakes involved in reacting to many presidential proposals, also making the Senate a more rigorous test for the theory.

Comparing partisan divisions on roll-call votes depending on whether issues were mentioned in the State of the Union address provides an initial test of whether presidential leadership exacerbates partisan divisions. Table 4.1 displays the average level of party polarization[9] on Senate roll-call votes between 1981 and 2000 for each major topic in the Policy Agenda Project classification scheme. For 14 out of the 19 functional categories, the average party difference was higher when presidents took a stand on the issue in the immediately preceding State of the Union address than when they did not. These higher levels of partisan division are statistically significant ($p < .01$) for 10 of the categories. Meanwhile, presidential leadership was only associated with lower levels of partisanship in five policy areas, and in these categories the differences were quite small and, in all but one case, statistically insignificant.

Presidential leadership was associated with increases in party difference scores of between 30 percent and 40 percent on votes in the areas
of social welfare, health and defense, as well as labor, employment, and
immigration. Partisanship was between 45 percent and 60 percent higher
when presidents led on education and government operations and on law,
crime, and family issues, as well as on community development and housing. In the areas of international affairs and foreign aid as well as space,
science, and technology, presidential position taking was associated with
increases in partisanship that were even greater than 65 percent.

Remarkably, presidential leadership appears to bring the two parties
closer together in only one area: civil rights ($p < .01$). In the study period,
it appears that President Reagan's support for the reauthorization of the
Voting Rights Act in 1982 and President George H. W. Bush's support for
the civil rights act of 1991—both announced in their State of the Union
addresses—may have facilitated unusual levels of bipartisan agreement
on civil rights issues.

Table 4.2 displays the average level of party division on ideological issues. Because this classification scheme was specifically designed to isolate

TABLE 4.1 **Presidential leadership and party divisions on Senate roll-call votes, by government
function, 1981–2000**

Government function	No presidential leadership (n)		Presidential leadership (n)		Difference
Macroeconomics	54.5	(498)	52.4	(176)	−2.2
Civil rights	41.9	(213)	26.8	(44)	−15.1**
Health	**46.6**	**(269)**	**65.6**	**(93)**	**19.1***
Agriculture	33.2	(274)	36.6	(19)	3.4
Labor, employment, immigration	**43.1**	**(280)**	**58.2**	**(94)**	**15.1***
Education	**50.5**	**(180)**	**75.0**	**(93)**	**24.5***
Environment	38.8	(124)	30.3	(38)	−8.5
Energy	33.8	(140)	36.1	(36)	2.3
Transportation	33.9	(254)	28.6	(22)	−5.3
Law, crime, family issues	**31.6**	**(234)**	**49.8**	**(109)**	**18.2***
Social welfare	**43.1**	**(186)**	**57.3**	**(124)**	**14.2**
Community development and housing	**40.9**	**(88)**	**62.8**	**(26)**	**21.9**
Banking, finance, domestic commerce	36.6	(232)	39.8	(54)	3.2
Defense	**35.1**	**(670)**	**49.1**	**(195)**	**14.0***
Space, science, technology	**32.3**	**(105)**	**62.8**	**(20)**	**30.5***
Foreign trade	29.3	(147)	21.0	(42)	−8.3
International affairs, foreign aid	**22.6**	**(551)**	**37.9**	**(69)**	**15.3***
Government operations	**37.6**	**(1177)**	**56.9**	**(199)**	**19.3***
Public lands and water management	39.4	(199)	46.9	(11)	7.5
Average for all votes	**41.3**	**(6699)**	**56.5**	**(1895)**	**17.1***

Note: Cells show the average Rice Index of party difference score for roll-call votes in each category.
Lines in bold are those in which presidential leadership is associated with higher levels of party conflict.
*$p < .05$; **$p < .01$; *** $p < .001$.

TABLE 4.2 **Presidential leadership and party divisions on Senate roll-call votes, by ideological issue category, 1981–2004**

Ideological issue categories	No presidential leadership (n)		Presidential leadership (n)		Difference
Economic	**58.8**	**(1495)**	**67.6**	**(736)**	**8.8*****
Social	43.9	(528)	44.2	(144)	.3
Hawk vs. dove	54.3	(234)	56.2	(134)	1.9
Government's share of the economy	**66.4**	**(353)**	**76.1**	**(156)**	**9.7*****
Regulation of economic activity	**52.7**	**(654)**	**62.3**	**(252)**	**9.6*****
Distribution of the tax burden	66.0	(140)	71.0	(125)	5.0
Redistributive programs	**55.8**	**(323)**	**65.3**	**(197)**	**9.5*****
Any of the above	**54.9**	**(2453)**	**62.8**	**(1141)**	**7.9*****
None of the above	**30.2**	**(4246)**	**43.9**	**(754)**	**13.7*****

Note: Cells show the average Rice Index of party difference score for roll-call votes in each category.
Lines in bold are those in which presidential leadership is associated with higher levels of party conflict.
$*p < .05; **p < .01; ***p < .001$.

the most divisive issues in American politics, it sets a higher bar for finding any additional effects of presidential leadership. As one would expect, presidential involvement is not associated with increases in partisanship as substantial as those evident using the Policy Agenda Project categories. Nevertheless, in every ideological category votes on issues mentioned by the president in the State of the Union address were more divisive along party lines than votes on issues not mentioned, though there was variation across categories in the magnitude and statistical significance of the effect. Among ideological issues, the effect of presidential leadership was greatest on issues involving regulatory policy, redistributive programs, and government's share of the economy ($p < .001$).

Presidential involvement has little influence on partisanship on votes dealing with social issues and the distribution of the tax burden ($p =$ n.s.). These are clearly party-defining issues regardless of whether a president demands action on them. Generally speaking, taxes and abortion sparked partisan division in the Senate at approximately the same levels regardless of their presidential agenda status. Nevertheless, taken as a group, votes on ideological issues became 13 percent more polarized along party lines when they were the focus of presidential attention ($p < .001$).

Do Presidents Prefer Polarizing Agendas?

Could these findings result from presidents preferring to raise issues that are inherently controversial? If presidents systematically focus their agendas on more polarizing issues, then the higher level of partisanship on presidential agenda items could potentially be the artifact of presidential agenda choices rather than congressional reactions to the president.

One simple way to test whether presidents deliberately steer their agendas toward the most divisive types of issues is to compare the average level of party polarization across the categories of issues mentioned in each State of the Union address with the average level of polarization across the categories of issues not mentioned. To do this, I draw on Baumgartner, Jones, and Wilkerson's State of the Union address dataset, which classifies every sentence in a State of the Union address by its policy content using the Policy Agenda Project classification scheme.[10] Using this, I was able to determine which major policy topics were mentioned in each State of the Union address from 1982–99 and then to compare the average level of party polarization across the topics mentioned with the average level of party polarization on the topics not mentioned. The results are displayed as table 4.3.

The data provide no support for the counter hypothesis that presidents disproportionately focus their addresses on polarizing topics. For 7 of the 18 years available in the dataset, the types of issues included in presiden-

TABLE 4.3 **Are presidential agendas focused on more party-polarizing types of issues?**

| | Average party difference on . . . | | |
Year	Topics mentioned in the State of the Union address	Topics not mentioned in the State of the Union address	*p*
1982	33.2	24.2	n.s.
1983	31.8	29.4	n.s.
1984	**30.3**	**33.2**	**n.s.**
1985	**39.4**	**50.6**	**n.s.**
1986	31.2	28.2	n.s.
1987	**27.1**	**31.7**	**n.s.**
1988	30.9	26.7	n.s.
1989	**32.1**	**40.6**	**n.s.**
1990	**36.8**	**42.8**	**n.s.**
1991	37.0	30.0	n.s.
1992	40.1	36.1	n.s.
1993	54.6	35.0	n.s.
1994	40.1	33.2	n.s.
1995	**52.5**	**60.2**	**n.s.**
1996	53.0	46.4	n.s.
1997	**43.0**	**45.3**	**n.s.**
1998	47.2	38.1	n.s.
1999	56.3	49.2	n.s.

Note: Cells show the average Rice Index of party difference scores for Senate votes on the issue topics that presidents included in their State of the Union addresses and on the issue topics that presidents did not mention in their State of the Union address. Data on the major topics mentioned and not mentioned are drawn from the State of the Union Address Dataset available at policyagendas.org. Years in bold are those in which the topics mentioned in the address were less controversial along party lines than the topics presidents did not mention.

tial addresses are actually *less* party polarizing than the types of issues that presidents declined to include in their agenda.[11] Seeking to tamp down partisan conflict actually seems like a good strategy for presidents facing a hostile Congress. However, in no Congress are the differences in party polarization between the types of issues mentioned and those not mentioned statistically significant. The data provide no evidence that the issue content of presidential agendas is more focused on party polarizing issues than the congressional agenda generally.[12]

Generally speaking, it appears that the types of issues incorporated into presidential agendas are broadly representative of the issues considered in Congress in terms of party polarization. Presidents do not shy away from partisan controversy, but there is no evidence that they actively seek it out.

Any reading of State of the Union addresses reveals that presidents devote significant portions of their agendas to relatively uncontroversial items. This is not to deny that presidents use their addresses to assert leadership on ideologically divisive matters, such as universal health care, Social Security personal accounts, and tax cuts. But presidents highlight many issues that do not raise issues of the role of government in the economy, redistribution across classes, the "culture war," the use of military force, or any of the ideological issues that tend to divide Democrats from Republicans. Examples of relatively noncontroversial issues that *regularly* appear as presidential agenda items include: space exploration; military pay and veterans' benefits; homeland security; grant program consolidations; medical research funding; and targeted tax credits for charitable contributions, care-giving, and education expenditures. Moreover, presidents do not confine themselves to leadership on major issues. For example, recent addresses have asked for congressional action on a regulation requiring V-Chips in new televisions, an initiative to permit public schools to require school uniforms, and a small grant program to encourage the development of biofuels out of woodchips and switchgrass. There is nothing in these data to suggest that the causal arrow runs in reverse, that is, that the higher levels of conflict on presidential agenda items are a result of presidents first anticipating the issues that will be more controversial and then actively building their agendas around those issues.

Modeling Party Polarization on Senate Votes

In order to assess fully the effect of presidential leadership on congressional partisanship, it is necessary to control for several potential causes of spurious correlation. Separate multiple regression models are estimated for the roll-call votes in each of the functional and ideological issue categories. The dependent variable is the Rice Index of party difference for each roll-call vote. Controls in the model take into account:

- *Votes on procedural matters and on amendments:* The congressional voting behavior literature has demonstrated that party-line votes are more likely to occur on procedural and parliamentary matters (Cox and McCubbins 1993; Theriault 2006) and on amendments (Roberts and Smith 2003; Rohde 1991). If a greater proportion of presidential agenda items are handled with procedural motions or amendments, then the higher level of partisanship on these issues might have nothing to do with presidential involvement. To control for this, the model includes *procedural* and *passage*, dummy variables coded as 1 when votes occurred on procedural motions and on final passage, respectively.
- *Growing partisanship over time:* Partisanship dramatically increased over the study's time period. Presidential agenda items would spuriously appear to be more partisan if more such votes in any category occurred in later Congresses than earlier Congresses. The models thus include a time trend, *year.*
- *Constituency change:* Overall levels of partisanship in congressional voting may also be affected by the number of senators representing states that strongly tilt toward one party. Previous studies have found that an increase in "safe seats" has exacerbated congressional partisanship (Jacobson 2004; Lowry and Shipan 2002). Constituency partisanship is measured by *safe seats,* a measure developed by Abramowitz, Alexander, and Gunning (2006) to capture the number of senators representing states that lean heavily toward their own party. This indicator is the number of states in which the presidential candidate of the incumbent senator's party ran at least 10 percentage points ahead of the candidate's national average.

Controlling for these potential causes of spurious correlation, tables 4.4 and 4.5 present separate regression results for roll-call votes in each of the functional policy categories and in each of the ideological issue categories. The findings displayed here confirm that the effects of presidential leadership evident in the bivariate analysis above are not the spurious result of any of these factors.

The control variables performed as expected. In nearly every category, votes on *procedural* motions were more partisan than votes on substantive legislation ($p < .05$). In almost every category, votes on final *passage* were less partisan than votes on amendments. Reflecting the growth in party polarization over the time period, *year* always took a positive coefficient that was usually statistically significant. Votes occurring in Congresses in which more senators held safe seats tended to be more partisan, with *safe seats* usually taking a positive coefficient, statistically significant in 7 of the 19 functional categories. Alternative specifications of the models (not shown here) were also attempted. The presence or absence of divided government does not modify these results.

The findings in table 4.4 strongly suggest that presidential leadership has a wide-ranging influence on congressional politics. Presidential involvement appears to spark intensified partisanship across most substantive areas of national policy: effects are especially pronounced on social welfare, education, health, international affairs, and defense.

Significantly, the policy areas where presidential leadership has no statistically significant effect on congressional partisanship tend to be those that are heavily distributive (Lowi 1964) in nature: transportation, agriculture, public lands and water, energy, and environment.[13] To a greater extent than most public policy, these programs are "tied to the land" in that they provide concentrated benefits to senators' geographic constituencies (Arnold 1990, 25–29). They are also the policy areas most often cited as examples of "iron triangles," self-serving networks of constituency-based interest groups, members of Congress, and career bureaucrats that cooperate together to thwart presidential influence (Lee 2005, 296–97). Presidents do attempt to assert leadership in these areas (as is evident from the numbers of cases found in the second column of table 4.1). However, these are policy areas where senators may be more concerned with providing for local constituents than with cultivating a collective party brand name. Members' votes in these areas are likely affected more by their electoral interests in "bringing home the bacon" than their interest in sustaining or embarrassing an administration.

The results displayed in table 4.5 reveal that presidential leadership has a measurable impact on the party politics of even the most ideologically divisive political issues, issues on which individual senators are likely to have relatively well-defined ideological preferences. *Redistributive* programs, as well as *economic* issues generally, tend to be more party polarized when presidents include them in their agenda. Holding all other variables in the model constant at their means, presidential leadership deepens the divide between the parties on *redistributive programs* by an estimated 18 percent[14] and on *economic* programs generally by an estimated 7 percent.[15] Similarly, although it was not apparent from the bivariate analysis shown

TABLE 4.4 Presidential leadership and partisan division in the Senate, by government function, 1981–2000

	Macroeconomics	Civil rights	Health	Agriculture	Labor, employment	Education	Environment	Energy	Transportation	Social welfare
Pres. leadership	-.46	**-7.38**	**14.16**	1.76	**6.92**	**20.62**	-5.44	2.78	-8.85	**15.28**
	(2.70)	(4.05)	(3.92)	(6.42)	(3.78)	(3.76)	(4.58)	(4.17)	(5.79)	(3.43)
Safe seats	**.69**	.31	**1.16**	.30	**.56**	.92	.99	**.97**	**-.64**	-.09
	(.19)	(.24)	(.30)	(.26)	(.26)	(.31)	(.32)	(.28)	(.26)	(.29)
Year	**1.39**	**2.41**	**.79**	.45	**1.44**	**.86**	**2.12**	**1.33**	**.53**	**1.27**
	(.19)	(.29)	(.32)	(.27)	(.31)	(.31)	(.35)	(.36)	(.27)	(.29)
Procedural	**15.75**	**8.69**	**17.90**	**9.40**	**17.49**	**23.74**	**15.33**	**7.05**	**6.56**	**28.49**
	(2.64)	(3.18)	(3.27)	(3.53)	(3.25)	(3.66)	(4.38)	(4.13)	(3.65)	(3.62)
Passage	.26	**-7.21**	-7.06	**-16.10**	**-11.51**	**-15.80**	**-18.08**	**-19.31**	**-25.00**	**-18.00**
	(3.28)	(4.48)	(6.20)	(4.70)	(4.84)	(6.28)	(5.23)	(6.12)	(4.55)	(4.92)
F	**24.67**	**18.07**	**19.58**	**7.52**	**18.69**	**26.48**	**22.87**	**10.22**	**13.89**	**33.51**
Adj. R^2	.16	.26	.22	.12	.20	.33	.42	.23	.20	.35
N	673	256	361	292	373	272	161	175	274	309

	Community developm't	Law, crime, family	Banking, finance	Defense	Space, science, technology	Foreign trade	Intern'l affairs	Gov't ops	Public lands, water
Pres. leadership	**23.45**	**13.71**	3.80	**12.86**	**25.63**	-7.48	**14.43**	**10.89**	-5.72
	(6.51)	(3.26)	(4.21)	(2.23)	(6.54)	(5.03)	(3.19)	(2.34)	(7.85)
Safe seats	-.02	.38	.25	.13	-.28	**.68**	**-.35**	**-.53**	**-1.10**
	(.45)	(.24)	(.27)	(.14)	(.39)	(.29)	(.16)	(.13)	(.29)
Year	.50	**2.06**	**1.32**	.26	**.79**	.30	.25	**.92**	**1.20**
	(.49)	(.27)	(.28)	(.17)	(.40)	(.34)	(.19)	(.15)	(.29)
Procedural	**14.50**	**18.80**	**15.01**	**18.64**	**18.05**	**14.73**	**21.40**	**29.43**	4.51
	(5.83)	(3.05)	(3.78)	(2.01)	(4.96)	(3.98)	(2.30)	(1.83)	(4.57)
Passage	-12.48	-2.33	**-15.58**	**-14.72**	-6.89	-3.77	**-8.43**	**-8.66**	**-33.66**
	(7.23)	(4.31)	(4.83)	(2.70)	(6.87)	(5.23)	(2.49)	(2.32)	(4.92)
F	**5.95**	**26.75**	**15.06**	**41.92**	**10.04**	**6.96**	**33.36**	**102.26**	**24.74**
Adj. R^2	.22	.28	.21	.20	.30	.16	.21	.27	.38
N	113	342	285	864	124	188	619	1375	209

Note: Dependent variable is the Rice Index for party difference for each roll call vote in the category. Entries are OLS coefficients (standard errors in parentheses) Coefficients in bold are statistically significant ($p < .05$). Vote classification scheme developed by Frank Baumgartner and Bryan Jones; data and codebook available at the Policy Agendas Project website (www.policyagendas.org).

TABLE 4.5 **Presidential leadership and partisan division in the Senate, by ideological issue, 1981–2004**

	Social issues	Hawk vs. dove	Economic issues	Gv't share of economy	Regulations	Distribution of tax burden	Redistributive programs	None	Any
Pres. leadership	-2.81	**5.52**	**4.43**	3.89	3.89	.20	**10.30**	**10.90**	**3.53**
	(2.19)	(2.32)	(1.27)	(2.74)	(2.09)	(3.50)	(2.38)	(1.16)	(.99)
Safe seats	.01	**-.32**	.05	-.07	-.46	.53	.002	.01	.03
	(.13)	(.17)	(.09)	(.20)	(.15)	(.28)	(.17)	(.06)	(.06)
Year	**2.19**	**1.42**	**1.51**	**1.58**	**2.00**	**1.56**	**1.09**	**.51**	**1.61**
	(.14)	(.20)	(.09)	(.16)	(.18)	(.27)	(.16)	(.06)	(.07)
Procedural	**10.37**	**10.68**	**8.74**	**6.95**	**9.12**	**6.65**	**14.20**	**25.01**	**10.11**
	(1.88)	(2.27)	(1.24)	(2.46)	(1.95)	(3.23)	(2.48)	(.92)	(.90)
Passage	**-10.07**	-.55	**-10.40**	-5.39	**-18.90**	1.84	**-21.36**	**-11.06**	**-12.85**
	(3.18)	(4.00)	(1.90)	(3.68)	(3.04)	(5.83)	(3.97)	(1.14)	(1.42)
F	**55.84**	**16.89**	**111.32**	**29.01**	**54.32**	**16.87**	**36.01**	**283.65**	**196.26**
Adj. R²	.29	.18	.20	.22	.23	.23	.25	.22	.21
N	671	367	2230	508	905	264	519	4998	3593

Note: Dependent variable is the Rice Index for party difference for each roll call vote in the category. Entries are OLS coefficients (standard errors in parentheses). Coefficients in bold are statistically significant ($p < .05$).

in table 4.2, presidential leadership also has a statistically significant effect ($p < .05$) on the politics of *hawk vs. dove* issues once the multiple regression model controls for other confounding factors. The gap between the parties grows by 10 percent on military policy votes when they involve presidential agenda items.[16]

The finding that senators' voting behavior on *social issues* is not much affected by presidential position-taking is consistent with previous scholarship reporting that party pressure has little effect on "conscience issues" such as abortion, affirmative action, gay rights, and school prayer (Ansolabehere, Snyder, and Stewart 2001a). Similarly, presidential involvement appears not to influence partisanship in votes on *government's share of the economy* or the *distribution of the tax burden.* On these hot-button issues, members may be more concerned to maintain a clear voting record than with how their votes reflect on a president's leadership.

When all votes involving ideological issues are grouped together (shown in the last column of table 4.5), presidential leadership still systematically widens the gap between the parties ($p < .001$). However, the effect of presidential leadership is greatest on issues that do not fit into any of the ideological categories identified. When all roll-call votes that fall into none of the ideological categories are grouped together, presidential agenda status is one of the best predictors of the overall level of partisanship, with party polarization increasing by fully 34 percent when presidents highlight them in their State of the Union addresses.[17] It appears that presidential leadership is most important to party politics when ideological principles are not clearly at stake and when lines of party cleavage are not already well established. On such issues, presidents help define what the parties stand for as members organize to support or oppose the president.

Presidential Leadership and Party Cohesion

A question not answered by the preceding analysis is whether the higher levels of party conflict on presidential agenda items occur because of changes in the behavior of the president's party, the opposition party, or both simultaneously. The theory advanced here is that members of both legislative parties have important political incentives as they react to presidential leadership. It is not only that members of the president's party are more inclined to support their party leader in the White House. Members of the president's opposition party are also expected to stiffen their opposition because of the political stakes involved in granting opposition presidents bipartisan support and policy victories. In order to shed light on this question, the cohesion of the two parties[18] is examined separately in tables 4.6 and 4.7.

Table 4.6 displays party cohesion among the two parties for each type of functional policy issue when presidents do and do not take a leadership role. Policy types in which presidential leadership simultaneously enhances cohesion in both the president's party and the opposition party are in bold. The results clearly show that the higher levels of party conflict on presidential agenda items (shown in table 4.1) are generally the result of simultaneous changes in both parties' behavior. All the domestic issues on which presidential leadership exacerbates partisan conflict exhibit enhanced cohesion among both the president's party and the opposition party. The increases in cohesion associated with presidential leadership are also similar within both parties. There is no clear pattern in which one party shows greater behavioral shifts than the other: on half of the issue types, the president's party enjoys a larger boost in cohesion when presidents take a leadership role; on the other half, presidential leadership prompts somewhat higher cohesion in the opposition party.

The only significant exception to the general pattern that presidential leadership is associated with increases in cohesion among both parties lies in foreign and defense policy. On defense and international affairs, presidential leadership sparks enhanced cohesion among the president's party without also leading to improved cohesion among the opposition party. It appears that the president's party rallies to his side on foreign affairs and defense, but the opposition party does not strengthen its cohesion in opposition. Overall party conflict is higher on defense and foreign affairs issues when presidents are involved (as shown in table 4.1), but this is the result of behavioral changes within the president's party, not the opposition. Perhaps in this limited sense, American politics still stops at the water's edge. As with the analysis of party conflict above, these findings are not the result of spurious correlation.[19]

Presidential leadership also affects the cohesion of both parties on many of the most ideologically-charged issues in American politics. The data shown in table 4.7 are also consistent with the theory that presidential involvement alters the political incentives of both parties. Generally speaking, both the president's party and the opposition party exhibit higher levels of cohesion on presidential agenda items, even when focusing on issues that are already divisive along ideological lines. The pattern

TABLE 4.6 **Presidential leadership and party cohesion, by government function, 1981–2000**

Government function	Cohesion of the president's party			Cohesion of the opposition party		
	No presidential leadership	Presidential leadership	Difference	No presidential leadership	Presidential leadership	Difference
Macroeconomics	39.5	36.0	-3.5	36.1	31.8	-4.4
Civil rights	21.4	3.9	-17.5***	28.2	21.3	-6.9
Health	**28.5**	**56.9**	**28.4***	**31.9**	**51.3**	**19.5***
Agriculture	18.8	25.3	6.4	18.7	22.9	4.2
Labor, employment, immigration	**25.8**	**44.1**	**18.3***	**28.5**	**40.0**	**11.4***
Education	**35.7**	**59.0**	**23.3***	**36.9**	**56.8**	**19.9***
Environment	17.9	14.2	-3.7	26.3	20.9	-5.4
Energy	25.1	29.1	4.0	12.3	8.1	-4.2
Transportation	18.2	15.6	-2.6	19.0	18.1	-0.9
Law, crime, family issues	**19.1**	**30.3**	**11.2***	**14.9**	**38.0**	**23.1***
Social welfare	**27.4**	**41.5**	**14.1***	**32.3**	**41.0**	**8.7***
Community development and housing	**21.9**	**41.2**	**19.3***	**26.7**	**52.3**	**25.7***
Banking, finance, domestic commerce	18.4	31.7	13.3*	22.5	17.1	-5.3
Defense	19.2	38.9	19.7***	22.6	27.1	4.4
Space, science, technology	**14.0**	**44.6**	**30.6***	**15.9**	**48.7**	**32.8***
Foreign trade	6.6	5.7	-.94	18.9	13.7	-5.2
International affairs, foreign aid	9.7	29.7	20.0***	13.9	13.0	-.9
Government operations	**21.9**	**40.0**	**18.1***	**22.8**	**45.2**	**22.4***
Public lands and water management	26.9	41.5	14.6	23.2	18.3	-5.0
Average for all votes	**23.4**	**40.9**	**17.5***	**24.8**	**36.8**	**12.0***

Policy types in which presidential leadership simultaneously enhances cohesion in both the president's party and the opposition party are in bold.

Note: Cells show the average party cohesion score for roll-call votes in each category; the methodology for calculating party cohesion is explained in note 18 of chap. 4. *N*s for each cell are the same as those shown in table 4.1.

*p < .05; **p < .01; ***p < .001.

TABLE 4.7 **Presidential leadership and party cohesion, by ideological issue category, 1981–2004**

	Cohesion of the president's party			Cohesion of the opposition party		
Ideological issue category	No presidential leadership	Presidential leadership	Difference	No presidential leadership	Presidential leadership	Difference
Economic	**39.7**	**54.4**	**14.7***	**42.6**	**50.8**	**8.2***
Social	27.1	24.7	–2.4	25.6	27.6	2.0
Hawk vs. dove	33.2	50.8	17.7***	36.5	26.4	–10.16**
Government's share of the economy	**50.8**	**64.8**	**13.9***	**48.6**	**59.3**	**10.8**
Regulation of economic activity	**30.2**	**48.8**	**18.7***	**36.4**	**48.0**	**11.7***
Distribution of the tax burden	53.7	63.9	10.2*	48.5	47.3	–1.1
Redistributive programs	**36.5**	**46.7**	**10.2**	**40.1**	**48.9**	**8.8**
Any of the above	**34.1**	**46.5**	**15.23***	**36.4**	**41.0**	**12.3***
None of the above	**17.2**	**32.4**	**12.4***	**18.1**	**30.4**	**4.05**

Policy types in which presidential leadership simultaneously enhances cohesion in both the president's party and the opposition party are in bold.

Note: The methodology for calculating party cohesion is explained in note 18 of chap. 4. *N*s for each cell are the same as those shown in table 4.2.

*$p<.05$; **$p<.01$; ***$p<.001$.

holds for economic issues generally, as well as for votes on redistributive programs, regulatory policy, and on government's share of the economy.

But just as presidential leadership does not provoke higher levels of conflict on social issues like gun control, death penalty, and abortion (table 4.2), it does not positively affect either party's cohesion in this issue area. Consistent with the results on military and foreign affairs issues in Policy Agendas Project categories (table 4.6), the higher levels of conflict on *hawk vs. dove* issues is the result of substantially higher cohesion within the president's party, not among the opposition (where the effect on cohesion is actually negative).

Overall, among the ideological issue categories, the effect of presidential leadership is consistently larger for presidential party cohesion than for opposition party cohesion, although the differences are not dramatic. On these issues, presidential leadership serves to attract additional support from within the president's own party to a greater extent than it repulses the opposition party, though, as above, the behavior of both parties differs in the presence of presidential leadership.

Perspective on Party Conflict over Time

The preceding analysis of Senate roll-call voting supports the theory that presidential leadership stimulates party conflict. Interestingly, the Senate's roll-call agenda has become progressively more occupied with presidential agenda items during the 1981–2004 period. Compared with earlier Congresses in the study, the contemporary Senate takes more votes on presidential agenda items as a proportion of the Senate agenda.

Figure 4.1 displays the percentage of Senate roll-call votes devoted to presidential agenda items in each session of Congress over the period. There is considerable year-to-year variability,[20] but over the period, each president's agenda occupied roll-call voting in the Senate to a greater extent than his predecessor's, without respect to unified or divided party control. Especially noteworthy is that President George H. W. Bush's agenda dominated the Senate roll-call agenda to a greater extent than President Reagan's, even though Reagan would generally be rated the more influential president. Regressing the percentage of Senate roll-call votes devoted to presidential agenda items on time reveals that for each additional year in the series, the percentage of Senate roll-call votes devoted to presidential agenda items increased by .63 ($p < .05$).[21] In the more recent Con-

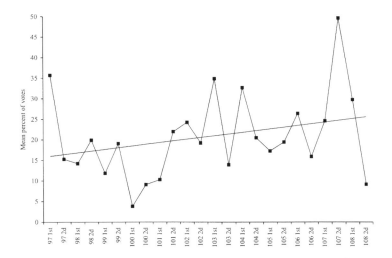

FIGURE 4.1. Presidential agenda items as a percentage of Senate roll-call votes, 1981–2004.

gresses, proportionally fewer Senate roll-call votes occurred on issues on which the president had not taken a stand one way or another.

The causes of this increased Senate attention to presidential agenda items are not apparent or easy to ascertain, and they were not anticipated at the outset of the research. The change could, in part, be a result of strengthened party organizations at the national level. That the president and the congressional parties engage in "conversation" over the same sorts of issues to a greater extent suggests more internal coordination and a less diffuse national agenda. With all due respect to Neustadt (1990), it may be that stronger parties-in-government have become better able in recent years to unite what the Constitution divides. Regardless of the underlying cause of the shift, it has the potential to explain some of the increase in Senate partisanship overall during the time period.

Can Congress's greater attention to presidential agenda items shed light on the higher level of party polarization in recent years? Multiple regression is employed to determine whether the increased proportion of the Senate roll-call votes devoted to the president's agenda can help account for the level of party polarization in the Senate, while controlling for other factors shown to affect partisanship above.

- The dependent variable is average party difference *per quarter* from the 97th Congress through the 108th Congress ($n = 96$). Use of quarterly data is appropriate because agenda content varies not just from year to year, but also within sessions of Congress.[22] It also allows me to boost the study's n, so as to improve model estimation.

- The key independent variable is the percentage of the Senate's roll-call agenda involving presidential agenda items.
- Control variables account for the percentage of votes dealing with ideological issues, which—as shown in chapter 3—generate far more party conflict than other types of issues. Similarly, a control variable accounts for the percentage of votes that were procedural.
- Changes in party strength are accounted for by the number of senators holding safe seats and the institutional strength of party leadership (as measured by the level of funding appropriated to leadership institutions, from fig. 1.1).
- A lag of the dependent variable corrects for autocorrelation in the error term.[23]

The results of the regression analysis are shown in table 4.8. Overall, the model accounts for 42 percent of the variance in Senate party polarization over the period.[24]

Presidential agenda-setting is not only associated with higher levels of partisan conflict on individual votes, it also helps account for the overall level of party polarization at different points in time. The positive coefficient for *presidential agenda items (%)* shows that the average distance between the parties increases when the Senate's roll-call agenda is more focused on issues important to the president. Increasing the proportion of *presidential agenda items (%)* from one standard deviation below to one standard deviation above the mean is associated with a 17 percent increase in the average level of party polarization, holding all other variables constant at their means.[25]

The control variables largely perform as expected, based on the preceding analysis. Periods when ideological issues constitute a larger share of the roll-call agenda show higher levels of partisanship ($p = .015$). A higher proportion of *procedural* votes produces more party polarization ($p < .001$). Increases in party strength over the time period—as measured by the strengthened party leadership institutions—are associated with wider average distances between the parties on roll-call votes. *Safe seats* takes the expected positive coefficient, but it is not statistically significant. These results are not affected by the presence or absence of divided government.[26]

There are undoubtedly many other important sources of congressional partisanship: the partisan and ideological composition of local constituencies (Brewer, Mariana, and Stonecash 2002; Jacobson 2000), the com-

TABLE 4.8 **Senate party polarization and presidential leadership, 1981–2004 ($n = 96$)**

	B (s.e.)
Presidential leadership	
Presidential agenda items (%)	.18***
	(.09)
Agenda content	
Nonideological (%)	−.17*
	(.08)
Procedural votes (%)	.19***
	(.08)
Party strength	
Number of safe seats	.06
	(.14)
Senate party leadership funds (millions)	3.33***
	(1.27)
Control for autocorrelation	
Party polarization (Lag 1)	.32***
	(.09)
Goodness of fit	
F	12.45***
Adjusted R^2	.42
Breusch-Godfrey	
LM Test (Lag 1)	.44
LM Test (Lag 2)	.84
LM Test (Lag 3)	5.89

Note: Dependent variable is mean level of party polarization (absolute difference between Democrats and Republicans voting yea) on all roll-call votes by quarter, 1981–2004.
*$p < .05$; **$p < .01$; ***$p < .001$, one-tailed tests.

position of the legislative agenda (Lee 2008; Roberts and Smith 2003), economic inequality in society (McCarty, Poole, and Rosenthal 2006), and the influence of party activists (Aldrich 1995; Burden 2001). But these findings strongly suggest that partisanship in Congress also has an endogenous source in interbranch interactions, as members of Congress react to and mobilize around presidential initiatives. Accordingly, a legislative agenda more centered on presidential leadership initiatives results in systematically higher levels of party conflict.

Although variation in attention to presidential agenda items is related to variation in overall party conflict, it is not clear why the Senate's roll-call agenda has become more focused on presidential leadership issues. Chapter 7 will give further attention to agenda change as a source of changes in party polarization in Congress. But a detailed account of changing levels of party conflict over time goes beyond the scope of this study. The theory being advanced both in this chapter and in the book as a whole is primarily a static one: partisanship has sources in electoral and power politics that go beyond the ideological policy differences between members of the two parties.

If presidential leadership shapes political incentives in Congress in the manner postulated here, the effect should not be confined to the contemporary era. Presidents would be expected to spark party conflict even at times when overall levels of partisanship in Congress are lower than they currently are. At least since presidents have been expected to advance a legislative agenda, it has always been politically useful for members of the party controlling the presidency to help the president avoid embarrassing policy failures. At the same time, members of the party not controlling the presidency have always operated under a different and contrary set of political incentives. In order to develop an argument for regaining power, they need to call into question the president's policy leadership. It is simply not possible to campaign against a president and his party while regularly voting in favor of that president's signature policy initiatives.

Reactions to presidential leadership are thus likely to provide a constant source of party conflict in Congress, even while the overall level of party conflict in Congress varies over time. Future research could extend the analysis backward in time or investigate temporal variation in the effects documented here. But it is important to note that it is not merely the changes in the level of party conflict over time that need to be better understood. Scholars also have an insufficient grasp of the reasons for the base level of party conflict during all time periods. The analysis provided here suggests that presidential leadership itself can account for some of that baseline amount of party conflict that is continually present in Congress.

Presidents, Parties, and Partisanship

Previous scholarship has not considered presidential leadership as an independent source of partisan conflict in Congress. Most research on the relationship between the president and Congress has focused on the ability of presidents to set the congressional agenda and to pass their legislative program (Bond and Fleisher 1992; Canes-Wrone 2001; Collier and Sullivan 1995; Edwards 1990; Kernell 1997). But presidents do more than influence the policies that Congress considers and adopts; a president's participation on an issue also affects its politics as members respond to the president on the basis of their shared or adverse political interests. Presidents are central political actors in legislative politics, and their intervention in policy debates has important effects on party politics.

When presidents propose a legislative program, they are doing more than suggesting a set of policy proposals for Congress to consider. They are also serving as the most visible public face of their political party. Members of Congress react to a president in both his capacity as chief legislator and as party leader. Members' opposed political interests appear to stimulate a certain amount of reflexive partisanship on presidential agenda items, with members of the president's party supporting the president for reasons separate from their agreement on the policy merits and members of the opposition disagreeing simply in order to deny the president political victories or the ability to claim bipartisan support for initiatives. Describing this kind of partisan logic, Sen. Lindsey Graham (R-S.C.) said, "If it's a Democratic idea, I have to be against it because it came from a Democrat. And vice versa" (quoted in Brownstein 2007, 12). Even if party politics is usually less crude and ruthless than Graham describes, political motives probably shape the burden of proof senators impose when evaluating presidential initiatives, with members of the president's party more likely to go along even before all policy doubts are resolved and members of the opposition more likely to resist unless they are overwhelmingly persuaded.

Legislators' attitudes toward the president influence their perceptions of his policy ideas. Representative George Miller (D-Calif.) observed, for example, that members' views of No Child Left Behind were significantly shaped by their attitudes toward President George W. Bush: "At the end of the day, it may be the most tainted brand in America. . . . There's more resentment that the law is connected with George Bush than anything else. It's the biggest anchor that you're trying to work with something that's considered his franchise." When considering the president's legislative proposals, members are likely to extend their general views of the president to the specific initiatives on the president's agenda. Their views of the president are undoubtedly deeply affected by their own partisan identification. Presidential leadership thus separates the partisans in Congress both because of their different responses to the president as a "source cue" and their opposing political interests.

Results presented in this chapter strongly suggest that partisan interests and attitudes systematically affect the Senate's response to presidential leadership. Both at the individual vote level and in the aggregate over time, the data support the inference that presidential leadership fuels congressional partisanship. A president mentioning an issue in the State of the Union address generally widens the distance between the parties on that issue in Congress, controlling for policy content. Both parties are simultaneously affected by presidential leadership, with the cohesion of the president's and the opposition party solidifying on issues the president champions. Increases over time in the proportion of the Senate roll-call agenda devoted to presidential initiatives can partly account for the higher levels of partisan conflict in the contemporary Congress.

These findings have at least three important implications for scholarly understanding of congressional parties and partisanship. First, members' willingness to support a policy idea can depend on who proposes it, not just on what it would do. Because party images are at stake, members may be willing to support a policy idea when offered by the leader of their own party but oppose it when put forward by the opposing party's leader. Not all types of issues were equally affected by these incentives. Notably, presidential politics appeared to have little influence on partisan conflict on the types of issues on which local constituency interests weigh more heavily in members' voting decisions. But behavior on most types of national policy exhibited patterns consistent with the political logic advanced here. Members' decisions on roll-call voting are the result not only of their views on the policy issues involved; they also take into account the politics of supporting or opposing particular presidents.

Second, presidential leadership can spark intense partisan disagreement on issues that might otherwise have been uncontroversial or relatively uncontroversial. As discussed in chapter 3, 39 percent of Senate votes on nonideological issues—matters on which liberals and conservatives have not staked out clear opposing positions—resulted in party-line divisions. But when those nonideological issues were featured as part of a president's agenda, they broke along party lines fully 56 percent of the time, as compared with only 36 percent of the time when they were not part of the president's agenda. Presidential leadership gives partisan structure to types of issues that are not otherwise defined by ideological cleavages. As shown by the regression analysis in table 4.2, presidential agenda status has its most dramatic effect on roll-call votes involving issues on which liberals and conservatives do not already have differentiated positions. On issues that otherwise tend to be relatively uncontroversial, presidential leadership appears to set the two parties more at odds.

Although it is impossible to prove a counterfactual, it is difficult to believe that the intense Senate controversy over the Community-Oriented Policing Services (COPS) program had nothing to do with its high profile as a presidential agenda item. The program implemented President Clinton's State of the Union address promise to "put 100,000 more police officers on the street," and it was mentioned in most of his addresses. The ultimate goal of the program—to improve the capacities of local law enforcement—is hardly a matter on which liberals and conservatives disagree. The COPS program is just one of many grant programs in the Department of Justice's Office of Justice Programs (OJP) to assist local law enforcement for various purposes, including technology, statistics, missing children, and crime victims. None of these other programs sparked controversy in the roll-call record. COPS was not the most expensive of the OJP's grant programs, and it was never the focus of a management or corruption scandal. Nevertheless, an examination of the Senate roll-call record indicates that the COPS program was one of most controversial intergovernmental grant programs of the 1990s. No fewer than eight roll-call votes were taken on the program, all breaking almost perfectly along party lines, with nearly every Democrat in support of the program and nearly every Republican opposed. Why should a relatively modest intergovernmental grant program spark such intense partisan controversy? The answer almost certainly has to do with the legislation's potential to improve Democrats' reputation on crime issues. "The COPS program allow[ed] Clinton to campaign on crime as a central pillar of his Presidency," and it was widely seen by both Republicans and Democrats as an effort to defuse Republican advantages on that issue (Johnston and Weiner 1996). Members should hardly be expected to be immune to these kinds of political calculations as they evaluate policy proposals.

Third, to fully understand congressional voting behavior, scholars need to take into account members' partisan political interests as well as their policy preferences. These findings suggest that a considerable amount of partisanship in congressional voting follows the logic of "whose ox is being gored." Although deeply held ideological differences between the parties account for much voting behavior in the contemporary Congress, partisanship also springs from contextual and strategic sources. Even if their policy preferences are philosophically fixed over the course of their political lives, members are also self-interested political actors with their electoral and power goals in mind. The perceived success or failure of a presidency has such a uniquely important effect on the political interests of both parties in Congress that they cannot fail to consider how their behavior will affect a president's prospects. Presidential leadership thus provides cues and strategic incentives that lead congressional partisans to take clearer stands in opposition to one another.

WITHDRAWN
WVU
LIBRARY

CHAPTER FIVE

The Partisan Politics of Good Government

Political leaders often see their strategic problem as one of choosing from a large number of potential issues those that will maximize their identification with positive values and their opponents with negative ones, rather than of positioning themselves in a space of ordered dimensions.—Donald Stokes, "Valence Politics"

Although it may at times be difficult to believe, there is actually a great deal of consensus in American politics on a broad range of basic political values. Everyone—liberals, conservatives, moderates, and nonideologues—believes that government should be honest, competent, responsible, and democratically elected. Government officials must not take bribes; elections ought to be determined on the basis of who received the most votes; no one should be above the law; government ought to gather, report, and use accurate information; taxpayer money should not be wasted; revenues and expenditures should balance over the long run; government contracts ought not to be distributed on the basis of patronage or inside connections. These norms may be violated from time to time, but their violation brings the risk of widespread condemnation.

Recognizing that some issues command universal consensus, Stokes (1963, 1992) famously distinguished between "position issues," on which candidates and parties take a range of positions along a continuum of alternatives, and "valence issues," on which everyone holds the same position. When government ethics becomes a political issue, there is no "procorruption" side. When considering the management of government programs, there is no "incompetence" side. No one favors waste, fraud, or abuse. "Many of the issues that agitate our politics do not involve even a shriveled set of two alternatives of government action," writes Stokes. "If we are to speak of a dimension at all, both parties and all voters [are] located at single point—the position of virtue in government" (Stokes 1963, 372).

Despite the lack of disagreement on policy goals, valence issues are enormously important for election outcomes. At different times, the public perceives that one party has weaker "bonds" or "valences" with universally held values of honesty, integrity, and competence than the other. Such perceptions are critical to the parties' fortunes. Indeed, Stimson (2004) finds that pragmatic, nonideological voters are the main drivers of opinion change in American politics. Unlike "the passionate" or "the uninvolved," pragmatic voters serve as "scorekeepers" who "sit on the sidelines as judges" and base their approval or disapproval of elected officials "almost wholly . . . on the quality of performance in office" (Stimson 2004, 168–69). A party perceived as corrupt or incompetent will lose support from these crucial voters and can lose seats or control of the government as a result.

This chapter analyzes partisan behavior on valence issues. In particular, I focus on "good government" causes, such as measures to fight corruption, uphold ethical standards, investigate failures, collect and report information, promote fiscal responsibility, ensure electoral integrity, and make government operations more efficient. These are not issues on which liberals and conservatives have staked out opposing positions; they are not matters of ideological disagreement in American politics. Yet, as will be shown below, some of the most highly partisan conflicts in Congress occur over precisely these issues. As on presidential agenda items, the electoral stakes for both parties are high when good-government issues are considered in Congress. Members understand that congressional handling of these issues does more than shape public policy; it can build up or tear down party reputations and affect electoral victory or defeat.

The parties in Congress do not passively wait to see how the public will evaluate their integrity and competence; they use the resources at their disposal—including agenda-setting, floor debate, and roll-call votes—to shape public perceptions of their commitment to good government. When considering good-government matters, party members cooperate to "maximize their identification with positive values and their opponents with negative ones" (Stokes 1992, 146).

Undermining the reputation of one's partisan opponents is often the more attainable goal. It is difficult for a party through its own actions to enhance its perceived linkages to positive values. Incorruptibility is obligatory rather than supererogatory, so a clean ethical record garners no special credit. The reputation for competence depends on policy outcomes that are affected by far more than a governing party's own actions. Not even prudent, capable government can guarantee a growing economy in a global marketplace.[1] By comparison, it is often much easier to build a public record that will undercut the public's perceptions of the opposition. All that is necessary is to investigate policy failures on its watch, scrutinize its officials for ethical lapses, and draw attention to any evidence of wrongdoing or incompetence. The result can be highly beneficial for a party and its members. Indeed, charges of corruption are one of the most potent weapons in electoral politics (Jacobson and Dimock 1994; Peters and Welch 1980; Welch and Hibbing 1997). In a two-party system, associating the opposition with mismanagement and failure will likely redound to a party's benefit. A basic logic of two-party politics is that one party's scandals and failures redound to the benefit of the other party.

Good-government causes thus present a highly profitable area for cooperative partisan endeavor. I argue that legislative behavior on these issues is shaped more by partisan teamsmanship than by members' individual policy preferences. When good-government issues are considered in Congress, parties unify around their shared electoral interests and common public relations strategies. Debates and votes on such issues should generally be viewed as "message politics" (Evans 2001) or "p.r. wars" (Sinclair 2006, 255–307), rather than straightforward policy decisions in which members vote for the position closest to their own preferred outcomes. Party coalitions appear to be held together by members' collective electoral interest in capitalizing on these issues rather than by spatial proximity on a left-right continuum.

I find that the two parties frequently stake out strongly opposed stands on good-government issues, even those on which there is broad consensus in the abstract. On average, parties are even more distinct in their voting behavior on good-government causes than they are on explosive social issues, such as abortion, gay rights, and affirmative action. Good-government issues tend to be either highly controversial along party lines or not at all controversial. On average, however, they are far more controversial than the typical matter considered in Congress. Compared with other issue types, internal party divisions on good-government issues are relatively rare. No other substantive issue type examined in this study—economic, social, or hawk vs. dove issues—was as likely to result in a unanimous party vote in the Senate, with 100 percent of Republicans on one side and 100 percent of Democrats on the other, as good-government issues. Relative to the other types of issues analyzed, the parties' voting patterns on good government are distinctly tribal.

Despite the level of conflict, however, the parties are often not *consistent* in their positions over time. The parties' positions on these issues are fluid and strategic. At one point, Republicans will take up a crusade for balanced budgets against Democratic opposition; at a later point, the parties reverse positions. Neither party is consistently a stickler on government ethics. Instead, the usual pattern is that Democrats press for far-reaching investigations into potential Republican wrongdoing and vice versa. Generally speaking, the president's fellow partisans in the Senate perceive fewer ethical problems with his nominees than do members of the opposing party. The politics of election reform and regulation and of gathering and reporting information tends to reflect the parties' transparent calculations of political advantage. In short, good-government causes elicit high levels of partisan division as each party attempts to undercut its opposition's reputation for efficiency, competence, fiscal responsibility, and integrity.

Defining Good-Government Causes

As discussed in chapter 3, good-government causes—efforts to improve government's integrity, efficiency, fairness, democratic accountability, and fiscal responsibility—cannot be classified on the left-right continuum, as it is understood in contemporary American politics. Under this heading, Congress considers:

- *Anticorruption rules for its own members:* lobbyist registration, conflict of interest regulations, campaign disclosure requirements, limits on gifts to members, and individual ethics cases involving members of Congress.
- *Anticorruption efforts aimed at executive agencies and government officials:* competitive bidding requirements, whistleblower protections, and scrutiny of individual officials and nominees for ethical shortcomings.
- *Measures to promote electoral integrity:* voting technology, recount rules, anti–voter-fraud measures, and limits on electioneering by government employees.
- *Improvements to the budget process:* procedural reforms, budget scoring of the sale of government assets, determinations of what programs should be on- or

off-budget. As long as these efforts do not attempt to bias outcomes in favor of either a larger or a smaller role for government (e.g., restricting tax increases or imposing spending limits), these measures are neutral with respect to ideology.

- *Information gathering:* conducting studies, creating independent commissions, publicly releasing reports and information.
- *Measures to improve government operations:* paperwork reductions, limits on administrative expenses, agency accounting procedures, requirements that government pay interest on overdue debts, administer an accurate census.

See table 5.1 for a more comprehensive list of good-government measures considered in Congress during the study period. Liberals and conservatives do not hold differing ideological views on good-government goals. Everyone believes in rooting out corruption, providing for efficient management of programs, ensuring that election outcomes are determined democratically, collecting information about government operations and policy problems, and formulating budgets that balance over the long term.

TABLE 5.1 **Types of good-government issues, 1981–2004 ($n = 631$)**

Anticorruption ($n = 140$). Includes votes on:
- competitive bidding in government contracting
- inspectors general and independent counsels
- whistleblower protections
- lobbying disclosure
- ethics cases involving individual government officials or nominees

Information ($n = 60$). Includes votes on:
- requests for studies
- requests or requirements for executive branch disclosure of information
- investigatory commissions
- testing and evaluation of government programs

Elections and electioneering rules ($n = 124$). Includes votes on:
- Hatch Act
- voter registration processes
- election machinery

Budget process and reform ($n = 209$). Includes votes on:
- budget assumptions
- procedural reforms (e.g., biennial budgeting)
- PAYGO
- placing programs on- or off-budget
- debt-limit increases
- budget scoring of the sale of government assets

Government operations ($n = 98$). Includes votes on:
- government accounting procedures
- census procedures
- requirements that government pay interest on overdue payments
- limits on unfunded mandates
- limits on administrative expenses
- putting government under same laws as private industry

How does Congress handle such matters? Agreement on abstract goals does not preclude disagreement over means or relevant facts.[2] In fact, good-government issues are typically very controversial in Congress. They regularly prompt hard-fought, emotional debates, such as Democratic attempts to require the Pentagon to provide Congress with progress reports on the Iraq war. The mere act of requiring the Department of Defense to report on progress toward benchmark goals in Iraq does not move war policy in a more liberal or conservative direction. Highlighting that the Bush administration has not met benchmarks, on the other hand, undercuts the administration's—and by extension, the Republican party's—reputation for competence and efficiency in its handling of the war. Similarly, investigations into no-bid contracts in Iraq serve partisan ends by (potentially) showing that the administrations' financial management of the war effort was marred by waste and abuse. Regardless of opinions on issues along the hawk vs. dove cleavage, everyone believes that government should be a good steward of the public purse.

Theorizing Legislative Behavior on Good-Government Causes

Although good-government causes do not map on a spatial continuum from left to right, they have great implications for each party's "brand name" with voters. A hard-hitting congressional investigation into government contracting that turns up widespread abuses can have devastating impact on a party's public image. Requiring official Pentagon reports that will reveal virtually no progress toward stated war policy goals can discredit an administration and its party. Extended congressional debates over a balanced budget amendment, raising the debt limit, or the use of pay-as-you-go budgeting indict the competence of the governing party and help make the case that it cannot fulfill a basic responsibility of governance.

In short, good-government causes are excellent vehicles for achieving partisan aims. Not all good-government issues considered in Congress will have implications for party brand names. But, generally speaking, this type of issue is ideal for appealing to the nonideological "scorekeeper" voter who has no passionate partisan commitments and who foremost expects competent performance from government (Stimson 2004, 168).

Congressional parties may actually find it much easier to organize and mobilize collective action on good-government causes than on ideologically divisive position issues. Position issues are inherently controversial.

A party pursuing a legislative agenda on such issues—for example, abortion, redistributive taxation, affirmative action—will inevitably alienate voters who do not support its policy stances. Valence issues elicit universal assent, and taking up the cause of good government only wins friends among the broader public: "Part of the appeal of valence-campaigning to the electoral strategist is that an artfully chosen valence issue need not cost *any* votes" (Stokes 1992, 158). No party hurts its reputation with voters for demanding tough ethics standards, promising honesty and accountability in government, proclaiming the need for a balanced budget, or denouncing waste, fraud, and abuse. Prosecuting a substantive legislative agenda on position issues can be electorally risky, particularly for members representing swing states and marginal districts. Party members' incentives to defect from collective goals may thus be lower on good-government causes.

In addition, collective action on good-government issues does not require centrist members to trade-off their individual policy preferences and collective party goals in the manner that partisan teamwork on position issues typically requires. On issues where alternatives can be ranged on a left-right continuum, centrist members face trade-offs in deciding whether to prioritize working with their fellow partisans or whether to vote in a way that is more consistent with their individual policy views. But, as Cox and McCubbins (2005, 46) observe, for issues that cannot "be formally represented as spatial or left-right policy dimensions . . . there would be no median legislator who had to sacrifice his strategic advantages for the sake of the party."

This chapter will proceed by examining voting patterns on good-government issues. First, the two parties' voting behavior on good-government issues is compared with their behavior on position issues that divide liberals from conservatives on economic, social, and foreign policy. Following the quantitative analysis, floor debates in specific good-government controversies are examined to shed additional light on the party politics of good-government causes. Senators' perceptions of the electoral stakes are clearly evident in party positioning on these issues.

Party Conflict on Good-Government Causes

Even though no one (other than crooks!) favors corruption, mismanagement, inefficiency, or election fraud, measures designed to address these and related matters are nevertheless highly controversial. When these is-sues are voted on, Republicans and Democrats are more likely than usual to take opposing sides. Figure 5.1 displays the mean party difference for all the votes in each category over the whole 1981–2004 period: good govern-ment, economic, social, and hawk vs. dove issues. Mean party difference is 14 percentage points higher on good-government issues than on the av-erage vote ($t = 10.1$, $p < .001$). Comparatively speaking, good-government issues are second to economic issues and tied with hawk vs. dove issues in the level of partisan disagreement they elicit.

Voting on good-government issues is considerably more partisan than on the social and moral issues so prominent in electoral and party poli-tics, including abortion, gay rights, and affirmative action. These two issue types made up a comparable proportion of the Senate's agenda during the study period, with roll-call votes on good-government issues ($n = 631$) occurring almost as frequently as on social issues ($n = 672$). Any moder-ately informed observer of American politics can identify the general po-sitions of Republicans and Democrats on hot button "values" issues, but the parties are actually considerably more distinct in Senate voting on good-government issues. Good-government issues were on average about 26 percent more party polarizing than social issues ($t = 6.6$, $p < .001$). Votes on government ethics, control of information, budget processes, election rules, and government operations show remarkable levels of partisan structuring, even though a close observer of American politics would have difficulty providing any summary description of the differences between the parties' overall stances on these matters.

Multivariate regression analysis is necessary to determine whether the higher level of partisanship on good-government issues is merely a result of spurious correlation. As discussed in chapter 4, a great deal of scholar-ship on congressional voting behavior has demonstrated that party-line votes are more likely to occur on procedural matters (Cox and McCubbins 1993; Cox and Poole 2002; Theriault 2006; Van Houweling 2003) and on amendments (Roberts and Smith 2003; Rohde 1991). If a greater propor-tion of good-government issues are handled with procedural motions or amendments, then the higher level of partisanship on these issues might have nothing to do with the substance of the issue. Similarly, fixed effects for individual Congresses are included to control for Congress-specific factors that could affect the overall level of partisanship in any given year (e.g., divided or unified control, the majority party's margin of control). Controlling for the overall level of partisanship in a Congress also ensures

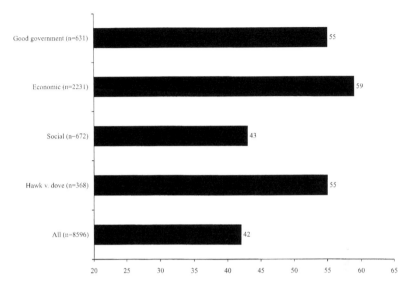

FIGURE 5.1. Mean party difference by issue type, 1981–2004.
Note: One-way analysis of variance shows that differences among these types of votes are statistically significant at $p < .001$ (F = 97.7, df = 4). Mean party difference is calculated by averaging the absolute difference between the percentage of Republicans voting yea and the percentage of Democrats voting yea for each roll-call vote in each category.

that the coefficient on *good-government issues* is not an artifact of the timing of good-government votes. Examination of the incidence of good-government votes reveals that they made up between 2 and 16 percent of Senate roll-call votes taken in any given Congress during the time period. There was no trend toward their becoming a larger or smaller share of the Senate roll-call agenda during the time period studied.

Table 5.2 presents the results of OLS regression models designed to rule out these potential causes of spurious correlation. Regression results displayed in the left column of table 5.2 reveal that good-government issues are more partisan than the typical vote, controlling for other factors likely to affect the level of partisanship. The dependent variable in the model is the party difference index score on each vote during the time period.[3] *Good-government issues* (a dummy variable coded as 1 if the vote involves this type of issue, otherwise 0) takes a positive, statistically significant coefficient ($p < .001$) in the model, indicating that, all else being equal, the parties disagree more on good-government issues than on the average matter considered in Congress.

TABLE 5.2 **Party difference on good-government issues, controlling for type of votes and routine matters** ($n = 8593$)

	B (s.e.)	B (s.e.)
Type of issue		
Good-government issues	11.4***	19.7***
	(1.3)	(1.3)
Economic issues	—	22.4***
		(.7)
Social issues	—	10.9***
		(1.2)
Hawk vs. dove issues	—	23.7***
		(1.6)
Type of vote		
Procedural	16.7***	14.8***
	(.7)	(.7)
Passage	−13.6***	−11.1***
	(1.0)	(.9)
Routine matters		
Appropriations	−2.8***	−.6
	(.8)	(.7)
Nominations	−16.0***	−11.1***
	(1.6)	(1.6)
Purely symbolic	−7.9***	−6.0***
	(1.3)	(1.2)
Congress		
98th Congress	−4.3**	−3.2*
	(1.5)	(1.4)
99th Congress	−1.1	−1.4
	(1.5)	(1.4)
100th Congress	−1.9	−1.8
	(1.5)	(1.4)
101st Congress	−1.7	−1.3
	(1.6)	(1.5)
102d Congress	4.6**	5.0***
	(1.6)	(1.5)
103d Congress	12.6***	12.2***
	(1.5)	(1.4)
104th Congress	17.5***	17.2***
	(1.4)	(1.3)
105th Congress	11.6***	12.5***
	(1.6)	(1.5)
106th Congress	16.3***	16.1***
	(1.5)	(1.4)
107th Congress	8.5***	8.4***
	(1.6)	(1.5)
108th Congress	22.8***	22.3***
	(1.5)	(1.4)
Constant	31.3***	22.4***
F	129.3***	172.6***
Adj. R^2	.20	.29

Note: Coefficients were estimated with OLS regression. The dependent variable is the party difference index for each roll-call vote, defined as the absolute difference between the percentage of Republicans voting yea and the percentage of Democrats voting year.
*$p < .05$; **$p < .01$; ***$p < .001$.

The control variables perform as expected ($p < .001$), with *procedural*[4] votes more partisan, and votes on final *passage* less partisan. Other routine matters, such as *nominations* and *purely symbolic*[5] matters, are also less partisan ($p < .001$). The inclusion of the fixed effects for each Congress confirm that these findings are not affected by increasing partisanship over time or any factor that is constant across a Congress, including divided or unified government, party leadership, and the margin of party control. The fixed effects coefficients also point to a generally rising level of partisanship. The omitted reference category is the 97th Congress, so the large positive coefficients for each Congress throughout the 1990s point to a rising level of partisanship, relative to the 1981–1982 time period, that cannot be explained by any of the other variables in the model.[6]

The right column of table 5.2 shows the results of an identical regression model of party difference that includes dummy variables for votes in the ideological issue categories: *economic, social, and hawk vs. dove.* Each dummy variable takes a positive, statistically significant coefficient ($p < .001$), indicating that the parties are more clearly distinct from one another in roll-call voting when these ideologically charged position issues are on the floor. In every case, the substantive content of the issue affects the level of party differentiation, controlling for the procedural posture of the vote and other considerations likely to affect voting behavior. As one would expect, the coefficient for *good-government issues* is larger ($p < .001$) in a model in which these polarizing ideological issues have been controlled for. The regression results confirm that after accounting for other factors affecting the level of party conflict, *good-government issues* are just slightly less polarizing than *economic issues* in the amount of partisanship they elicit, equivalent to *hawk vs. dove issues*, and about twice as partisan as *social issues*.

Good-government issues are not only at least as partisan as most of the position issues that are already known to divide the parties, they are also more likely to divide the Senate perfectly along party lines, with 100 percent of Republicans voting in opposition to 100 percent of Democrats. Considering the individualism characteristic of the Senate (Baker 2001; Sinclair 1989) and the ideological and stylistic diversity among members of both Senate parties at any given time, it is remarkable that unanimous party line votes ever occur. Indeed, among all the Senate roll-call votes taken between 1981 and 2004 that could be classified into one of the substantive ideological categories ($n = 3,271$)—economic, social, foreign policy—there were only 65 perfect party line votes. But there were 44 perfect party line votes on good-government issues alone, even though this category comprises one fifth as many votes ($n = 631$).

Figures 5.2, 5.3, 5.4, and 5.5 show the frequency distribution for the party difference index for each type of issue. Unlike any of the other issue types, the distribution of the party difference index for good-government issues (fig. 5.2) is strikingly bimodal. In other words, good-government issues are either not controversial along party lines or they divide the parties almost perfectly. When good-government issues are partisan, they are *highly* partisan. Nearly a quarter of all good-government votes have party dissimilarity scores of 90 or more, and fully 7 percent of them are unanimous party votes. At the same time, nearly 10 percent of votes on good-government issues exhibit no partisanship whatsoever (with scores of 0 on the party dissimilarity index). To a greater extent than on the other issues, the parties vote as blocs on good-government issues. Sometimes, both parties are on the same side. At other times, they are on opposing sides. But the parties are less likely to be internally divided on good-government causes than on other issues.

As above, multivariate analysis is necessary to determine whether the parties' distinctive behavior on good-government issues is the result of spurious correlation. When other characteristics of the votes involved are controlled, is voting behavior on good-government issues really distinctive? I estimate a multinomial logit model of party voting with a dependent variable that can take three values: a perfectly unanimous party vote, not a party vote, and a nonunanimous party vote.[7] The models include all the same controls as in the OLS regression models shown in table 5.2 along with dummy variables reflecting the substantive type of issue involved. The full results of the multinomial logit model are available in Appendix C.

To illustrate the substantive implications of the multinomial logit estimates, I calculate the predicted probabilities of the three different vote outcomes for each type of issue: good government, economic, social, and hawk vs. dove. The results are displayed in table 5.3. All else being equal, good-government issues are more likely than any of the position issues to produce a pure party-line vote, with no defections in either party. The predicted probability of a unanimous party vote, $p = .05$ ($p < .001$), is not high, but it is five times as likely to occur on a good-government issue as on any of the ideological position issue categories. Unanimous party votes are vanishingly rare on social issues, $p = .003$ ($p < .001$). Holding all other factors affecting party conflict constant, merely switching the issue content of a roll-call vote from an economic issue to a good-government cause is estimated to increase the probability of a unanimous party-line vote by 200 percent.

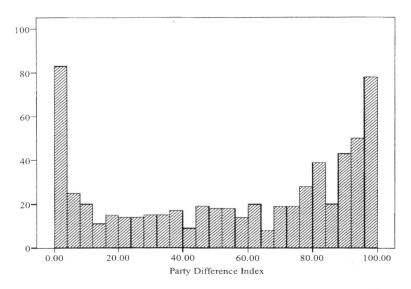

FIGURE 5.2. Frequency distribution of the party difference index on good-government issues.

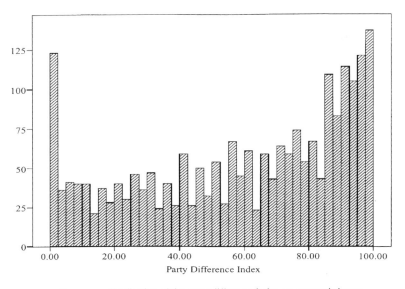

FIGURE 5.3. Frequency distribution of the party difference index on economic issues.

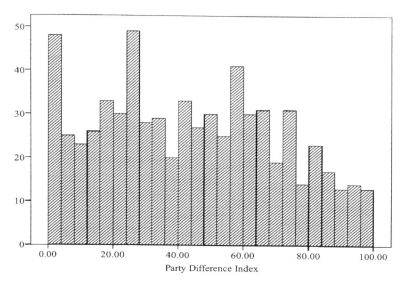

FIGURE 5.4. Frequency distribution of the party difference index on social issues.

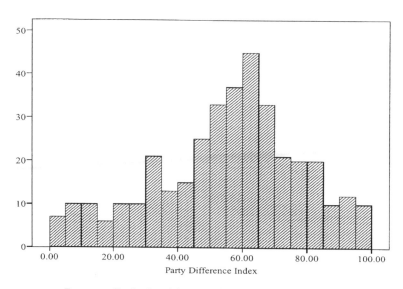

FIGURE 5.5. Frequency distribution of the party difference index on hawk vs. dove issues.

TABLE 5.3. **Effect of issue type on the predicted probabilities and predicted changes in probabilities of party votes and unanimous party votes ($n = 8593$)**

	Unanimous party vote (s.e.)	Party vote (s.e.)	Not a party vote (s.e.)
Type of issue			
Good-government issues	.05 (.01)***	.60 (.02)***	.35 (.02)***
Economic issues	.01 (.00)***	.68 (.01)***	.31 (.01)***
Social issues	.003 (.002)***	.59 (.02)***	.37 (.02)***
Hawk vs. dove issues	.01 (.01)	.79 (.02)***	.20 (.02)***
Change in probability			
From economic to good gov't	.03 (.01)***	−.08 (.01)***	.04 (.02)
From social to good gov't	.04 (.00)***	.01 (.03)	−.06 (.03)
From hawk to good gov't	.03 (.01)*	−.18 (.03)***	.15 (.03)***

Note: Computed by the author from the multinomial logit analyses in Appendix C using CLARIFY.
Entries are predicted probabilities and predicted changes in probabilities. All control variables are held constant at their sample means.
*$p < .05$; **$p < .01$; ***$p < .001$.

The empirical evidence is consistent with an argument that the parties act as teams on good-government issues. When these issues are controversial, senators take sides along party lines. What leads them to do so? In the case of these issues, it is particularly unsatisfying to answer that their "preferences" align in a way that follows their party affiliation, because the content of those preferences is so unclear. The policy goals at stake—efficiency, competence, integrity, fiscal responsibility, and fair elections—are valence issues on which there is no disagreement in principle. Nevertheless, members disagree on these issues, and they tend to do so along party lines. In the next sections, I examine floor debate and position taking in particular good-government policy disputes in order to shed light on the nature of the partisan disagreements. In the context of the systematic analysis of roll-call data, the content of these disputes reinforces the teamwork thesis. The parties' substantive positions on these issues are flexible over time in substantive terms but consistent with their collective political incentives. Party members' behavior on these issues, as in reacting to presidential leadership, is powerfully influenced by their common interests as fellow partisans.

Party Positioning on Good-Government Causes

As Sen. Phil Gramm (R-Tex.) stated during a debate over Hatch Act reform in 1990,[8] "I guess the question we have to ask ourselves here is, are we reforming or are we really engaged in partisan politics on the floor of the U.S. Senate." Sen. Gramm's question can be asked of many congressional debates over good-government causes. On the surface, they are about universally shared values, about "reform." But beneath the surface, the partisan stakes are high. During congressional debates on good-government causes, party reputations for competence, ethics, and honesty are on the line.

A close look at these floor debates reveals that good-government issues raise the partisan stakes in two general ways. First, good-government debates are closely intertwined with "message politics" (Evans 2001) in which one party is systematically calling into question the trustworthiness or competence of the other. Debates over ethics violations, the need for and scope of investigations, and the collection and release of information regularly involve circumstances where one party and its members are evidently on the defensive. Similarly, debates over the budget process or over government operations often center on fiscal or management problems for which one party is perceived as bearing greater responsibility. In such cases, members of both parties have strong incentives to work collectively either to protect their party's reputation or to prosecute the case against the opposition.

Second, good-government debates can implicate the parties' interests directly. When Congress considers legislation related to the management or conduct of campaigns and elections, its actions can potentially affect the parties' electoral prospects. Even though everyone participating in these debates professes the same basic values—honest elections free of fraud and coercion—partisan mistrust colors the deliberations. Reforms are always scrutinized for potential partisan bias. During debates on these matters, senators regularly express concerns that, in the words of Sen. Mitch McConnell (R-Ky.), the other party wants "to redraw the political playing field to their advantage."[9] In these cases, fellow partisans cooperate to protect or advance their most basic interests, their prospects for winning and holding office.

Ethics and investigations

During the debate over the confirmation of Sen. John Tower (R-Tex.) as secretary of defense, Sen. George Mitchell (D-Maine) said, "Let us refrain from self-righteousness. . . . Let us all recognize, as I said earlier, that if we stay here long enough and make enough speeches, we are going to find ourselves on opposite sides of the same issue."[10]

When government officials or nominees are suspected of corruption, incompetence, or ethical improprieties, a proponent of good government would recommend further investigation and, if the evidence warrants, rejection of the nomination or removal from office. Examination of Senate disputes over ethics charges and investigations, however, reveals that these cases generally break down along party lines. Debates on such matters repeatedly raise the same competing claims. Where members of one party see clear evidence of wrongdoing, members of the other usually see unsubstantiated allegations. Where members of one party see grave abuses, members of the other see, at most, mere peccadilloes. Where members of one party see the need for a full investigation, members of the other party tend to see a partisan fishing expedition. Members of Congress all profess the same good-government values, but, in practice, their considered judgments in particular cases closely correlate with their party affiliation.

Nominations controversial for good-government reasons are those in which the nominee's ethics or qualifications are in dispute and the nominee's views on policy matters do not arise in the Senate debate.[11] Many battles over judicial and executive branch nominations are fought out on good-government grounds in which the question before the Senate is whether the nominee meets standards of ethics and competence.[12] Conflicts of interest are a particularly common concern. On average for all the nominations in this study controversial for good-government reasons ($n = 39$), overwhelming majorities of the president's party continued to support his nominee, as compared with just around half of the senators from the opposing party.

President George H. W. Bush's nomination of Sen. John Tower to be secretary of defense is one of the most famous cases. Controversy over Tower centered entirely on allegations of alcoholism, womanizing, and conflicts of interest in his relationships with defense contractors. Sen. John Warner (R-Va.) rejected the allegations against Tower as "a cobweb of fact, fiction, and fantasy" and contended that the Senate should defer to the president's choice.[13] Democrats pointed to more than four hundred FBI interviews containing evidence against the nominee. The Senate Armed Services Committee recommended against confirmation on a straight party line vote.[14] Tower's nomination was then rejected on a nearly unanimous party vote in the Democratic-controlled Senate, with all Republicans except one supporting the nomination and all but three Democrats rejecting it.

In the context of the debate, Majority Leader Mitchell took note of the differing standards in use for evaluating Republican and Democratic nominees: "Many of my colleagues on the Republican side have made the most dramatic reversals of positions imaginable on this issue, and I predict to them that if and when there ever again is a Democratic President, a proposition of which there is much doubt among many people, they will be back on the other side of the issue, where they were in 1977."[15] To this, Sen. Warner replied, "As we look at these windows of history, depending on whether there is a Democrat or a Republican in the White House, indeed we can come up with statistics as the majority leader represents."[16]

Disputes over the need for and scope of investigations into particular ethics cases generally follow a similar script, with the parties in profound disagreement about the merits of the case. In the summer of 1994, for example, Senate Republicans pressed the Democratic controlled Senate to set up a special committee to investigate the Whitewater affair, which centered on President Bill Clinton's involvement with an Arkansas thrift, Madison Guaranty, and a failed real estate investment. Republicans demanded an open-ended investigation to be conducted by a special committee with the authority to look into distantly connected matters, including the death of Vincent Foster, a Clinton White House aide who had committed suicide. These Republican proposals were rejected on the Senate floor by unanimous party vote,[17] although Democrats authorized the Banking Committee to conduct a much narrower investigation into whether there had been improper contacts between White House staff and bank regulators.[18] The committee's report concluded that no laws or ethical standards had been violated; minority Republicans dissented from the report.[19] Once Republicans gained control of the Senate after the 1994 elections, they established a Special Committee on Whitewater with subpoena power, authorized $950,000 for staff salaries, and gave the committee a broad investigatory mandate. This committee's final report concluded that the Clinton administration had improperly attempted to undermine the law enforcement investigation into both Madison Guaranty and Foster's death.[20] The Democrats on the committee issued a dissent that concluded that President Clinton had not misused his office as either president or governor of Arkansas.

The Senate disputes over Whitewater provide a stark blueprint of how congressional debate over ethics and investigations so often unfold. In principle, everyone professes to believe that government should be managed in an ethical manner by competent public officials. But when asked to evaluate allegations and evidence in the same cases, Republicans and Democrats drew radically different conclusions. The pattern was repeated on perhaps the grandest possible scale in President Clinton's second term with independent counsel Kenneth Starr's investigation into allegations that Clinton had committed perjury and obstruction of justice in the context of a sexual harassment lawsuit. The evidence in favor of impeaching President Clinton and removing him from office was laid out in a 445-page report (Starr 1998) and over a month-long trial in the Senate in January 1999. On the Senate roll-call votes on two articles of impeachment, no Democrat voted in favor of either article, while 81 percent of Republicans voted in favor of one article and 90 percent in favor of the other.[21] Disputes about the ethics or competence of particular officeholders tend to draw the clearest possible distinctions between the parties.

Control of information

Congressional debates over whether to conduct a study or release a report often occur in circumstances where one party stands to benefit more than the other from the gathering or release of the information. Official government reports—from inspectors general, independent commissions, congressional committees, and government agencies—can greatly influence both media narratives and the congressional agenda. It is neither liberal nor conservative to require an investigation into the circumstances of the release of Iranian hostages or the government's response to Hurricane Katrina, or to seek to declassify the 9/11 Commission Report. Nevertheless, when information is expected to be more favorable to the interests of one political party, decisions about pursuing or releasing it are likely to be decided along partisan lines. Members of Congress are aware that information is a powerful weapon, and they seek to wield it to shape public perceptions of government performance.

During the 108th Congress, Senate Democrats continually demanded information from the Bush administration related to the conduct of the war in Iraq. They sought reports on the costs of the war and the contributions of foreign countries,[22] the status of detained enemy combatants,[23] the progress of Iraqi reconstruction efforts,[24] the role of executive branch policymakers in the development and use of intelligence relating to Iraq,[25] and the anticipated U.S. military force needed in Iraq.[26] These requests for reports were made by Democrats as amendments to the 2004 Defense

Appropriations bill, and Republicans and Democrats were in near universal disagreement on all of them. Every one of the roll-call votes on these amendments had party difference index scores in excess of 92, and two were unanimous party-line votes.

The debate that unfolded allowed Democrats as a bloc to advance a message that the Bush administration was failing to live up to basic good-government values of transparency, accountability, and fiscal responsibility.[27] They were able to complain about the administration's lack of candor and stonewalling in providing information to Congress. They denounced the high cost of the war and compared it unfavorably to the 1991 Persian Gulf War, in which the United States enjoyed more financial and military support from coalition countries. They complained about war profiteering and sole-source contracts to Halliburton. It was not in the collective interests of Senate Republicans to have such a debate, and the release of such reports would be unlikely to reveal information politically beneficial to their party. Republicans did not speak at any length on these amendments, but they explained their opposition to the reports as saving the administration from duplicative and unnecessary briefings and paperwork.

Requests for information or the release of reports do not necessarily cause partisan contention. Members of Congress will often agree across party lines on the need for additional information on particular subjects, such as on the benefits of mammography[28] or on the effects of violent video games and other entertainment.[29] As with good-government matters generally, votes on information control tend to be either noncontroversial or highly controversial along party lines. But when one party's interests are clearly on the line, it is not surprising that members of Congress react accordingly.

Fiscal responsibility

Debates over budget reform—balanced budget amendments, pay-as-you-go requirements, and other procedural matters—are frequently vehicles for one party to impeach the fiscal management of the other. Everyone involved in these debates professes commitment to fiscal responsibility, but the two parties regularly disagree about process, including such matters as how to calculate the size of the federal budget surplus or deficit, which programs to put on-budget or off-budget, and how to score the sale of government assets for purposes of meeting budget targets. Debates on these issues are often highly technical, involving citation of competing economic authorities. Nevertheless, the vote breakdowns in the Senate are highly partisan.

A general pattern evident in these debates is that the party out of power in the presidency prefers bleak budget pictures; the president's party prefers a more favorable outlook. The party out of power wants a full budgetary accounting of all the administration's expenditures; the party in power takes a less stringent view. Under President George H. W. Bush, Democrats sought to put the cost of the Savings and Loan bailout on budget; Republicans opposed it.[30] Under President Reagan, all Republicans opposed a Democrat-sponsored resolution to remove the revenues dedicated to the Social Security Trust Fund from calculations of the budget deficit, a move that would have put the federal budget much deeper into the red.[31] Republicans demanded more transparency in establishing the costs of President Clinton's bailout of the Mexican economy in 1995.[32] Along the same lines, the party out of power typically complains about excessive spending in emergency appropriations legislation, and it disputes whether or not items included in these bills really are "emergencies."[33]

One recurring issue in this vein is whether the Congress should rely on budget estimates produced by the Office of Management and Budget (OMB) or the Congressional Budget Office (CBO). CBO's assumptions are more conservative than OMB's and thus the use of CBO estimates generally results in a less favorable budget picture (Fessler 1989; Schatz 2005).

During President George H. W. Bush's tenure in office, Republicans preferred to determine whether deficit reduction targets had been met using OMB estimates rather than CBO's. On May 3, 1989, for example, 98 percent of Republicans voted against a resolution stating that Congress should use the CBO economic and technical assumptions in calculating the federal deficit while 98 percent of Democrats voted for it.[34] The sponsor of the resolution, Sen. James Exon (D-Neb.) stated, "This amendment offers truth. It reveals that if more realistic CBO assumptions were used ... the budget in 1992 would be $134.8 billion, a full $106.8 billion over the promised deficit."[35] Sen. Pete Domenici (R-N.M.) contradicted the Democrats' contention that CBO estimates were more accurate than OMB: "Mr. President, if there is some assumption here that the Congressional Budget Office of the United States is a better predictor of economic indicators in the United States than the Office of Management and Budget, I am here to tell you that that is not true."[36]

During President Clinton's tenure in office, a dispute over the relative merits of CBO and OMB estimates was central to the impasse that led to the government shutdowns in 1995 and 1996 (Rubin 1995). But this time, the parties' positions were reversed. "We're going to balance the budget in seven years, and we're going to let the Congressional Budget Office do the arithmetic to make sure that all the numbers add up, and that's it," said House Budget Committee Chairman Rep. John Kasich (R-Ohio).[37] In 1995, there was not a Senate vote directly on the issue, but when a number of key senators declared their positions, a partisan role-reversal was fully in evidence. Sen. Domenici went on the record in support of using CBO's numbers: "You get to a balanced budget using the Congressional Budget Office's more conservative, historically more accurate, economic assumptions than those prepared by OMB."[38] Meanwhile, Democrats who had voted to use CBO estimates in 1989 spoke in favor of allowing greater flexibility on that point in 1995. Sen. Bob Kerrey (D-Neb.) indicated that the matter of budget estimates figured in his vote on the failed continuing resolution that led to the government shutdown: "I voted against the continuing resolution for precisely that reason. This Congress should not bind the president to use numbers that are developed by the Congress."[39]

Generally speaking, the party out of power expresses greater alarm at the state of the nation's finances than the party in power. Debates on the budget process present the party out of power with opportunities to call into question the competence of the party in power. As Sen. Exon (D-Neb.) noted in arguing in favor of a conservative approach to calculating the budget deficit, "This amendment will hammer home the point that President Bush's compromise agreement does not reduce the deficit as much as claimed."[40] The party out of power generally does want to hammer home the point that the party in power is not managing the nation's finances competently, and it uses floor debate and roll-call votes to do so.

Regulating elections and campaigns

"I heard it said, and it is part of the Record, that one reason the other side is opposed to [the Motor Voter Act] is that they will never be in the majority again. That gives me enough incentive to be for it. But that is not my idea. That is not why I am for this. I just want people to have the opportunity to vote," claimed Sen. Wendell Ford (D-Ky.)[41]

When Congress considers regulations of elections and campaigns, the public policies it makes can directly affect members' own political interests. These issues come up with great regularity. There were extended battles in the Senate over campaign finance regulations in 1991, 1993, 1997, and 2001,[42] over voter registration procedures in 1991, 1992, 1993, and 2002, over federal employee involvement in elections in 1990 and 1993, and over election administration in 2002. As a good-government matter, all members profess support for free and fair elections and lawful democratic participation. Nevertheless, policies related to these ends tend to be highly controversial. Votes on such matters as federal employee involvement in elections, the design and distribution of voter registration forms, the type of election machinery used, and the rules governing provisional ballots consistently break on party lines. The public record on these debates is filled with examples of members suggesting that the other party wants to rewrite the rules to its own advantage. Members' fears may be exaggerated or unwarranted, but the parties view one another with great suspicion on these matters.

The Hatch Act, which limits federal employees' participation in partisan political activity, is a recurrent source of controversy. Designed to ensure that government employees are not coerced into providing election support in order to retain their jobs, the law was passed in 1939, at a time when less than one-third of the federal workforce were professional public servants. The professionalization of the federal civil service has rendered the law in some respects outdated, but efforts to revise it invariably spark partisan controversy. Federal civil servants are perceived as disproportionately Democratic in party affiliation, in part because public employee unions' campaign contributions go overwhelmingly to Democratic candidates. "The federal work force is a major potential source of manpower in campaigns," as Rep. Alfred R. Wynn (D-Md.) explained, "No question that it's likely to be an asset to the Democratic party" (Alston 1993).

Consistent with these perceptions of the partisan tilt of the federal workforce, Senate Democrats overwhelmingly favor proposals that would relax regulations on the political activities of federal employees, and Republicans overwhelmingly oppose them.[43] The floor debates clearly show that members perceive that these regulations have the potential to help or hurt their parties. During consideration of Hatch Act reform in 1993, a number of Republicans entered into the *Congressional Record* a *New York Times* editorial that argued, "Senate Democrats seem determined to get Federal civil servants in the business of hustling political contributions from their co-workers."[44] During the 1990 debate, Sen. Phil Gramm (R-Tex.) proposed that the Senate extend the same rules governing federal employees' political activities to members of the armed forces: "If this amendment fails, I guess I am going to begin to wonder if maybe there is an objective here to pick and choose, based on the plain, old partisanship . . . of the various members of the branches of our Government."[45]

Debates over rules governing voter registration are similarly contentious. During the 1992 and 1993 consideration of the Motor Voter Act, a measure that would require states to allow citizens to register to vote while applying for or renewing a driver's license or other public services, Republicans charged the Democrats with pursuing a partisan agenda. "It is just another one of the many politically motivated—but politically correct—measures that we have come to expect around here," said Sen. McConnell (R-Ky.).[46] Democrats responded by accusing Republicans of being afraid of the voters. Sen. Ford said, "I am not afraid of the people. I am not afraid of their voice and what they think."[47] "The political fears of the Republicans were unfounded and really pathetic," said Sen. Mitchell (D-Maine); "They don't have enough confidence in their own candidates and their own positions, so they try to prevent the registration of more voters" (Sammon 1993b).

As during consideration of the Hatch Act, members of Congress were very sensitive to the political leanings of affected groups. Republicans were especially suspicious of proposed provisions in the Motor Voter law requiring state welfare offices to make voter registration forms available. "Why is it that we are selecting the welfare population?" asked Rep. Jack Kingston (R-Ga.); "Why do we not just say, 'Hey look: When you go to sell your stock and go down to Merrill Lynch, you can register to vote. That would increase voter participation. But that is not what this bill is all about'" (Sammon 1993a). In the Senate, Republican senators offered an amendment that would require all members of the Armed Forces to be registered to vote, suggesting that failure to support this bill would be tantamount to hypocrisy, "Mr. President, any opposition to this amendment contradicts directly the majority leader's words of yesterday. The men and women who serve in the military should be given every opportunity to register to vote and to vote."[48] On a tabling motion, 98 percent of Democrats voted to kill the measure while 95 percent of Republicans supported it.[49] The mean party difference on all Senate votes ($n = 25$) related to the Motor Voter law was 85.

Senate debate over election reform in 2002 affords additional examples of the partisan suspicion that pervades congressional consideration of campaign and election regulation. Republicans put Democrats on the defensive during this debate with measures aimed at preventing voter fraud. Concerned that these measures would disproportionately burden Democratic voters, Democratic senators objected. Of the requirement that first-time voters who registered by mail provide some proof of identity, Sen. Charles Schumer (D-N.Y.) said, "On the surface, that sounds to be a very reasonable requirement. But once you begin to scratch the surface, you discover it could easily disenfranchise countless eligible voters."[50] Sen. McConnell quoted from a *Wall Street Journal* editorial that portrayed Democrats as favoring voter fraud: "Dogs and dead people don't have the constitutional right to vote, but more of them are going to start turning up at the polls if Senate Democrats, led by New York's Charles Schumer, have their way."[51] The mean party difference on all Senate votes related to the 2002 Help America Vote Act ($n = 11$) was 91.

Partisan disagreement on campaign and election regulation mirrors voting behavior and debate on other good-government causes, just as intense partisan disagreement coexists with bipartisan agreement on values. There is no evidence in the record that Democrats and Republicans disagree about the desirability of preventing voter fraud, the value of democratic participation, or the need to prevent partisan exploitation of civil servants. Nevertheless, both parties clearly analyze this type of legislation with careful attention to provisions that might harm their electoral prospects.

Partisan Interests and Good-Government Causes

After the Senate Judiciary Committee authorized subpoenas to investigate the 2006 firings of eight U.S. attorneys, Sen. Tom Coburn (R-Okla.) remarked, "This is about who can make someone bloody, who can make someone look bad" (quoted in Schor 2007, 4). Generally speaking, these are the political stakes when Congress considers good-government causes. No one denies that the administration of justice should be above partisan politics. Everyone agrees that it would be inappropriate for the attorney general to fire U.S. attorneys because they indicted too many Republicans or too few Democrats. The question is thus not about differing policy preferences on which members of Congress might be ranged on a continuum from left to right. Instead, the central question, as in the consideration of most good-government matters, is whether both parties are equally competent or ethical. In such conditions, one party has great electoral incentive to work collectively to undercut the reputation of its opposition. And a party on the receiving end of such efforts will cooperate to defend its collective reputation.

Agreement on ultimate values is what defines good-government causes as valence issues. But this agreement does not by any means preclude contentious partisan politics in Congress. Members of Congress do not passively wait to see which party might obtain a valence advantage by being perceived by the broader public as more committed to common values. Instead, members work together as partisan teams in service of their common electoral interests. Fellow partisans cooperate to undercut the opposing party's brand name and to enhance their own. They seek to make the opposition party's nominees appear ethically compromised and to expose wrongdoing. They pursue politically beneficial investigations into the Whitewater scandal or the response to Hurricane Katrina. They demand reforms to eliminate government inefficiencies and root out waste, fraud, and abuse. They use the legislative tools at their disposal—floor speeches, roll-call votes, and investigations—to advance their shared interests.

Despite the importance of valence issues in the literature on mass voting behavior, congressional scholars have given relatively little attention to them. Instead, as shown in chapter 2, contemporary legislative scholarship has become preoccupied with ideological models of voting behavior, with scholars attending almost exclusively to congressional behavior and lawmaking on issues that can be conceptualized on the left-right continuum. A few congressional scholars have focused on how candidates or parties who enjoy valence advantages with the public will position themselves on left-right issues (Ansolabehere and Snyder 1998; Enelow and Hinich 1982; Groseclose 2001; Moon 2004), but there has been no serious work on valence issues themselves. Instead, the dependent variable of scholarly interest in studying congressional policymaking is usually the extent or outcome of ideological conflict (Cox and McCubbins 2005, 171–97; Erikson, MacKuen, and Stimson 2004, 284–382; Krehbiel 1998).

The analysis of Senate roll-call voting behavior reveals that the parties strongly disagree on policies where no competing values are at stake: measures to fight corruption, uphold ethics standards, investigate failures, collect information, promote fiscal responsibility, ensure electoral integrity, and make government operations more efficient. Good-government causes divide Republicans from Democrats more deeply than the typical matter considered in Congress. In fact, Republicans and Democrats disagree with one another as much on these issues as on matters that separate liberals from conservatives on the grounds of economic, social, or foreign policy. Over the period examined, 1981–2004, good-government issues were considerably more divisive along party lines than the explosive social issues of race, abortion, and gay rights. No other substantive type of issue was as likely to produce a perfect party-line vote in the Senate with all Democrats on one side and all Republicans on the other.

Compared with ideological questions, party positioning on good-government causes is fluid and tactical. It is easy to summarize the parties' general tendencies on position issues: Republicans tend to be more conservative than Democrats on social and economic issues and more hawkish in foreign policy. Analysis of floor debate reveals that parties exhibit little consistency over time on good-government causes. Instead, members take positions that are consistent with their partisan self-interest.

Neither party reliably stakes out a more rigorous stance on government ethics or on the need to investigate government failures and abuses. Instead, members of the potentially advantaged party pursue the case. When presented with evidence of government failure or ethical shortcomings, the advantaged party demands a full accounting and mobilizes resources to investigate. The disadvantaged party resists the release of information damaging to its reputation and denounces the opposition for playing partisan politics.

Neither party is consistently the champion of balanced budgets. Instead, fiscal irresponsibility is a criticism that one party, usually the one not controlling the presidency, levels at the other. Members exploit debates over budget process to make a case that their partisan opposition cannot be trusted to manage fiscal affairs responsibly and competently. This pattern was noted as long ago as 1951 in Julius Turner's seminal *Party and Constituency: Pressures on Congress.* "Republican denunciations of bureaucratic waste and inefficiency are as much a part of the American scene as hot dogs and apple pie. Examination of the roll-calls, however, leads to the conclusion that party positions on this issue have been almost entirely dependent upon the question of who controlled the government," wrote Turner (1951, 56). "With Democrats in the White House, Republican opposition to bureaucracy was clear. . . . With Republicans in the White House, on the other hand, Democratic congressmen led the assault on bureaucratic growth." Rather than trying to shoehorn debates over balanced budgets into an ideological framework, issues of fiscal responsibility and debates over waste, fraud, and abuse should be understood in the context of their implications for parties' claims to good government and thus to maintain control of the government.

In focusing so heavily on position issues, legislative scholars have neglected the congressional politics of governmental performance. Since

Stokes (1963) articulated the distinction between position and valence issues, scholars in other political science fields have explored the way the two types of issue affect mass voting behavior and election outcomes. But the dominance of the concept of "ideology" has led scholars of legislative politics to give little attention to this type of issue. Party brand names are greatly affected by whether the party in power is perceived to execute policies successfully. Party reputations are strengthened or weakened by whether its officeholders are seen as ethical. By viewing congressional politics as primarily about legislating on position issues, the literature has systematically deemphasized the congressional politics of scandal, investigation, process, information control, and public relations.[52]

Good-government issues lie at the heart of party politics in Congress. Indeed, these causes elicit the rawest forms of partisan politics as members call into question their opponents' integrity and competence. A focus on the congressional politics of good government highlights the ways in which party conflict is opportunistic and focused on electoral advantage. The politics of good government, ironically, is hardball.

CHAPTER SIX

Procedural Partisanship

Intraparty Dealmaking and Partisan Bloc Voting

"Every Republican in Congress today . . . is a member of a team, one which he joined of his own free will. . . . He has a vote, like every other member . . . in the selection of the quarterbacks. A successful team is one which executes the signals called by the duly chosen quarterback. Differences of opinion as to the choice of a particular play are ironed out in the huddles before the plays are called, not afterward. Team play is," as former RNC Chairman Carroll Reece put it, "the first essential of success" (quoted in Berdahl 1949, 207). As ideological coalitions, party members work together because their individual policy preferences are relatively proximate to one another. But as institutionalized *teams*, party members cooperate with one another and come into conflict with their party opponents for reasons that extend far beyond ideology.

For parties, "success" means more than passing legislation that reflects their members' policy preferences. Legislative parties must also succeed in winning elections and in organizing to manage the business of the institution. Previous chapters have focused on the ways that senators use floor politics to advance their party's electoral goals as well as to make policy. Members of the president's party work in concert with the president to build a reputation for coherent and effective leadership; the opposition party seeks to undercut the president and to make the case for change. Members exploit good-government causes to enhance their own party's reputation for integrity and competence and, just as important, to undermine the opposing party's claims to these qualities.

This chapter examines the partisan politics of floor procedure in the Senate, another significant source of partisan contestation. The outcome of procedural conflicts determines, among other things, which proposals will come up for a vote on the merits and when they will do so. As with presidential agenda items and good-government causes, the parties' images are very much at stake in decisions about the content of the floor agenda. The majority party wants to focus debate on its party "message," issues designed to put the party in a favorable light. The minority party contests the majority's use of the floor for public relations, seeks to change the subject to its own message and issues instead, and attempts to force the majority party to take votes on difficult or divisive political issues. The minority party can succeed by embarrassing the majority party, without achieving its own policy goals at all.

In addition to electoral considerations, procedural votes also directly raise questions about power, that is, about control over floor proceedings. Procedural battles not only determine what policies will be considered; they are about "who calls the shots." Even in the less majoritarian Senate, the majority party expects to be able to set the floor agenda, and individual members of the majority party generally have a stake in their party leaders retaining this basic prerogative. At the same time, the minority party persistently challenges the majority's control. Partisan conflict on procedural matters is a struggle over who will control the agenda and the flow of business on the Senate floor, not simply a contest between the two parties' policy preferences. Indeed, political power has value independent of the purposes to which it is put, and partisan power struggles over control of the floor can occur even when the Senate is considering matters that are entirely noncontroversial in policy terms. The power stakes alone can spark partisan conflict, separate from any specific policy or ideological disputes that divide the parties.

In light of the important partisan interests at stake in procedural politics, this chapter offers additional reason to look beyond ideology to understand party politics in Congress. Since Fenno (1973), scholars have distinguished between legislators' electoral, policy, and power goals. So far, the argument of this book has centered primarily on the ways that the parties' sense of shared *electoral* fate sparks partisan conflict. The parties react to presidents and to good-government issues with an eye to how floor votes and debates will affect their party's overall public image. Procedural decisions, however, implicate members' power interests as much as their electoral interests. In addition to their significant policy consequences, procedural controversies are always also about control of the chamber.

Analysis presented here shows that members' policy preferences alone cannot account for the extremely high levels of partisan conflict on procedural matters. Instead, the evidence strongly suggests that partisans act as teams on procedural matters, teams in pursuit of common electoral and power interests, not simply as ideological coalitions. First, analysis of roll-call voting patterns reveals that procedural votes are far more controversial along partisan lines than one would expect based on issue content. Indeed, procedural votes are highly partisan, *regardless* of underlying issue content and even when the issues at stake are otherwise not at all divisive. In fact, party divisions are just as deep on procedural and parliamentary matters that do not involve ideological issues as they are on substantive votes involving the most ideologically divisive issues in American politics.

Second, analysis of floor debates involving procedural controversies sheds further light on procedural partisanship. In Fenno's terminology, it becomes clear that members' electoral and power goals, as well as their policy preferences, profoundly shape their handling of procedural matters. The content of floor debate affords little evidence that party cooperation on procedure is the result of Senate leadership pressure. Instead, it strongly suggests that partisans engage in a great deal of *willing* cooperation on procedural matters in order to further their parties' collective interests.

Third, an analysis over time reveals that the heightened levels of partisan conflict in the contemporary Senate are to a great extent the result of improved team play on procedural matters. Party conflict on procedural votes has increased dramatically, including procedural conflicts involving issues that do not implicate liberalism and conservatism. Even outside the sorts of issues on which senators might "polarize" along the ideological continuum in American politics, contemporary Senate parties are simply better-organized teams who, when faced with procedural choices, "execute the signals called by the duly chosen quarterback" to a greater extent than they did in the past.

Senate Procedure and Party Conflict

A very large proportion of roll-call votes in the Senate occur on procedural matters. During the study period, fully 42 percent of all Senate votes were taken on motions[1] rather than on direct policy questions of whether to adopt an amendment, pass a bill, approve a nominee, ratify a treaty, amend the Constitution, or override a veto. Most common is the motion to table, a nondebatable motion that can be made on any pending question which, when agreed to, stops further consideration of the underlying matter. Motions to table alone made up 28 percent of all Senate roll-call votes. Well over a third of all amendments that received Senate roll-call votes, 43 percent, were dealt with on tabling motions, and more than a quarter of all pending questions were subjected to motions to table. Motions to waive the Budget Act represented 5 percent of all Senate roll-call votes during the study period.[2] Motions for cloture made up another 5 percent.

Procedural votes have one well-known characteristic: they usually break on party lines (Cox and McCubbins 1993; Den Hartog and Monroe 2006; Marshall, Prins, and Rohde 1999; Theriault 2006). Figure 6.1 displays the dramatic differences in levels of partisanship on procedural and substantive votes.[3] The figure's two bars show the percentage of party-line votes occurring on procedural and substantive votes; the line tracks the mean party difference on these two types of votes. Fully 73 percent of all procedural votes pitted a majority of Democrats against a majority of Republicans, while only 37 percent of substantive votes divided along party lines. The mean party difference score across all substantive votes was 31.7, compared with 56.1 for procedural votes.

Why is there such sharp partisanship on procedural votes? The high level of partisanship on procedural matters is often noted (Ansolabehere, Snyder, and Stewart 2001a; Cox and Poole 2002; Snyder and Groseclose 2000), but the scholarly literature offers surprisingly little in the way of explanation.

The most common explanation offered is that party leaders are more influential on procedural matters than on substantive votes. This topic is discussed most often in the literature on "party effects." In this literature, party effects are generally defined as leaders' ability to use positive or negative incentives to induce members to bow to party discipline against their own policy preferences (Krehbiel 1993; McCarty, Poole, and Rosenthal 2001; Snyder and Groseclose 2000). Heightened leadership influence on these votes is generally thought to stem from the lower public salience of procedural votes. Scholars have long hypothesized that members are more willing to support their parties on matters that are less visible to constituents (Smith 1989; Theriault 2006; Van Houweling 2003).[4] Procedural and parliamentary votes do tend to receive less media attention than substantive votes (Theriault 2006). Given the difficulties constituents have in learning about and understanding procedural votes,

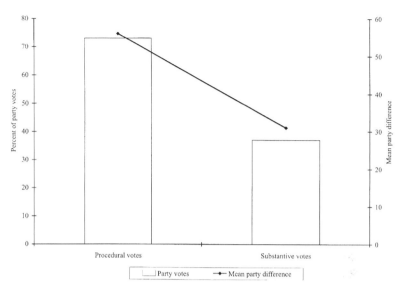

FIGURE 6.1. Partisanship on procedural and substantive votes in the Senate, 97th–108th Congress.

senators' "voting leeway" (Fenno 1978, 151–57) on such matters is un-doubtedly greater.

Taken on its own, though, freedom from constituency pressure would also allow senators to vote according to their own personal policy prefer-ences, rather than obeying dictates from leadership. In light of the lim-ited sanctions and inducements available to Senate leaders (Baker 2001, 93–96), it is difficult to imagine the majority or minority leader routinely whipping fellow senators into line against their own policy preferences, even on low salience votes. Senators' motivations undergirding their dif-ferent behavior on procedural and substantive votes are impossible to as-certain with any degree of certainty. But the *Congressional Record* offers many occasions when senators justify their votes on procedural matters, and these discussions can shed light on these votes. As will be shown be-low, senators often explicitly state that their considerations on procedural votes are different from on substantive votes, and they often explain that they are willingly going along with party leadership on such votes, despite disagreements on some substantive matters of policy.

An alternative to party pressure as an explanation for the higher level of partisan conflict on procedural matters is that procedural devices are disproportionately used to handle contentious matters. Senators may prefer to rely on procedural mechanisms to dispose of divisive or controversial issues, rather than taking votes on them directly. If so, then the higher level of partisanship on procedural votes would simply be an artifact of the more divisive nature of the underlying issues dealt with using procedural tactics.

Procedural votes are often, as Oleszek (2007, 234) explains, "a classic ploy to avoid being recorded directly on politically sensitive policy issues. . . . [If] a procedural vote can be arranged to kill or delay a controversial bill, it is likely to win the support of senators who may prefer to duck the substantive issue." Procedural motions afford legislators some cover. In voting to table an amendment, Sen. Robert Byrd (D-W.V.) noted, "A senator can say that his vote was not on the merits of the issue. . . . he can . . . assign any number of reasons [for his vote], one of which would be . . . so that the Senate would get on with its work."[5] Sen. Edward Zorinsky (D-Neb.) complained about the ambiguity: "A motion to table is really a neat and cute method of avoiding one's duty as a U.S. Senator. . . . it is an attempt by some to have it both ways."[6] Given that procedural votes can enable senators to dispose of controversial issues without taking a clear stand, senators may make use of them to handle ideologically charged matters.

Controlling for the type of issue being considered can illuminate whether the higher level of partisanship on procedural votes is a consequence of the more controversial nature of the issues that are handled procedurally. Scholarship examining party conflict on procedural matters, however, generally does not take account of issue content. Without an independent measure of the issue content of procedural and substantive votes, however, it is not possible to adequately interpret differences in how members behave on procedural and substantive votes. The higher levels of partisanship on procedural matters may be a result of either senators' different political incentives or of the different types of issues involved.

Figure 6.2 compares the issue composition of procedural and substantive votes. The data reveal that, to a very limited extent, senators do prefer to use procedural votes to handle ideologically controversial matters. A larger proportion of procedural votes than of substantive votes dealt with issues that were controversial along liberal-conservative lines. However, the differences are not at all dramatic: 42 percent of substantive votes occurred on matters in the ideological categories identified in the study, while 48 percent of procedural votes dealt with such matters.[7] The disparity

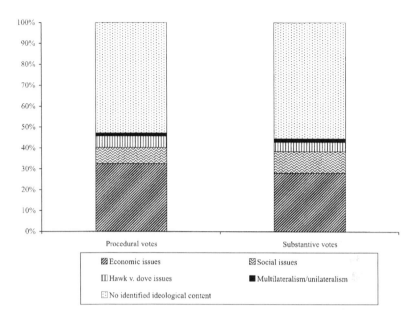

FIGURE 6.2. Issue composition of procedural and substantive votes in the Senate, 97th–108th Congress.

is mainly driven by the economic category. Economic issues constituted a larger proportion of procedural votes, 32 percent, than of substantive votes, 26 percent.[8] Social issues, by contrast, make up precisely the same proportion of substantive votes as of procedural votes, 7.6 percent. Hawk vs. dove issues are only slightly more prevalent among procedural votes, 5.4 percent than among substantive votes, 4.3 percent. These modest differences in the types of issues being handled by procedural and substantive votes simply cannot account for the strikingly dissimilar levels of partisanship that occur on the two types of votes.

Instead, partisanship is more pronounced on procedural votes than on substantive votes, *controlling for issue type*. Put differently, the same types of issues divide the Senate more deeply along party lines when they are considered as procedural matters than as substantive policy questions.

Figure 6.3 displays the proportion of procedural and substantive votes that divided along party lines, controlling for whether the underlying issue was classified in any of the ideological issue categories identified in the study. For more refined analysis, table 6.1 divides procedural votes into two categories to distinguish between motions that are very closely

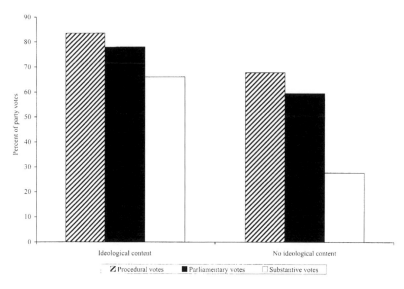

FIGURE 6.3. Effect of procedural posture on the likelihood of a party vote.

linked to a particular question of public policy and those that deal more with control of the parliamentary situation generally. For purposes of this analysis, I define votes on the types of motions that are most directly connected to particular policy questions (the motion to table, to recommit, and to waive the Budget Act) as "procedural votes." Votes on motions that deal more with the overall parliamentary situation (to proceed to consider a measure, to appeal the ruling of the chair, for cloture, to adjourn, for attendance, to waive the rules of the Senate) are termed "parliamentary votes."[9]

The data reveal that procedural and parliamentary votes are almost always partisan, *regardless* of whether the underlying issue involved any of the conventional sources of disagreement between liberals and conservatives. Procedural votes on nonideological matters were twice as partisan on average as substantive votes on nonideological matters.[10] In fact, procedural votes on *non*ideological issues were approximately just as controversial along party lines as substantive votes on ideological issues.

The decision to frame an issue procedurally or on the merits has an enormous impact on Senate behavior. Among substantive votes, ideological issues are far more partisan than issues not involving ideologically contentious matters. But among procedural votes, party divisions occur at dramatically high rates regardless of policy content. On average in the study, substantive votes on ideological issues were 139 percent more partisan than substantive votes on nonideological issues. But when issues were framed procedurally, ideological content does not make a great difference for partisanship: 68 percent of procedural votes on nonideological issues were party votes and 83 percent of procedural votes on ideological issues were party votes, a mere 22 percent increase in partisanship that can be attributed to the more controversial nature of the underlying issues. Similarly, parliamentary votes divided along party lines more than three-quarters of the time when they occurred on ideologically controversial matters but also fully 60 percent of the time when they occurred on issues not connected to conventional understandings of liberal-conservative differences.

Indeed, procedural votes break more starkly along party lines than substantive votes on some of the *most* ideologically explosive issues. Substantive votes relating to ideologically charged policy questions sparked party-line votes 66 percent of the time, a level of partisanship slightly *lower* than that on procedural votes on *non*ideological issues (68 percent). Unlike substantive votes, procedural votes generally break on partisan lines regardless of whether they deal with any ideologically contentious issue.

Table 6.1 displays the mean level of party differentiation for substantive, procedural, and parliamentary votes within each type of ideological issue. When nonideological issues appear as straightforward policy questions, they tend to be relatively uncontroversial. But when they appear as procedural matters—thus implicating power over the floor agenda—they are far more likely to break along party lines. The mean party polarization

TABLE 6.1 **Mean party difference by type of vote, controlling for ideological content**

	Substantive votes	Procedural votes	Parliamentary votes
Any economic policy issue	55.5	67.6	67.7
Government's share of the economy	65.5	72.9	74.6
Regulation of private economic activity	47.5	59.7	66.4
Distribution of the tax burden	64.7	71.1	73.5
Redistributive social programs	50.1	71.3	61.8
Social issue	40.7	47.8	49.8
Hawk vs. dove issue	49.6	55.4	79.6
Multilateralism vs. unilateralism	39.4	38.6	48.3
No identifiable ideological content	21.7	51.0	48.0
Any ideological content	50.8	62.3	63.2

Note: Analysis of variance reveals that the higher levels of partisanship on procedural and parliamentary votes are statistically significant ($p < .001$) for every category of vote.

on procedural votes dealing with nonideological issues is much greater than party polarization on substantive votes on nonideological issues—51 compared to 21.7. This finding provides strong support for the inference that partisan team play can organize party conflict, even when ideological differences do not.

Moreover, the average party difference score on procedural votes on nonideological issues is considerably higher than the typical level of partisan disagreement on substantive votes involving social issues, such as abortion and gay marriage (mean party difference of 40.7). Indeed, the parties disagree on procedural matters not involving ideological issues at levels comparable to those seen on substantive votes on economic regulations (47.5), redistributive social programs (50.1), and hawk vs. dove issues (49.6). The only substantive ideological categories that exhibit higher levels of partisanship than procedural votes on *non*ideological issues are those involving the distribution of the tax burden (64.7) and government's share of the economy (65.5).

Framing a vote as a procedural or parliamentary matter greatly increases the extent of partisan disagreement for every issue category aside from multilateralism vs. unilateralism.[11] When regulatory issues are structured as procedural or parliamentary questions, for example, they are at least 30 percent more partisan on average than substantive votes on the same category of issue. Procedural votes on redistributive social programs are 42 percent more partisan than substantive votes on redistributive social programs.

A more detailed look at how the procedural posture of a vote affects Senate behavior is provided in table 6.2, which displays the level of partisan disagreement on substantive, procedural, and parliamentary votes across the functional issue categories in the Policy Agendas Project (see chap. 4). On the same types of issues, procedural votes are on average 75 percent more partisan than substantive votes. The difference between procedural and substantive votes ranges from a 30 percent increase in partisanship on civil rights to a 117 percent increase in partisanship in votes dealing with government operations. Increases in partisanship are equally pronounced on parliamentary votes, controlling for issue content.[12] Using both the ideological classification scheme as well as the Policy Agendas categories, I find that senators are far more likely to break along party lines when issues are framed as procedural or parliamentary matters than they are on the same types of issues when they occur as straightforward votes on substantive policy.

TABLE 6.2 **Mean party difference by type of vote, controlling for issue topic**

	Substantive votes	Procedural votes	Parliamentary votes
Macroeconomics	45.2	63.2	64.5
Civil rights	37.0	47.8	34.7
Health	42.2	61.5	54.1
Agriculture	25.2	39.1	49.6
Labor, employment, immigration	37.9	60.0	58.1
Education	45.7	75.2	68.5
Environment	24.5	50.5	47.9
Energy	25.7	37.3	50.1
Transportation	24.8	37.1	51.9
Law, crime, family issues	30.0	51.0	44.5
Social welfare	35.0	67.9	74.7
Community development and housing	38.1	60.0	36.1
Banking, finance, domestic commerce commerce	27.1	51.5	41.1
Defense	28.7	49.8	60.4
Space, science, technology	26.5	50.0	46.4
Foreign trade	18.9	39.5	23.0
International affairs	16.6	38.7	50.7
Government operations	28.9	62.9	64.4
Public lands and water management	27.0	54.0	54.3
Average	37.7	56.3	55.3
n	5011	2741	842

Note: Analysis of variance reveals that the higher levels of partisanship on procedural and parliamentary votes are statistically significant ($p < .001$) for every category of vote.

Based on this analysis, there is virtually no evidence that procedural and parliamentary devices are disproportionately used to dispose of controversial matters. It is not that the issues dealt with using procedural and parliamentary devices are inherently more partisan; instead it appears that Senate behavior on issues *becomes* more partisan when they are presented as procedural or parliamentary questions. The same types of issues generate very different reactions from senators depending on whether they come to the floor as procedural or substantive questions.

After discounting the supposition that procedural votes are more partisan because of the types of issues involved, the fundamental question remains unanswered: Why are procedural and parliamentary matters so highly partisan? Do members just take party or leadership cues on procedural votes? Sen. Bob Packwood (R-Ore.) once observed, "This is a procedural vote, and in the Senate we traditionally stick with the leadership on such votes."[13] If this is so, *why* do senators "traditionally" do this? Is it "leadership pressure," as the party-effects literature posits? Or are there other considerations that prompt this highly patterned behavior?

Why Are Procedural and Parliamentary Votes So Partisan?

In order to shed light on the reasons that procedural and parliamentary votes are so much more partisan than substantive votes, I turn to an examination of debates in the *Congressional Record* in which procedural options are discussed. These discussions further reinforce the inference drawn from the quantitative analysis above that senators' policy preferences alone cannot explain their decisions on procedural and parliamentary questions. Furthermore, the evidence from the *Record* suggests that these decisions are also not primarily the result of "pressure" from leadership, although leaders often do play a major role in these discussions. Instead, I will argue that party-line voting on procedural and parliamentary matters is better understood as a kind of partisan team play. When handling these matters, partisans *willingly cooperate* in their common electoral and power interests. This cooperation is not always easy to achieve, but the *Record* provides little evidence for the supposition that leadership incentives (rewards and sanctions) are the primary mechanisms by which party cohesion is achieved.

Rather than leadership pressure, there appear to be three major reasons for the higher levels of partisanship on procedural and parliamentary votes. First, it is clear that senators simply do not regard procedural votes as equivalent to substantive votes, even on occasions when the two types of vote can achieve the same substantive policy outcome. Senators draw sharp distinctions between procedural and substantive votes, and they do not view procedural votes as straightforward expressions of their views on policy questions. Procedural and parliamentary votes have implications for their parties' electoral and power interests, and in casting these types of votes members take into account broader issues of party strategy, not just their individual policy preferences.

Second, procedural and parliamentary devices are frequently used to protect complex agreements among majority party members from minority party floor obstruction and challenge. In such cases, majority party members do not vote their personal policy preferences on each individual amendment but stand together as a bloc to support a deal worked out, in a partisan setting, off the Senate floor. Majority party senators will often cut a deal amongst themselves, sometimes after difficult internal negotiations. They are then able to monopolize decision-making power by voting down any amendment that would undermine that agreement, even when those amendments raise issues on which there were differences of opinion within the majority party. Indeed, it is clear that sometimes the majority party's strategy is simply to vote to table any and all amendments, regardless of what is being proposed.

Third, partisanship on procedural motions is frequently the result of conflict over agenda control. It is not unusual for intense procedural conflict to occur during debates on issues that are otherwise *entirely* uncontroversial. Minority party members frequently instigate procedural conflict during floor consideration of legislative issues that command broad bipartisan support. By raising issues and amendments that the majority party does not support considering at that time, the minority party attempts to wrest control of the floor agenda from the majority. In response to these efforts, the majority bands together to protect their party leadership's agenda-setting prerogatives. A measure will frequently pass with few votes in opposition, even though a great deal of procedural wrangling occurred during its floor consideration. In other words, party conflict over the agenda can occur in the absence of partisan disagreement over the substantive policy issues on the floor. Each of these causes is examined in more detail below.

Procedural votes are viewed differently

Senators recognize fundamental differences between procedural votes and substantive votes "on the merits." During floor debate, senators regularly distinguish between votes on tabling motions and substantive "up or down" votes. Tabling an amendment generally has the same practical effect on policy outcomes as voting an amendment down, but senators proposing amendments *much* prefer to have a vote on the merits of the language rather than on a tabling motion. "If there is a motion to table—I hope there will not be," said Sen. Jesse Helms (R-N.C.) during a debate over the 1989 Department of Defense Authorization Act, "I hope there will be an up or down vote on it, but that is up to the managers of this bill."[14]

Procedural votes obfuscate the underlying policy question, even if they do not eliminate it entirely. Motions to table are not comparable to the special rules in the House of Representatives that allow members to avoid being recorded on particular issues at all. "Obviously," as Sen. Mitchell (D-Maine) observed in asking for support on a series of tabling motions, "you will be on record at least on a motion to table."[15] Even though a roll-call vote on a motion to table does put senators on the record, senators recognize that procedural votes allow for more alternative explanations than substantive votes. "When an amendment is tabled or rejected on the pending legislation," explained Sen. Arlen Specter (R-Pa.), "it does not mean that those who vote in favor of tabling the amendment disagree with the substance of it, if it were presented as a freestanding bill."[16]

Given the ambiguities involved in interpreting procedural votes, amendment sponsors clearly recognize that votes on procedure will simply not have the desired effect of forcing senators to take a public stand on the issue. "A motion to table can be interpreted—often is interpreted—as a procedural vote," Sen. Russ Feingold (D-Wisc.) said during a debate over a resolution involving President Clinton's intervention in Kosovo; "On something this important, we should be voting on the merits of the language."[17] Sen. Edward F. Kennedy (D-Mass.) objected to a unanimous consent request for consideration of a Patient's Bill of Rights on the basis that it "does not guarantee a clear vote or final action. The Republican leadership could meet this requirement simply by having procedural votes. . . . Under this proposal, the American people will never find out where the Senate stands on patient protections."[18]

It is not unusual for senators to assert that they might be able to muster the votes for a particular measure if they could get a direct vote on the substantive issue but nevertheless to expect defeat if it is handled as a procedural matter. During a debate over President Reagan's veto of the Fairness in Broadcasting Act of 1987, Sen. Bob Packwood (R-Ore.) complained that the Senate would have sustained the veto had a direct vote been permitted on the matter: "There are the votes to sustain the veto," said Packwood, "So, as the Democratic Party does not want to give the President a victory, they are going to move to refer the veto message to the Commerce Committee." "I do not know how many votes I might have had on the Democratic side on a veto who will stick with the leadership on the vote to re-refer," Packwood continued, "That is the procedure. That is the politics of it." Sen. Bob Dole (R- Kans.) lodged a similar complaint: "We think we have the votes, and we think the leadership on the other side has the process. . . . We cannot beat the majority on procedural votes, and many colleagues on the other side, for reasons that are probably very good, have decided to stick with the leadership on procedural votes. I have learned how things work here. If you are in the majority, you control pretty much the flow of legislation and what happens."[19]

Numerous examples in the *Congressional Record* also make it clear that majority party leaders generally expect that they can rely on support from fellow partisans on procedural votes. Leaders will indicate that time is running short and state simply that it "may be necessary to start tabling the amendments because we need to complete action on the bill."[20] In making statements like these, leaders clearly assume that tabling motions will indeed save floor time. But such an assumption only makes sense if leaders have confidence that the motions will usually be adopted. Otherwise, tabling motions would only lead to *more* time-consuming roll-call votes as leaders are voted down first on the tabling motion and then have to proceed to debate and then, eventually, a second roll-call vote on the merits. But it is not unusual for leaders to ask colleagues to "join in tabling the amendments that come up, so we can proceed and get on with this."[21]

The data show that leaders are not mistaken in expecting they will receive this kind of routine support on tabling motions. Figure 6.4 displays the success rate of amendments considered on the merits and amendments handled with tabling motions. Over the study period, 54 percent of amendments considered on the merits received at least majority support in the Senate; in most Congresses the success rate for amendments considered as substantive votes was around 60 percent. Amendments subjected to tabling motions, by contrast, almost always failed. Motions to table received majority support fully 80 percent of the time on average. In other words, only 20 percent of amendments handled with a motion to table received sufficient support from the Senate to avoid summary dismissal.

Speaking of members' behavior on procedural votes, Sen. Dale Bumpers (D-Ark.) complained, "My proposed amendment ought to get 100 votes in the U.S. Senate, but it will not. People will walk up to the door and up to the manager and say, 'What is our vote on this?'" Well, they will not have to ask, they know what their vote is. They know there has been a motion to table every single amendment."[22] In short, members do appear to "know what their votes are" on tabling motions and on procedural matters generally.

Senators' own public record discussions of procedural matters make it clear that legislative scholars are on shaky ground if they attempt to interpret members' behavior on procedural votes as uncomplicated "revealed policy preferences." Although senators' decisions on procedural questions are undoubtedly affected by their policy preferences, senators emphasize that they simply do not see procedural votes as a straightforward expression of their views on the merits of policy questions. To assume that senators' policy preferences inform their decisions on procedural matters in the same way as they affect their substantive policy decisions is to reject

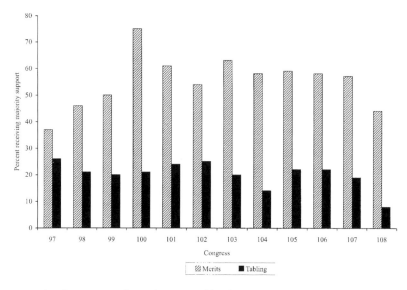

FIGURE 6.4. Success rates of amendments considered on the merits and amendments handled with tabling motions.
Note: Figure compares the percentage of amendments that received majority support when considered as "up or down" votes on the merits with the percentage of amendments that received majority support for further consideration when subjected to a tabling motion.

out of hand what senators themselves have to say about the differences between procedural and "up or down" votes. Beyond senators' own perspectives, further examination reveals that procedural decisions serve important *political* functions for senators, in addition to their effects on public policy. Senators have power and electoral interests at stake as they consider procedural matters. These political interests greatly complicate any assumption that senators' votes on procedure are solely driven by their policy views on the underlying issue.

Voting the "big picture"

Procedural votes are frequently used to protect complex agreements that could unravel in an open amending process. Senators regularly meet in settings in which deals are struck among fellow partisans, such as in majority party caucus, partisan task forces, or rump sessions of a standing or conference committee. After an agreement is reached across a set of issues, senators who support the package must then uphold the whole agreement during floor consideration despite the differences of opinion that exist among members of the group. Even when they might personally support a particular amendment, voting in favor of it can endanger the overall agreement. Indeed, in some cases, the whole deal may come apart unless all aspects receive protection from amendment. Because Senate procedure does not allow the majority to use special rules to prohibit the offering of troublesome amendments, all parties to an agreement must vote together as a bloc to table any and all amendments that would substantially alter the terms of the deal. In short, to protect intraparty agreements, senators must be willing to table amendments that they might personally prefer.

Senators often recognize that it is preferable for partisans to work together to arrive at the best policy that the team as a whole can support, rather than hashing out everything on the floor where the preferences of the opposing party have more potential influence. Thus, partisans come to an understanding within their own ranks and then support that deal against challenges. Sen. Harry Reid (D-Nev.), majority leader of the U.S. Senate, has said, "I've tried to create the reality that we are a team, and if we are going to be able to do some of the things we want to do on a policy basis, we have to stick together" (quoted in Brownstein 2007, 346). Individual senators must be willing to play along with the team—even at the cost of some sacrifice of their own personal preferences—in order to push through the best agreement that the team as a whole will support. A party that wants to obtain a reputation for coherent policy leadership simply must develop facility at cutting and sustaining these kinds of deals.

Senators may thus "vote the big picture" on procedural and parliamentary matters, rather than evaluating their policy preferences on each proposed amendment individually. Even when a senator might favor an amendment on the merits, she may well be prepared to vote to table it if it threatens the passage of a difficult agreement that has been worked out. Sen. Bob Dole (R-Kans.) explains the logic: "I know the Senator . . . was there about 10 or 12 hours a day for 3 weeks, and I think four or five others were, trying to hammer out an agreement. We did not agree on everything, but we did make an agreement that where there was a consensus or where there was an agreement, that the leadership would support the agreement. . . . it seems to me that we ought to, in this instance, *notwithstanding the difference of opinion*, support the leadership."[23]

Leaders regularly ask for members' support on procedural votes, even if they may disagree on the policy merits, by telling them that this is the best deal they are likely to get. Senate Majority Leader Tom Daschle

(D-S.D.) illustrated this type of appeal in a debate on the Uniting and Strengthening America (USA) Act of 2001: "My difficulty tonight is not substantive as much as it is procedural. There is no question, all 100 of us could go through the bill with a fine-tooth comb and pinpoint those things which we could improve. . . . While I may be sympathetic to some amendments offered tonight . . . I hope my colleagues will join me tonight in tabling this amendment and tabling every other amendment that is offered."[24] In response to Daschle's request above, Sen. Pat Leahy (D-Vt.) replied, "There are parts I would do differently. . . . I have high regard for the Senator from Wisconsin, and I would have loved to have had his amendment. . . . I can tell you right now, if we start unraveling this bill, we are going to lose all the parts we won and we will be back to a proposal that was blatantly unconstitutional in many parts. So I join, with no reluctance whatsoever in the leader's motion."

In light of the simple fact that a complex legislative package usually requires members to concede on some issues in order to win on others, members are often prepared to vote to table amendments that they favor in order to pass the package intact. "As far as I am concerned," Sen. Robert Byrd (D-W.V.) remarked in a debate on a continuing resolution, "I am willing to follow these [bill] managers down the barrel of a cannon. I may like the amendment. But I am ready to support them on tabling amendments."[25]

Procedural votes are sometimes used to push forward bipartisan deals reached in conference committee or in other bipartisan settings. Indeed, the entire leadership of a committee and a subcommittee, chairs and ranking members alike, may announce that they intend to move to table all amendments. As Sen. Sam Nunn (D-Ga.) replied to a request from a senator seeking consideration of an amendment to a Department of Defense Supplemental Appropriations package, "The leadership has already made it clear that six of us, the two leaders, Senator Warner, Senator McCain, and Senator Glenn, managers of the benefits package, and I have already agreed we will be moving to table all amendments."

But given the high levels of partisanship on procedural motions, it is clear that, in most cases, the two parties are not equally satisfied with the terms of the agreements being protected by tabling motions. Indeed, majority party members clearly use procedural maneuvers to protect explicitly partisan programs worked out in settings where minority party legislators have had little input. During the four-month-long conference committee negotiations over the Medicare Prescription Drug Improvement and Modernization Act of 2003, for example, only two of the seven Democrats who had been appointed to the conference committee were actually permitted to participate in the negotiations. Meetings at which key decisions were made were open only to legislators whom conference chairman Representative Bill Thomas (R-Calif.) viewed as part of "the coalition of the willing" (Inglehart 2004, 827). Once a deal was reached, all senators who were satisfied with the overall legislative package had to defend it, even when senators offered amendments involving issues on which there were differences of opinion among those who had signed off on the deal.

When proposed legislation involves a difficult compromise among majority party members, the minority party will often attempt to exploit divisions within the majority party. The debate over the balanced budget constitutional amendment in 1997 provides an example of how the tabling motion is used to protect agreements arrived at within the majority party. In writing the language of this amendment, Republicans had to work out several thorny issues.[26] One controversy involved the treatment of the Social Security Trust Fund. Some Republicans thought that Social Security should be exempted from the amendment because surpluses in Social Security were being used to mask the size of the deficit; failing to exempt Social Security would give constitutional legitimacy to the practice. For other Republicans, it was necessary to include Social Security in calculating the overall deficit so that balanced budget requirements would not exact unacceptably large spending cuts or tax increases. Another contentious matter was whether to include a provision in the amendment requiring a supermajority vote to raise taxes, which had been provided for in the 1982 draft of the balanced budget constitutional amendment and which many Republicans favored.

After reaching agreements on these and other issues, Sen. Orrin Hatch (R-Utah) indicated that Republicans intended to vote as a bloc to table any amendments: "With regard to tabling, we have always done it and intend to table the amendments if we can, and that is a right that we have. . . . it is just a matter of procedural choice, which I—and I just want to make it clear up front—will probably do on all, if not most all, amendments that come before the body on this matter."[27] To protect the consensus language, Republicans went on to table on party line votes all but one of the 14 amendments[28] Democrats sought to offer, including amendments on complicated matters such as how to handle Social Security funds, whether the balanced budget requirement should be waived during wartime, and whether Congress should concede so much power over fiscal policy to the federal

courts—all difficult issues for supporters of the balanced budget amendment. On each of these tabling motions there was nearly unanimous (>95
percent) Republican support for tabling and at least 70 percent support
among Democrats for continuing debate. As Hatch explained, "Everybody
knows [this version of the amendment] is the only one that has a chance
of passage. Everybody knows we have to keep amendments off or we lose
Senators here or Senators there."[29] In other words, if every senator who
wanted to pass the Balanced Budget Constitutional Amendment voted his
own individual policy preferences on every issue involved, no single draft
of the Amendment would have sufficient votes for passage.

After assenting to work together as a team in support of their agreement, senators may take little interest in the policy content of proposed
amendments. The Bankruptcy Abuse Prevention and Consumer Protection Act of 2005 was passed with party bloc voting of this kind. Senate Republicans sought to avoid conference committee negotiations by passing a
bill that House Republicans would accept in full, and House Republicans
had indicated that they would not accept any deviations from their version
of the legislation. All Senate amendments, regardless of content—even
those intended to correct problems in the legislation—were rejected along
nearly unanimous party lines: "In each case, the core rationale for rejection was not the worth of the amendment but that the House Republicans
would not accept it" (Mann and Ornstein 2006, 144). Sen. Hatch himself
had encountered this kind of bloc voting when serving in the minority
party in 1988 during debate over legislation requiring companies to notify
workers in advance of plant closures: "I have some other amendments
that will, hopefully, clarify other ambiguities in this bill, because what I am
trying to do is . . . to clarify [the bill], and if I have to live with it, I might
as well try to make it the best bill I possibly can."[30] But most amendments
(11 out of 17) were summarily tabled on party line votes, leading Hatch to
protest, "I think basically because there is a kind of party politic here that
is leading to tabling anything that is brought up, then I am not sure that
there is anything we can do to clarify or straighten out this bill."[31]

When party bloc voting of this kind occurs, it is generally not legitimate
to interpret senators' votes on each amendment as a sincere indicator of
their policy preferences on that issue. Instead, senators are voting "the
big picture." Supporters of the deal have come to the conclusion that the
best agreement possible has been reached, and they simply vote to protect
the overall package from challenges. The key policy decisions were made
elsewhere, off the Senate floor, and floor procedure is being used to ratify

a preexisting agreement. Opponents of the deal are likely to attempt to raise issues that were divisive or controversial within the supportive coalition, but sincere voting on all amendments would just allow opponents to pick apart the negotiated settlement. Unless senators who support the deal cannot think even one move ahead in this game, they will stand united against such ploys.

Partisan battles over agenda control

The parties often disagree strongly over procedural matters because of the power stakes involved, not because the two parties strongly disagree in policy terms on the specific policy issue being considered on the floor. Highly partisan procedural battles can occur in the context of passing popular measures that have broad, bipartisan support. Even if there are not significant policy or ideological disagreements over a measure, minority party members may seek to wrest control of the floor agenda in order to change the subject of floor debate to the minority party's priority issues or to force majority party members to take difficult votes on related (or even unrelated) matters. A great deal of partisan wrangling on procedural matters during floor debate does not necessarily indicate that there are any wide or important policy differences between the parties on the underlying issue.

For example, a lengthy, highly partisan floor battle occurred on an initiative with strong bipartisan support at the start of the 104th Congress. One of the Republican majority party's top priorities, listed in the Contract with America, was a measure to apply the same employment laws governing the rest of the country to Congress itself, extending the protections of the Civil Rights Act, the Americans with Disabilities Act, the Age Discrimination in Employment Act, and other employment nondiscrimination measures to the employees of the legislative branch. In no sense could one claim that granting all these protections to a new class of employees moved national policy in a conservative direction, and the measure eventually passed the Senate with 98 yea votes. Nevertheless, along the way, Democrats offered a series of amendments designed to cause political pain for their party opponents. Democrats submitted proposals to ban senators from accepting any gifts greater than $20 in value, to cut congressional pay in the event of a budget sequester, and to deny senators the ability to transfer frequent flyer miles from official travel to personal use, among other efforts designed to make the case that the majority party was not serious about congressional reform.[32] None of these amendments would have moved policy in either a liberal or a conservative direction, either. Nevertheless, all eleven Democratic-sponsored amendments were handled with procedural motions, all but two with highly polarized party line votes.

As in this example, procedural decisions always have implications for agenda control. Given their interests in maintaining their party's prerogatives in this area, majority party members must generally muster most of the votes to cut off debate. Meanwhile, when minority party members propose an amendment, they are likely to gain support from other minority party senators for consideration of their amendments. After all, even if other minority party members may not favor a particular amendment on the merits, they are still free to support a fellow partisan by voting against the motion to table in support of allowing debate on the amendment to continue. Although voting to table an amendment is often equivalent to killing it, voting against a tabling motion is in no sense equivalent to adopting an amendment. A minority party senator's vote against a tabling motion is a very low-cost way to curry favor with a party colleague, especially given that motions to table usually succeed in shutting down debate anyway. Partisanship on motions to table often stems from calculations as simple as these, and the differing policy preferences of liberals and conservatives may play little or no causal role.

That procedural votes primarily serve the majority party's purposes is immediately evident in aggregate voting behavior. Figures 6.5 and 6.6 display the overall level of majority and minority party support for amendments considered on tabling motions and for amendments considered on the merits. Figure 6.5 clearly reveals that most votes in favor of tabling amendments come from the majority party. The typical pattern on these motions is that most members of the majority party support tabling amendments, while most members of the minority party resist doing so. On average on motions to table, fully three-quarters of the majority party votes in favor of tabling, whereas only about 40 percent of the minority party votes in support. For comparison purposes, figure 6.6 shows the level of majority and minority party support when amendments receive votes on the merits. A very different pattern is in evidence here. Most members of both parties support amendments when they receive up or down votes. In general, the minority party is more supportive of amendments that receive direct votes on the merits than the majority party is, but in most years the typical amendment garners majority support within both parties.

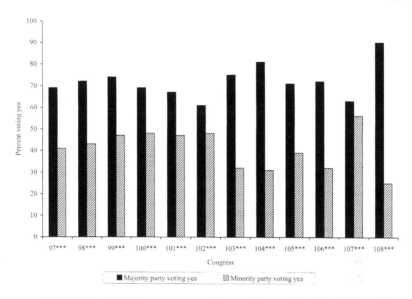

FIGURE 6.5. Majority and minority party support for amendments subjected to tabling motions. *Note: T*-tests were conducted to determine if these differences are statistically significant: *p* < .05; **p* < .01; ***p* < .001.

The wide disparities in Senate voting behavior between amendments considered on tabling motions and amendments considered directly on the merits strongly point to the use of tabling motions as a mechanism of majority party agenda control. The majority party uses tabling motions to manage what issues will come up for a substantive vote on the merits. By bloc voting on tabling motions, the majority party can ensure that amendments will not receive an up or down vote unless they command strong support within the majority party.[33]

Agenda control is important to the majority party for political reasons, regardless of whether the issues on the floor are controversial in policy terms. Whether or not senators have different policy preferences on an issue being considered, the minority party in the Senate can attempt to hijack any legislative vehicle and turn it to their own partisan purposes. Minority-party amendments can serve many purposes: exposing internal divisions within the majority party, forcing the majority to go on record on contentious issues, changing the subject to other topics, or simply as a means of delay and obstruction. It hardly matters whether the minority party's proposals are objectionable to the majority in ideological or policy terms; the majority party will likely resist minority members' amendments simply because to

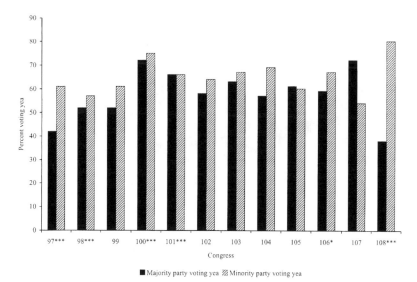

FIGURE 6.6. Majority and minority party support for amendments considered on the merits.

permit open debate on them is effectively to allow the minority party to set the floor agenda. To retain control of the floor, majority party leaders frequently move to dispose of amendments by tabling motions or (less frequently) attempt to invoke cloture to limit amendments altogether.

Nevertheless, any must-pass legislation provides the minority party with an opportunity to challenge the majority party's agenda control. Bills to increase the statutory debt limit are not ideological issues in the sense that they are merely permission for the federal treasury to pay the bills for funds that have already been spent. The alternative to a debt-limit increase is national default, a ruinous outcome for everyone, liberals and conservatives alike. The ideological shape of overall fiscal policy is set elsewhere. But high levels of partisanship on debt-limit votes occur because this must-pass legislation offers a ripe opportunity for the minority party to grandstand and excoriate the party in power for policy failures. For example, when a debt-limit increase was brought to the Senate floor in May 2003, Democrats proposed amendments to restrict the Department of the Treasury from any delays in investing payments to the Social Security Trust Fund, to reinstate the pay-as-you-go rule requiring revenue neutrality in all new taxing and spending legislation, and to reduce the size of the increase in the debt limit, among other proposals. It is quite clear that these amendments were designed mainly to make a political point, not to actually affect policy outcomes. Debates over "pay go," as discussed in chapter 5, are excellent vehicles for impeaching the fiscal management of the party in power. Debates over the size of the debt-limit increase are ways to highlight the governing party's profligacy. Similarly, amendments to limit the treasury secretary's flexibility in staving off default are designed to prompt "good government" debates about the legal limits of the treasury secretary's office and whether the current treasury secretary has exceeded his authority. Regardless of content, Republicans held together to shut down debate on all Democratic amendments. There was a series of nearly perfect party-line votes on amendments before the debt-limit increase was passed on May 23, 2003.[34]

Similarly, minority party members regularly attempt to use appropriations bills, especially emergency supplementals or continuing resolutions, as vehicles for their agenda. Even when there is no ideological controversy over the spending levels in the appropriations bill itself, there may nevertheless be many partisan votes on amendments on completely unrelated matters. Even when these unrelated matters are themselves not ideologically controversial, majority party members are still not likely to relish the opportunity for a minority party senator to usurp the majority's agenda-setting prerogatives. Whether or not an amendment may be objectionable on ideological or policy grounds, majority party senators are still likely to insist that regular order be followed.

As in each of the preceding examples, the power and electoral stakes involved in agenda control can create partisan controversy entirely separate from the merits of legislative proposals. Intense partisanship on procedural matters does not necessarily indicate that there are wide disagreements on policy. Republicans fought against Democratic amendments to the 1995 Congressional Accountability Act not because there were ideological differences between the parties on whether congressional pay should be cut in the presence of a budget sequester or whether members should be able to receive gifts larger than $20 in value, but because Republicans did not want to allow the minority to dictate the terms of the legislation or the debate. Similarly, the majority party votes to table minority amendments on votes to increase the debt limit because they do not want to allow the minority to use the legislation as a platform to force embarrassing votes and criticize their fiscal management. Procedural partisanship does indeed reflect policy differences, but it is also often a power struggle divorced from policy itself.

Improving Procedural Teamsmanship

Pundits and legislative scholars alike regularly interpret rising partisanship in Congress as "polarization," implying that the parties have moved
farther apart on the ideological continuum. But as has been argued
throughout this book, more highly organized partisan bloc voting is not
necessarily equivalent to "polarization." With more effective internal coordination, consultation, and leadership, parties can become more adept
at pursuing their collective electoral and power interests, whether or not
they are more opposed to one another in terms of political ideology. In
other words, parties can improve their team performance, separate from
changes in the preexisting levels of ideological consensus among individual
Republicans and Democrats. In other words, team play and ideological
polarization are analytically distinct dimensions of legislative behavior. It
is necessary to disentangle the two in order to adequately interpret congressional partisanship.

Figures 6.7 and 6.8 display mean party difference for procedural and
substantive votes over time, controlling for whether they involved any of
the ideological issues in this study. Over the period, the parties came into
increasingly intense conflict over procedural matters regardless of the nature of the underlying issue. As shown in figure 6.7, procedural votes on
nonideological issues were 72 percent more partisan in the 108th Congress
(2003–4) than they were in the 97th Congress (1981–82). Unquestionably,
ideological polarization occurred; the parties grew considerably farther
apart on both procedural and substantive votes involving ideological issues. But partisanship was higher on *everything*, regardless of ideological
content. In many Congresses, including in the 108th, there was actually
little difference in the extent of party conflict on procedural votes on ideological and nonideological issues.

Table 6.3 displays the results of a simple analysis in which the levels of
party differentiation in different categories of roll-call votes are regressed
on year. Over the period, Senate parties came into increasingly intense
conflict over procedure regardless of the nature of the underlying issues.[35]
Indeed, the coefficients reveal that partisanship increased more on procedural votes involving nonideological issues than on substantive amendments on ideological issues. The trend line for party conflict was steeper
for procedural votes on ideological issues than on nonideological issues:
party conflict increased by 2 percentage points per year on procedural
votes on ideological issues ($p < .001$), while party conflict increased by 1.5

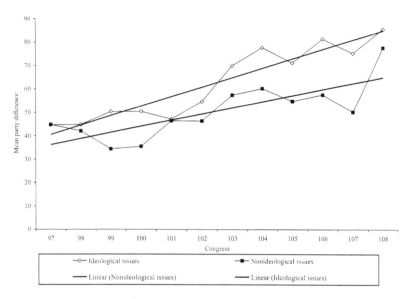

FIGURE 6.7. Senate party differentiation on procedural votes on ideological and nonideological issues.

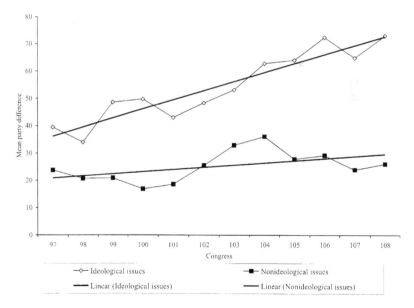

FIGURE 6.8. Senate party differentiation on substantive votes on ideological and nonideological issues.

TABLE 6.3 **Trends in party differentiation in the Senate, 97th–108th Congress**

Types of vote	Issues with ideological content (s.e.)	Issues without identifiable ideological content (s.e.)
Procedural votes	2.05*** (.10)	1.46*** (.11)
Parliamentary votes	1.65*** (.41)	.86** (.34)
Amendments (not procedural)	1.39*** (.11)	.50*** (.10)
Passage votes	1.90*** (.26)	.25* (.10)
All votes	1.77*** (.07)	.63*** (.06)

Note: Entries in the table are coefficients for a time-trend variable in separate regressions with dependent variable of mean party difference for each type of vote.
*$p < .05$; **$p < .01$; ***$p < .001$, two-tailed tests

percentage points per year on procedural votes on nonideological issues ($p < .001$). Even so, the parties have engaged in more bloc voting across the board. Partisanship increased on every category of vote, whether or not it involved any of the issues that differentiate liberals from conservatives in American politics.

As a final perspective on the heightened partisanship of the contemporary Congress, figure 6.9 breaks out the contributions that each type of vote made to the overall level of party conflict in each Congress between 1981 and 2004. The top line in the figure tracks the average level of party conflict across all votes each Congress (the same data displayed in figure 3.3), with the stacked areas beneath the top line showing the proportion of overall conflict contributed by procedural and substantive votes on ideological and nonideological issues.[36] The bottom two areas in the figure illustrate the percentage of overall party conflict that can be attributed to the differences between Republicans and Democrats on conventional left-right issues (both procedural and substantive votes). The top two areas (shown in stripes) display the proportion of party conflict that occurred on procedural and substantive votes on issues that could not be classified in any of the ideological categories.

The most important point conveyed in figure 6.9 is the extent to which intensifying partisanship has been a general phenomenon, not confined to the sorts of issues one thinks of when commentators speak of "ideological polarization" in Congress. Regardless of the extent of overall party conflict in any given Congress in the study, about half of all conflict between Republicans and Democrats took place on issues that did not fall into any of the broad categories identified as left-right disputes in this study. Party structuring increased on all types of votes, whether or not they dealt with matters related to senators' individual preferences on a left-right continuum.

In light of these coinciding trends, scholars need to distinguish between higher levels of partisanship that reflect real partisan divergence on policy matters and partisanship that occurs as a result of strengthened teamwork. The extensive recent literature on rising partisanship has generally not done so. As a result of this scholarship, we have a better sense for how member replacement (Fleisher and Bond 2004; Roberts and Smith 2003; Theriault 2008), electoral pressures (Jacobson 2004; Lowry and Shipan 2002; Rohde 1991), and economic forces (McCarty, Poole, and Rosenthal 2006) have all contributed to the shifts. But only by examining the types of issues on which the parties have diverged is it possible to determine the extent to which "ideological polarization" is an appropriate way to conceptualize and understand what has occurred. Although this book cannot offer

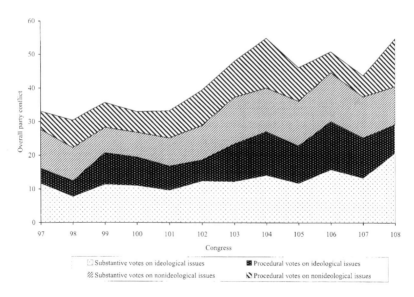

FIGURE 6.9. Sources of party conflict, by Congress.
Note: Stacked areas show the contribution of each type of vote to overall party conflict in the Senate.

a comprehensive account of all the reasons for the increase in partisanship, its approach of distinguishing among the different underlying sources of party conflict sheds light on what legislative partisanship means.

Conclusion

Although the different ideological orientations of Republicans and Democrats are a powerful source of party conflict in Senate politics, partisanship has many other roots beyond individual members' proximate policy preferences. Party conflict also grows directly out of members' willingness to cooperate as partisan teams in pursuit of their opposed electoral and power interests.

In particular, the markedly high levels of Senate partisanship on procedural and parliamentary matters go far beyond the ideological disagreements between liberals and conservatives. Procedural and parliamentary disputes boil down to who will control the Senate floor, and far more than policy is at stake in the outcome of these struggles.

Majority party members do not want only to advance their ideological visions through legislation, they also want to retain control of the floor in order to improve public perceptions of their party. Minority party members do not want only to move policy in an opposing ideological direction, they also want to challenge the majority's control for the benefit of their own electoral interests.

We should also not discount the likelihood that legislators value power as a good in itself. The majority party seeks to maintain control of the floor as a matter of right, not just for specific policy purposes. Individual members of the majority party generally enhance their own influence by ensuring that their party retains effective control of the floor agenda.

Members of the minority party are frequently dissatisfied with the subjects on the agenda because the majority party does not allow them to raise popular issues that they want to use to improve their own party's electoral prospects. Minority party members are thus not reluctant to exploit bipartisan or noncontroversial bills as legislative vehicles to change the subject and to force the majority to take votes on difficult or embarrassing issues. In other words, an underlying issue might be *entirely uncontroversial* from an ideological point of view, but the minority party attempts to use the amending process to steer the floor agenda to topics that serve its own political purposes. For its part, the majority party has reason to resist the minority's efforts to hijack the floor, regardless of the policy content of the alternative issues that the minority is raising. To allow the minority to change the subject is to grant the minority control over the floor agenda. The power stakes themselves give rise to partisanship, even when meaningful policy disagreements alone might not do so.

In addition, procedural partisanship is a result of the simple fact that minority party members have not had satisfactory input into the legislative package brought to the floor; majority party members have reserved key decisions for themselves. In Carroll Reece's terms, quoted at the start of the chapter, the "differences of opinion as to the choice of a particular play [were] ironed out in the huddles before the plays are called." Or, put differently, the majority party "usurped the power, theoretically resident" in the institution as a whole (Cox and McCubbins 1993, 2) to work out a partisan deal that its members then support against challenges of any kind. There is no reason to think that copartisans can only cooperate as teams on issues that tap into shared preferences on the liberal-conservative continuum.

A policy may be unsatisfactory to the minority for ideological reasons, but it also may be unsatisfactory simply because the minority party's constituency interests have not been adequately taken into account or because during the drafting of the legislation the majority party did not grant sufficient credit-claiming opportunities for members of the minority party. Via intraparty communication and negotiation, majority party members can cut a deal among themselves, permitting little or no input from the minority party. If the majority party can then hold together in bloc voting on procedural matters, it can block minority party efforts to amend or influence the package. It is no surprise that such strategies would engender partisan conflict, regardless of the ideological stakes involved.

Senators "execute the signals" of their leaders on procedural and parliamentary votes because doing so is "the first essential of success" in controlling the floor agenda. Control over the floor agenda has vitally important political uses, in addition to its effects on the ideological direction of public policy. To reduce all party disagreements to "ideology" is to assume away all of the political motives that make partisan team play a valuable strategy for members of Congress.

CHAPTER SEVEN

Agreeing to Disagree, or Disagreeing to Agree

Agenda Content and Rising Partisanship

According to John Aldrich (1995, 292), parties-in-government are "designed to select, out of all possible ways of forging majorities, those ways that align with partisan cleavages." Political ideology is integral to party politics, even if different views on the role and purpose of government are not the sole cause of interparty conflict. Republicans and Democrats hold systematically different positions on economic, social, and military policy issues. The findings presented in chapter 3 unequivocally show that issues that divide conservatives from liberals in American politics are also among the most divisive along partisan lines. The presence of these ideological issues on the roll-call agenda greatly increases the likelihood and intensity of partisan conflict.

The extent to which the congressional agenda centers on ideological cleavage issues, however, is not a "given." That agenda is not fixed, and Congress does not revisit the same policy issues year after year (Adler and Lapinski 2006; Baumgartner and Jones 1993): "The choice of what to vote on is just as much a legislative decision as is which policy option to choose" (Rohde 1992, 34). Members of Congress do not merely cast votes as individual legislators reacting to issues put before them. They also collectively choose the issues comprising the congressional agenda in the first place.

This chapter focuses on the variation in the presence of ideological issues on the Senate agenda. It argues that the strengthening of the "parties as teams" discussed in previous chapters has also promoted a legislative agenda on the ideological questions that most reliably differentiate the parties from one another. Improved team coordination results in greater partisan structure on votes even when they do not involve ideological distinctions—as on good-government causes, presidential agenda items, and overall procedural control of the chamber. But more effective team play also allows parties to better exploit their ideological differences as well. This chapter presents evidence that a substantial portion of the rise in Senate conflict between the 1980s and the first decade of the twenty-first century can be explained by changes in the content of the Senate agenda. The sorts of ideological issues that were most divisive along partisan lines in earlier periods became progressively more prominent on the congressional agenda. Meanwhile, the ideological issues that tended to divide the parties internally in earlier periods became a smaller proportion of the agenda. In short, the content of the Senate agenda has been altered in ways that facilitated higher levels of partisan voting.

The Uses of Ideology

Ideology is not important for congressional politics only insofar as individual members have personal beliefs that lead them to take predictable positions. Ideology is also important because it is institutionally *useful* for legislative parties and leaders. Both parties have an interest in focusing debate on issues that unify their members internally and that distinguish them from their opponents. Ideological issues in American politics unquestionably serve important political functions.

Debates on cleavage issues reinforce the parties' raison d'être. As the American Political Science Association's influential Committee on Political Parties (1950, 14) report noted, once a party cleavage exists, each side "works to keep it deep." Cleavage issues enable parties to present a clear alternative to their opponents. Democrats and Republicans have a vested interest in preserving established conflicts. As E. J. Dionne (1991, 16) has observed, the parties benefit politically even when these conflicts interfere with practical problem solving and consensus-building: "Since the 1960s, the key to winning elections has been to reopen the same divisive issues over and over again. . . . old resentments and angers are stirred up in an effort to get voters to cast yet one more ballot of angry protest." Just as for decades after the Civil War, both Republicans and Democrats campaigned waving the "bloody shirt" and reigniting old wartime passions (Sundquist

1983), contemporary Democrats and Republicans profit politically from reliable party cleavages. Parties remain relevant when the issues that differentiate them from one another stay at the center of national politics and congressional decisionmaking.

Party leaders also have powerful incentives to organize debate on cleavage issues. Internal party consensus allows a wider scope for leadership action, empowering party leaders (Cooper and Brady 1981; Sinclair 1995). Members entrust their leaders with greater authority when they have confidence that these powers will be used to advance partisans' common objectives (Rohde 1991). As a natural corollary, leaders themselves will thus prefer to maintain their power by avoiding or suppressing issues that have the potential to weaken or tear apart partisan consensus (Cox and McCubbins 2005).

These institutional incentives are what led E. E. Schattschneider (1975, 65) to term "organization" the "mobilization of bias." Decisions about legislative agendas developed in partisan settings are biased in favor of particular types of issues and against others, compared with the agendas that would emerge from deliberations in bipartisan committees or committees of the whole. Agendas developed through party institutions will suppress issues that divide the parties internally and emphasize those that follow existing lines of party cleavage. Hence, Schattschneider's famous aphorism: "some issues are organized into politics while others are organized out" (69).

If party organizations are a mobilization of bias, they are far more mobilized in Congress today than in the past. As shown in chapter 1, the parties-in-government have become stronger as institutions over the past 25 years. Congress has greatly enhanced staffing and financial support for its party leadership organs, increases that far outstrip those for other legislative branch purposes. Stronger, better-staffed leadership offices sponsor more meetings, task forces, and party retreats. They are also better able to generate more research and talking points to advance the party's agenda. With enhanced resources, leaders and leadership staff can play a more active legislative role, forging policy proposals, developing party messages, brokering compromises among committees, and even rewriting legislation (Milligan 2004; Sinclair 2000). Taken together, improved leadership resources help fellow partisans in their efforts to plot and execute common legislative strategies (Sinclair 1995, 2005; Smith 2005).

This chapter argues that the stronger, more institutionalized parties of the contemporary Senate have helped alter the content of the Senate agenda in ways that foster higher levels of partisanship. The Senate's issue agenda has been modified to better "align with partisan cleavages" (Aldrich 1995, 292) and thus to serve better the political interests of party leaders and party institutions.

Agenda Content and Party Agenda Control

Party coordination on agenda-setting does not occur primarily because party leaders regularly strong-arm individual senators into voting with their parties against their own personal preferences. Particularly in the Senate, party leaders lack the institutional and procedural resources that allow House leaders to effectively control the floor agenda (Sinclair 2000; Smith 2007). Nevertheless, as examined in chapter 6, there is significant party coordination on agenda-setting in the Senate. To achieve their common electoral and policy goals, partisans work out deals among themselves, and then individual members willingly support these agreements against challenges. To do so, members are often prepared to set aside their personal views on particular policy questions in order to sustain the overall agreement.

The power of parties to set the legislative agenda thus extends far beyond institutional and procedural mechanisms. "Power may be, and often is, exercised by confining the scope of decision-making to relatively 'safe' issues" (Bachrach and Baratz 1962, 948). Agendas are often set through "nondecisions" (Bachrach and Baratz 1963), as well as through the explicit exercise of gatekeeping and other procedural prerogatives.

"Nondecisions" occur in congressional agenda-setting when rank-and-file members willingly *acquiesce* in legislative strategies developed in consultation with fellow partisans or by party leaders.[1] They also occur when members adjust their own actions in *anticipation* of what party leaders and fellow partisans will support. Institutionalized party leadership thus does much more than perform whip functions or exert procedural control over the chamber. It functions as a central channel for the intraparty communication and negotiation necessary for party members to formulate a consensus policy agenda. The existence and institutionalization of parties promote nondecisions in the legislative process.

This kind of agenda control is impossible to observe directly. Unlike the visible forms of agenda power that political scientists often study, such as leaders' use of rules and procedures to limit debate and block amendments, agenda-setting by nondecision does not involve an explicit action or choice taken in public view. Instead, this kind of agenda control can only be inferred from that which is empirically observable—the changed issue agenda that results from it.

Party Conflict and Cohesion on Ideological Issues

Although agenda *control* cannot be directly observed, agenda *content* can be. Is the contemporary legislative agenda different from that of earlier eras? If so, is it more focused on the central ideological issues that reliably differentiate the parties from one another?

Party cohesion varies systematically across different types of ideological controversies. Table 7.1 displays Republican and Democratic cohesion across the three major dimensions of left-right contention: economic, social, and military issues. Cohesion levels are shown for each issue type for the whole time period in the study (the 97th through the 108th Congresses) as well as for separate Congresses (grouped in threes). A remarkably clear picture emerges. For both parties in every time period, economic issues always produce higher levels of cohesion than social issues. The difference is dramatic: cohesion levels are on average 60 to 75 percent higher on economic issues than on social issues. "Republicans tend to squabble, but when it's fiscal issues, when it's economic issues, we tend to come together," observed former Senate Republican Leader Trent Lott (R-Miss.), "That's what makes us Republicans" (quoted in Chait 2007, 31). There is more variation in party cohesion on military policy. For Republicans, military issues engender about the same level of cohesion as economic issues. For Democrats, military issues tend to be more internally fractious than economic issues.

Similarly, different types of issues are not equally party polarizing. Table 7.2 displays the mean party difference for each issue type over the whole period, as well as for groups of three Congresses. Economic issues were considerably more party polarizing than the other issue types. Although news media coverage yields a different impression, economic issues consistently produced much deeper party cleavages than social issues. Consistent with Lott's observation above, economic issues appear to be the "safest" for internal party unity and partisan differentiation.

The two parties were more clearly opposed on economic issues than on social issues in every time period. Across the entire period (shown in the

TABLE 7.1 **Senate party cohesion by issue type**

Average party cohesion on	97th–99th Mean	100th–102d Mean	103d–105th Mean	106th–108th Mean	97th–108th Mean
Economic policy					
Democrats	22.3	37.7	52.5	60.9	44.6
Republicans	31.8	20.9	55.5	64.1	45.1
Social issues					
Democrats	14.8	22.8	34.2	47.3	27.1
Republicans	14.5	17.5	31.5	53.0	25.5
Hawk vs. dove					
Democrats	22.0	38.6	26.9	58.5	27.8
Republicans	37.5	49.4	52.3	62.4	44.6
F					
Democrats	3.4*	16.1***	24.7***	9.5***	71.4***
Republicans	28.2***	26.2***	31.9***	4.1*	68.9***

Note: Ns are the same as in table 7.2. Party cohesion is based on the Rice Index of Party Similarity, the absolute difference between the percentage of a party voting yea and the percentage of a party voting nay, but adjusted for votes that exhibit high cohesion merely because the issue is uncontroversial. See note 18 in chap. 4 for more details.
$*p < .05; **p < .01; ***p < .001.$

TABLE 7.2 **Mean party difference by issue type**

Party difference on	97th–99th Mean (n)	100th–102d Mean (n)	103d–105th Mean (n)	106th–108th Mean (n)	97th–108th Mean (n)
Economic policy	44.5 (528)	49.8 (465)	70.5 (597)	75.6 (641)	61.7 (2231)
Social issues	31.6 (200)	38.5 (193)	51.7 (182)	65.7 (97)	44.0 (672)
Hawk vs. dove	47.8 (184)	61.5 (96)	60.6 (71)	71.8 (17)	55.0 (368)
F	27.6***	25.6***	36.4***	5.93***	99.7***

Note: Cells show for each type of issue the average Rice Index of Party Difference (the absolute difference between the percentage of Republicans voting yea and the percentage of Democrats voting yea).
$*p < .05; **p < .01; ***p < .001.$

far right column of the table) the average difference between the parties on economic issues was 62 percentage points. The average difference between the parties on social issues was 44 percentage points. Hawk vs. dove votes were consistently explosive, with an average difference between the parties of 55 percentage points. In each time period, economic issues were always at least 13 percent more party polarizing than social issues, and in some periods as much as 40 percent more polarizing. Similarly, since the end of the Cold War, economic issues have divided the two parties more clearly than military issues. Analysis of variance shows that the differences of means across issue categories are statistically significant for the whole time period ($p < .001$), as well as for each set of three Congresses taken separately ($p < .01$). By comparison, the parties took less opposed positions on social issues, including abortion, school prayer, drugs, homosexual rights, and flag burning.

The data also reveal a striking increase in party polarization within each of the categories. Average party differences increased by at least 42 percent for each type of issue. Despite the increased partisan differentiation on social issues, the parties nevertheless remain more divided along economic lines than on any other ideological issue. It may be, as Brownstein (2007, 197) observes, that average voters in recent years "classif[y] themselves as liberal or conservative less by their attitudes on material questions such as taxes, trade, or social spending than by their views on cultural issues and other nonmaterial concerns." But Republicans and Democrats in the U.S. Senate remain more divided on economics than on any other type of ideological issue.

These varying levels of partisanship across different issue types indicate that levels of party polarization can indeed be affected by the relative mix of issues being considered in Congress. A roll-call agenda more centered on economic issues is likely to be more party polarizing, even without any changes in individual members' policy preferences.

Agenda Content over Time

Changes in agenda content can thus help account for higher levels of Senate partisanship. Figure 7.1 plots the percentage of roll-call votes represented by each issue category for every Congress from 1981 to 2004. The pattern is quite clear: economic issues made up a substantially larger proportion of Senate roll-call votes in the later Congresses. In the 97th–98th Congresses, economic issues constituted 20.7 percent of the total roll-call agenda but fully 32.1 percent of the agenda during the 107th and 108th Congresses, a 55 percent increase. Meanwhile, social issues declined as a proportion of the agenda. They made up 8.4 percent of the roll-call agenda during Reagan's first term, but only 4.4 percent during George W. Bush's first term, a decline by nearly half. Hawk vs. dove issues have also declined

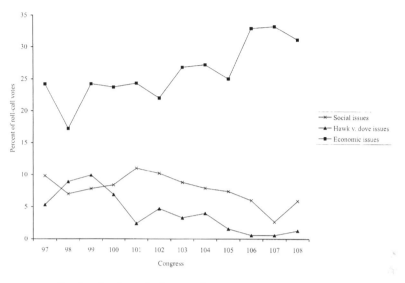

FIGURE 7.1. Senate roll-call agenda change, 1981–2004.

on the agenda, with a substantial drop-off in hawk vs. dove votes coinciding with the end of the Cold War.

As the proportion of roll-call votes on social issues declined, the range of distinctive policy controversies within this category narrowed. In the 1980s the social issue agenda regularly encompassed a wide array of issues: affirmative action, busing, school prayer, sex education in school, out-of-wedlock childbearing, criminal sentencing, school vouchers, arts funding, drugs, needle-exchange programs, and AIDS policy. At the turn of the twenty-first century, the social issue agenda in the Senate was focused on comparatively few topics: largely "right to life" (abortion and stem cell research) and homosexual rights issues, with occasional battles over school vouchers.

This smaller social issue agenda may help explain the narrowing gaps between economic and social policy issues on both party cohesion and party conflict that are evident in tables 7.1 and 7.2. The issues on the social issue agenda in later periods may have been selected by the more active party caucuses and prioritized by party leaders ("cherry picked") precisely because they reliably differentiate the parties and do not divide the parties internally. In other words, as social issues declined as a proportion of roll-call votes generally, the issues left remaining on the social issue agenda may disproportionately have been those that better served

partisan purposes. A more fine-grained analysis of the content of the social issue agenda over time would be needed to determine whether this
kind of issue selection helps to explain increased partisan conflict on social
issues.

By contrast, the scope of legislative conflict on economic issues widened. Not only did economic issues generally take up more of the agenda
in later Congresses, the effect was not confined to one type of economic
policy issue. The proportion of roll-call votes in three of the four subcategories of economic issue—regulatory policy, government's share of the
economy, and distribution of the tax burden—went up as well. Unlike
social policy, the number of distinct issues on the economic issue agenda
was larger in 2004 than in 1981.

Over the time period, an increasing percentage of roll-call votes thus
took place on the type of issue that has consistently created the deepest
line of cleavage between the two parties, while the percentage of votes on
less polarizing issues declined.

External Pressures on the Senate Agenda

The argument being advanced in this chapter is that political considerations affect the content of the Senate agenda, with stronger parties better able to direct the agenda in ways that highlight issues that unify their
members and to suppress issues that divide them internally. If, however,
the Senate agenda were merely a product of broader political and policy
conditions outside the institution, then it could not be understood as a
strategic choice. To address this concern, I collected data to track environmental factors that could potentially cause the Senate to devote more
attention to economic, social, or military policy issues.

One might expect that economic policy controversies would be more
dominant on the Senate agenda during periods of economic trouble or
budgetary strain. To determine whether tough economic times lead senators to focus more on economic issues that are disputed along left-right
lines—such as the minimum wage, unemployment benefits, and other
social welfare programs—I correlated economic agenda content with the
year-to-year change in gross domestic product (GDP) and with the size of
the deficit or surplus as a percentage of GDP. The results are shown in the
scatterplots in figures 7.2 and 7.3. These data provide no support for the inference that economic troubles force senators to confront their ideological

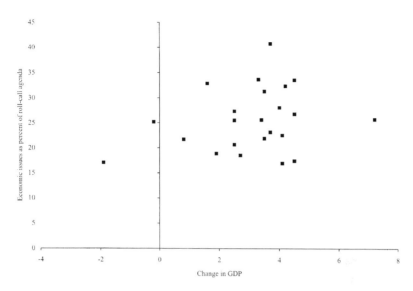

FIGURE 7.2. Economic pressures and the Senate roll-call agenda, 1982–2004.

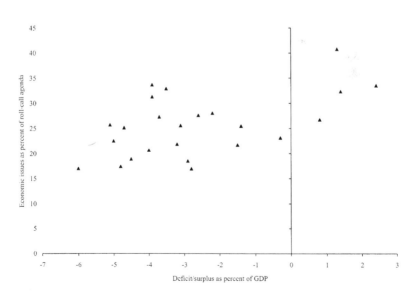

FIGURE 7.3. Deficits and the Senate roll-call agenda, 1982–2004.

disagreements to a greater extent than in other periods. Indeed, the effect of deficits is slightly the reverse of what one might expect:[2] the Senate roll-call agenda centered more on economic controversies during times of budget surplus.[3] There is no systematic relationship between GDP growth or contraction and the proportion of roll-call votes involving ideologically controversial economic issues.[4] Although a time series this short can only be suggestive, the data provide remarkably little support for any suspicion that more ideological controversies over economic issues occur because of budgetary constraints or difficulties in the broader economy.[5]

Similarly, one might also expect that the Senate's social issue agenda would react to events in the "culture war" outside the Congress, with senators likely to devote more agenda space to such issues when more such controversies are occurring in the broader political environment. To assess whether this might be the case, I employ a measure of culture war events developed by Horowitz (2006). This measure is a count of notable events in the culture war drawn from timelines compiled by major news organizations and various advocacy groups active on social issues. It tracks controversial Supreme Court decisions, bombings at abortion clinics, ballot initiatives on sexual issues, and other flash points for controversy. Figure 7.4 displays a scatterplot of this measure with the percent of the Senate roll-call agenda devoted to social issues. As with the economic data above, the content of the Senate agenda does not directly or closely track trends in the broader political environment.[6] Years that are more eventful in terms of the culture war do not generate a Senate agenda more centered on social issues.[7]

Finally, it is possible that hawk vs. dove issues take a more prominent place on the Senate agenda during times of military conflict. To determine whether this is the case, figure 7.5 displays a scatterplot of the number of named foreign military operations in a year with the share of the Senate agenda occupied by hawk vs. dove issues. As in the case of the economic and social policy agendas, the propensity of the Senate to hold roll-call votes on military policy issues does not easily correlate with external events. Neither a greater nor a smaller percentage of the roll-call agenda is devoted to military issues during years when more military operations are ongoing.[8] Although the number of military operations bears no direct relationship to the share of the Senate agenda made up by hawk vs. dove issues, it is clear that such issues did comprise a larger proportion of the Senate roll-call agenda prior to fall of the Berlin wall in 1989. The end of the Cold War correlates with a diminished focus on the hawk vs. dove cleavage.[9] But

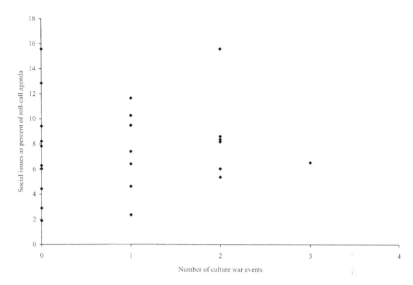

FIGURE 7.4. Culture war events and the Senate roll-call agenda.

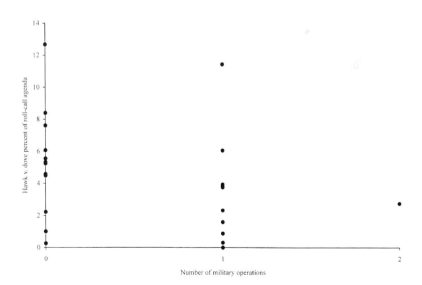

FIGURE 7.5. Military operations and the Senate roll-call agenda.

the proportion of the agenda devoted to such issues is no simple reflection of whether U.S. troops are engaged in combat operations.

The content of the Senate roll-call agenda simply does not bear a simple or direct relationship to changing pressures on the Senate. Important, highly relevant political events do not routinely translate into changes in the content of the Senate agenda. The Senate's agenda is collectively determined by senators themselves, and it is not a straightforward reflection of external pressures.

Agenda Content and Party Conflict over Time

The mobilization of Senate parties over the past 25 years has coincided with systematic changes in the Senate roll-call agenda. Can these changes in the legislative agenda help account for higher levels of party conflict in the contemporary Senate? The findings above showed that the two parties were most distinct from one another when battling over economic issues of taxation, redistributive social programs, economic regulations, and government's share of the economy. If economic issues constitute the main line of cleavage between the two parties, then an agenda more focused on these issues will elicit higher levels of partisan divergence.

The content of the policy agenda is not, however, the only source of change in Senate party conflict. To isolate the effects of agenda change, multivariate analysis is necessary to control for other possible causes of rising partisanship.

CONSTITUENCY CHANGE: To account for changes in constituency partisanship, the model includes the Abramowitz, Alexander, and Gunning (2006) "safe seats" indicator used in chapter 4 (see table 4.4), the number of states in which the presidential candidate of the incumbent senator's party ran at least 10 percentage points ahead of the president's national average. By this measure, fully 21 senators held "safe seats" in the 108th Congress, compared with only 5 senators in the 99th Congress. I expect higher levels of overall partisanship when more senators represent safe seats.

LEADERSHIP RESOURCES: In addition, the expanding role of Senate party leadership may have affected party polarization. Increased funding enables leadership staff to maintain a more pervasive presence in the institution, monitoring activity in committees and lobbying senators and their personal staffs at crucial points in the legislative process. Resources appropriated for leadership offices (as shown in fig. 1.1) serve as a proxy for the strength of legislative party leadership.

AGENDA CONTENT: The model includes six variables measuring agenda content.

- *Economic issues (%)*, *Social issues (%)*, and *Hawk vs. dove (%)* track the percentage of the total roll-call agenda in the Senate that can be classified as involving the issues in each of these ideological categories.
- *Procedural votes* are (1) motions that would table or recommit a bill or amendment and (2) motions that determine whether a bill or amendment can be considered under Budget Act rules.
- *Parliamentary votes* are all those involving rules of procedure or control of the floor, such as motions to proceed, cloture, and appeals of the ruling of the chair.
- *Presidential agenda items* are votes on policy initiatives on which the president took a position in the State of the Union address immediately preceding the vote. As examined in chapter 4, presidential agenda items tend to spark higher levels of partisanship.

Multiple regression is employed to determine whether the content of the agenda affects the level of partisanship in the Senate.

The dependent variable is average party difference per quarter from the 97th Congress through the 108th Congress, as shown in figure 7.6 ($n = 96$).[10] The heavy line in figure 7.6 shows mean party differences by Congress, and the lighter line shows mean party differences on a quarterly basis. The figure uncovers considerable variation in party polarization within each Congress. Senate membership and constituency context—or any other factor that remains constant (or nearly constant) over the course of a Congress—may constrain partisanship to a specified range, but there is clearly considerable fluctuation within those parameters.

A lag of the dependent variable is also included in the model.[11] There are substantive reasons to expect that party conflict is likely to have a self-reinforcing logic. Intense partisan battles can intensify resentment and mistrust between the parties (Jacobson 2004).

The content of the roll-call agenda has important effects on the level of partisanship. Table 7.3 displays results from two regression models: the first column presents a model containing only the lag of party polarization and the party strength variables; the second column shows the full results, with the agenda content variables included. Taking agenda content into

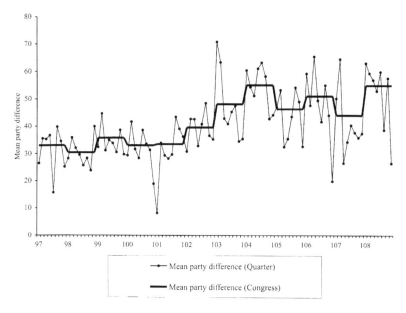

FIGURE 7.6. Mean party difference, by quarter and by Congress.

account significantly improves the model's ability to explain variation in party polarization over time.[12] Adjusted R^2 is boosted from .24 to .52, and residual mean square is reduced by 37 percent over the model containing only the party strength and lag variables.[13]

The presence of economic issues on the agenda substantially widens the divide between the parties. With all other variables in the model held constant at their means, the model predicts ($p < .001$) that mean party difference will be 64 percent higher when economic issues comprise their maximum proportion of the roll-call agenda compared with when they compose their minimum share.[14] A roll-call agenda focused on economic issues is systematically associated with higher levels of aggregate partisanship.

The negative coefficient for social issues suggests that the suppression of social issues on the agenda may also have led to greater overall partisanship, although it just misses conventional levels of statistical significance ($p < .07$). The parties do tend to take opposing positions on these issues, but—as shown in the party cohesion analysis in table 7.1—more members defect from their party's position on social issues than on economic issues, making the parties less distinct when these issues are being considered.

Two of the additional agenda content measures also perform as expected. Party difference is greater ($p < .01$) when more votes are taken on *procedural* matters. Senate parties are more clearly differentiated when the agenda includes more motions to table, recommit, or to waive the Budget Act. Moreover, the partisan divide is wider when presidential agenda items constitute a larger component of the agenda (see chap. 4).

The model also reveals that other factors besides agenda content affect the overall level of Senate partisanship. Inflation-adjusted increases in funding for party leadership offices are associated with rising partisanship.

TABLE 7.3 **Senate party conflict as a function of agenda content, 1981–2004 ($n = 96$)**

	Model 1 B (s.e.)	Model 2 B (s.e.)
Agenda content		
Economic issues (%)		.34***
		(.09)
Social issues (%)		−.18
		(.14)
Hawk vs. dove (%)		.06
		(.22)
Presidential agenda (%)		.13**
		(.05)
Procedural votes (%)		.22**
		(.08)
Parliamentary votes (%)		.15
		(.09)
Controls		
Number of safe seats	.01	−.01
	(.16)	(.14)
Senate party leadership funds (millions)	4.07**	2.83*
	(1.50)	(1.44)
Party polarization (Lag 1)	.31***	.30***
	(.10)	(.08)
Goodness of fit		
Adjusted R^2	.24	.52
Residual sum of squares	10405.64	6107.11
Degrees of freedom	91	85
Residual mean square	114.34	71.84
Improvement over Model 1 (in percentage)		37.17
F (agenda variables)		9.97***
Diagnostics		
LM Test (Lag 1)	1.49	2.47
LM Test (Lag 2)	1.65	2.50
Durbin's alternative test for autocorrelation	3.56	2.24

Note: Dependent variable is mean level of party polarization (absolute difference between Democrats and Republicans voting yea) on all roll-call votes by quarter, 1981–2004. The coefficients are least-squares regression estimates. *$p < .05$; **$p < .01$; ***$p < .001$, one-tailed tests.

Better staffed, more generously funded party leadership institutions may help intensify partisanship in the Senate. Larger leadership staffs can improve communications and facilitate better internal party negotiations. A cursory glance at the documents produced by the Democratic and Republican Senate leadership offices shows that they devote a lot of resources to developing arguments and information to be used against their partisan opponents. But this finding should be interpreted with caution because of a time trend component in the variation.[15] It is possible that *leadership funds* may merely stand in for an omitted variable also associated with time.[16] The variable performs no better than a year counter in the model.[17]

The positive coefficient on the lag of mean party difference ($p < .001$) suggests that there is indeed a self-reinforcing logic to partisanship. Party divisions appear to aggravate party antagonism in subsequent periods.

The increase in the number of senators representing states that are safe for their parties does not appear to drive party polarization. The number of senators representing states that lopsidedly favor their party has increased, along with party polarization, but the two trends do not correlate with one another, once other factors are controlled for.

Discussion

Changes in agenda content can account for a considerable portion of the rise in Senate partisanship over the past quarter century. Between the first terms of Presidents Ronald Reagan and George W. Bush, party conflict increased from a mean party difference of 32 percentage points across all votes in 1981–84 to a mean party difference of 49 percentage points across all votes in 2001–4, a 55 percent increase. Based on the regression results (shown in the second column of table 7.3), it is possible to calculate how the actual changes in agenda content between the two periods affected overall partisanship while holding other variables constant at their means (King, Tomz, and Wittenberg 2000). Differences in agenda content alone between the two periods can account for an increase in party conflict of 6.3 percentage points.[18] Given that the actual increase in overall party conflict between the two eras was 17 percentage points, the growth in partisan conflict attributable to agenda change would be 37 percent of the total increase.

To explain the rise in partisanship in Congress, scholars have looked primarily to explanations based on electoral and membership change. Studies have shown that congressional parties have become more polarized as a result of changes in constituency context, including the realignment of the South (Hood, Kidd, and Morris 1999; Lowry and Shipan 2002; Rohde 1991), the decline of split-ticket voting (Jacobson 2000), and the homogenization of congressional constituencies (Brewer, Mariana, and Stonecash 2002; Oppenheimer 2005). Membership change has also contributed to increased partisanship (Brady and Han 2004; Roberts and Smith 2003) as members with bipartisan voting records have disproportionately retired and suffered defeat (Fleisher and Bond 2004; Theriault 2008).[19]

External forces are not the whole story. After all, the Congress as a body chooses what issues will be voted on in the first place. Policy issues before Congress are not exogenous to the institution. Findings presented in this chapter show that the twenty-first-century Senate agenda was systematically different from that during the early 1980s. The ideological issues that were most divisive along party lines during the 97th Congress comprised a substantially larger part of the congressional agenda in the 108th Congress. Even without changes in external influences, those differences alone help account for intensified party conflict. Had the senators of the 97th Congress taken votes on the same issues presented to the 108th Congress, party conflict would have been higher. Had the senators of the 108th Congress voted on the same issues before the 97th Congress, party conflict would have been lower. The roll-call agenda of the early twenty-first century was simply more focused on issues that better promote internal party unity and two-party differentiation than that of the 1980s.

Substantive agenda content can thus serve as a vitally important *internal* factor affecting the degree of party conflict. Rising partisanship is not simply "polarization" of individual members along a preexisting ideological spectrum. It also results from a congressional agenda that devotes more time to debating party cleavage issues and less time to issues that do not differentiate the parties from one another or that divide the parties internally.

Scholarship on legislative agenda control has been heavily focused on procedural mechanisms (Bach and Smith 1988; Cox and McCubbins 1993, 2005; Den Hartog and Monroe 2008; Theriault 2006). But these long-term changes in the content of the Senate agenda also suggest that meaningful partisan agenda control can take the form of nondecisions (Bachrach and Baratz 1962, 1963)—the willing acquiescence and cooperation of individual members in collective party strategies—rather than through leaders' enforcement of rules or exercise of formal authority. By collaborating in partisan settings, members develop common floor strategies and consensus policy agendas. They play up issues on which fellow partisans agree and play down issues that divide their parties internally. They look for issues that allow them to showcase differences with their party opponents.

Party institutions are thus not important merely as mechanisms to enforce party discipline or to select leaders who monopolize gatekeeping positions in the legislative process. They are also important as a means of sharing information and facilitating negotiation among fellow partisans. Although this behind-the-scenes collaboration and consensus-building is not visible using the methods that empirical social scientists typically use, nondecisions will produce observable biases in the content of the legislative agenda. And, in fact, as Senate partisans have engaged in more of these collaborative activities in recent years, the Senate agenda has become more directed toward the types of ideological issues that most predictably generate clear partisan differences. Concurrent with the institutional strengthening of Senate parties over the 1980–2004 period, the Senate's roll-call agenda became progressively more focused on party cleavage issues.

Legislative partisanship itself is not a result of forces beyond the control of its members. Congress has discretion over the types of issues that predominate on its agenda, and the choice of issues in turn affects the extent to which the parties find themselves in disagreement. The extent of partisanship in roll-call voting is, in important respects, a consequence of the legislative agenda that party leaders and individual members select and prosecute.

CHAPTER EIGHT

Beyond Ideology

Returning to Politics

In *Federalist* 10, James Madison observes that partisan conflict springs from many sources: "The latent causes of faction are thus sown in the nature of man. . . . A zeal for different opinions concerning religion, concerning government, and many other points, as well of speculation as of practice; an attachment to different leaders ambitiously contending for pre-eminence and power . . . have, in turn, divided mankind into parties" (Hamilton, Jay, and Madison 1987, 124).

This study focuses on two central sources of party conflict in Congress: members' "opinions concerning government" and the competition "for pre-eminence and power." Although a great deal of party conflict in Congress derives from members' ideological orientations, continuous partisan struggles for power and elected office also create strong ongoing incentives for partisan conflict. Parties in Congress contend with one another not only because their members have different *beliefs* and *preferences*, but because they have opposed political *interests*. This book has shown that political competition exacerbates party conflict in the U.S. Senate far beyond what would occur solely on the basis of individual members' diverging views on the proper role and scope of government.

In recent years, political scientists and journalists have heavily emphasized the role of ideology in structuring party conflict in Congress. Chapter 2 tracked the increasing dominance of ideological concepts in explaining legislative partisanship, both in the scholarly literature and in political journalism. Although early scholarship on Congress made no use of these concepts, nearly all scholarly articles published on Congress in recent years draw on "ideology" for analytical traction. Indeed, it is not unusual for contemporary analysts both inside and outside academia to literally *equate* party conflict in Congress with party polarization on the ideological continuum. They have adopted methodologies explicitly assuming that partisan patterns in congressional roll-call votes can be reduced down to members' individual policy preferences. This applies to all approaches that scale roll-call votes, as well as *National Journal*'s widely used ideological ratings scheme. When Republicans and Democrats vote on opposite sides in Congress, the assumption is that members' policy preferences are the driving reason.

By focusing so intently on ideology, contemporary scholarship and journalism have systematically obscured the fact that partisans' diverging interests also engender partisan conflict. Knowing that Republicans tend to be conservative and Democrats tend to be liberal simply does not tell us everything there is to know about party conflict in Congress. To understand partisanship in Congress, it is necessary to pay attention to *politics*.

To do so, this study begins with a view of legislative parties as political institutions. Given their stake in these institutions, fellow partisans in Congress have compelling collective electoral and power interests, in addition to their common policy goals. Even in periods when the congressional parties have difficulty forging policy consensus, these common interests facilitate a great deal of internal party cooperation, as well as provide extensive grounds for contention with their party opponents.

Considering the importance of partisan cues to voters, party members have an ever-present interest in both fostering an attractive image for their own party and in undercutting the reputation of the opposition party. Party members are not judged solely on individual performance, but also on the perceived success or failures of the party to which they belong. Members thus always have a common interest in exploiting control of the floor agenda to send partisan political messages to voters. The majority party wants to demonstrate its collective ability to control the agenda; the minority contests this power. The level of policy agreement among legislative partisans varies from era to era, and contemporary parties in the United States are unquestionably more ideologically coherent than they were in the 1950s and 1960s. But regardless of the extent of policy consensus within the congressional parties, partisans' common interests form a foundation for a considerable amount of intraparty coordination and interparty conflict. Collective action problems create some obstacles to the achievement of partisans' common goals, but, as discussed in chapter 1, these problems can easily be exaggerated in the context of the small groups involved in legislative parties and the selective benefits that legislators can gain from working with their parties.

In order to differentiate empirically the role of ideology and partisan interests in structuring party conflict, this book began with the simple observation that not every issue considered in Congress raises ideological questions, at least as "ideology" is conventionally understood in American politics. As broad as "liberalism" and "conservatism" are as concepts, they cannot be expanded to cover every policy issue. Congress debates and legislates on many issues that bear no relationship to the policy differences that distinguish liberals from conservatives. Given this variation in the ideological content of policy issues before Congress, it then becomes possible to ask whether or not party conflict is largely confined to ideological issues. If the parties come into conflict on issues in which it is not possible to specify in advance which position (yea or nay) is the more liberal or conservative alternative, then it is necessary to look beyond ideology alone for sources of partisan structure. The only way to determine the extent to which ideology drives partisan conflict is to pay attention to the substantive content of the issues before Congress. Patterns in roll-call votes do not interpret themselves.

Differentiating votes by the types of issues at stake makes it possible to establish a baseline for a "normal" level of partisanship on particular issues at different times. This baseline was then used to ascertain how political factors—such as the president's involvement in the issue or its procedural framing—modify the level of party conflict on particular votes. When the presence of political incentives systematically intensifies partisan conflict relative to its baseline on a given issue, I infer that this "excess" partisanship goes beyond party members' usual policy differences on that type of issue. Disaggregating votes in this way reveals that divisive ideological issues become even more distinctly partisan when political factors provide additional incentives for party conflict. But political considerations can and do make otherwise noncontroversial issues partisan, as well.

The logic of the study and its principal findings are summarized in table 8.1. In broadest terms, issues are divided into those that can be understood using conventional understandings of liberalism and conservatism in American politics and those that cannot. "Ideological issues" include all

TABLE 8.1. **Differentiating partisan and ideological controversy in Congress**

	Ideological issues	Other issues
Party-line vote	Party cleavages driven by members' diverging preferences on economic, social, and military issues • Party cleavages on ideological issues intensified by political factors (e.g., presidential leadership, procedural framing) • The proportion of ideological issues on the congressional agenda affected by party coordination	Party cleavages driven by political factors, including • Partisan strategies on good-government causes • Partisan responses to presidential leadership • Party coordination on procedural and parliamentary control
Not party-line vote	• Extremist or consensus proposals on economic, social, and military issues	• Uncontroversial issues

votes dealing with the distribution of the tax burden, regulations of private economic activity for public purposes, government's share of the economy (budgets, across-the-board spending cuts, tax increases or reductions), social programs to redress inequalities, social issues (e.g., abortion, separation of church and state, gay rights, affirmative action, crime), the amount of resources devoted to the U.S. military, the use of military force, and support for international treaties and multilateral institutions. As laid out in chapter 3, the research design was structured to isolate roll-call votes dealing with issues on which liberals and conservatives have clearly staked out opposing positions. Drawing this basic distinction then makes it possible to cross-tabulate the ideological content of issues with whether or not roll-call votes on those issues divided along party lines.

Looking first at the ideological issues that divided the Senate along party lines (top left cell of table 8.1), this study confirms that ideology is indeed a very powerful predictor of party conflict. In this respect, the conventional wisdom is not wrong. Of all roll-call votes from 1981 through 2004 involving any of the ideological issues, nearly three-quarters, that is, 72 percent, divided a majority of Republicans from a majority of Democrats. A great deal of party conflict can easily be traced back to party members' diverging ideological preferences. A majority of all roll-call votes that divided along party lines, at least 55 percent, occurred on issues that had obvious left-right implications.

Interestingly, there were relatively few votes on ideological issues that did not elicit a party-line vote in the Senate (bottom left cell of the table). Only 28 percent of votes raising ideological issues failed to divide a majority of Republicans from a majority of Democrats. These votes involved proposals that can be described as either "consensus" or "extreme"; in other words, proposals in this category were ideologically motivated but either bipartisan or so far outside the mainstream that they were rejected by majorities of both parties. An example of an extreme proposal is Sen. Jesse Helms's (R-N.C.) amendment requiring that the Senate reexamine Dr. Martin Luther King Jr.'s ties to the Communist Party before authorizing a holiday in his honor.[1] Others were so uncontroversial that, even though they involved an ideological issue, there was broad bipartisan consensus on the matter—for example, a resolution reaffirming support for keeping "under God" in the Pledge of Allegiance.[2] Clearly, however, the overwhelming majority of ideological issues that received a roll-call vote in the Senate were also ones that overlapped with partisan cleavages.

Most important, however, this study reveals that party conflict *regularly* occurs on issues that do not involve conventional ideological distinctions in American politics. Other issues account for a very substantial amount of partisan conflict in Congress (top right cell of the table): fully 45 percent of roll-call votes on issues not involving typical left-right cleavages divided the Senate along party lines. Republicans and Democrats disagree about a lot more than liberals and conservatives do.

This study also identifies three political factors that systematically engender partisan conflict even in the absence of disagreement over the ideological direction of public policy: "good government" causes, presidential leadership, and procedural control of the agenda.

Debates over good-government causes—defined as measures to improve government ethics, investigate government or policy failures, promote government transparency, enhance fiscal responsibility, ensure electoral integrity, or make government operations more efficient—speak directly to issues of competency and integrity that are central to the political parties' public image. Even though there is no ideological dispute on the basic values involved in these issues, the parties exploit them to enhance their own or to attack their opponents' reputation. Information is wielded to partisan effect. Investigations and official reports are typically supported by the party that expects to benefit from them and opposed by the party whose image would be harmed. The party not responsible for spending wants to debate matters of fiscal responsibility or "waste, fraud and abuse," and seeks a strict accounting of annual deficits and the national debt. The president's partisan opposition screens presidential nominees for any conflict of interest or ethical failing, real, suspected, or imagined. Both parties try to position themselves as more committed to government ethics than their opponents.

Charges of corruption and incompetence form the basis of many partisan conflicts in Congress (see chap. 5). Indeed, these issues spark some of the highest levels of party conflict. In the study period, unanimous party-line votes—with all Republicans on one side and all Democrats on the other—were more likely to occur on these issues than on any of the ideological issues. Good-government issues were generally far more divisive along party lines than the hot-button social issues on which the contemporary parties' positions are so clearly defined.

No less important than good-government matters, presidential leadership has an enormous impact on the parties' collective image. Presidential leadership on an issue raises the political stakes for both parties. Members of the president's party want to protect the president from embarrassment and help make the case that their president is a strong and effective leader; in short, they have political reason to want the president to win, even when they might have misgivings about the merits of the president's proposed policies. Members of the opposition party need to make a case for a change in party control of the presidency; thus they want to undermine the president's reputation for leadership and call into question his ability to govern. Rather than setting aside any qualms they might have, the president's partisan opponents have political incentive to actively look for reasons to resist his proposals. As a consequence, presidential leadership becomes an important political factor leading the parties to define themselves in opposition to one another. Whether or not the proposal involves an ideologically divisive issue, presidential leadership can spark partisan division.

Analysis presented in chapter 4 revealed that presidential leadership is systematically associated with higher levels of party conflict on most areas of national policy. The effects were evident on issues raising conventional ideological disputes as well as those that do not (hence presidential leadership is listed as an important political factor affecting party conflict in both left and right columns of table 8.1). Relative to baseline levels of partisanship when issues were not part of the president's agenda, most issues, even those already controversial along left-right lines, tended to become more partisan when presidents involved themselves. But presidential leadership had its greatest influence on party conflict on issues on which liberals and conservatives had not already staked out clear positions in opposition to one another. In terms of the policy issues most affected, presidential leadership had marked effects on partisan contention in the areas of social welfare, education, health, international affairs, and defense. Policy issues where presidential leadership had no measurable impact tended to be those on which members' local constituency interests are likely to receive greater weight, such as agriculture, public lands, and transportation.

A third important political factor affecting party conflict in Congress is whether or not the question before the body involves agenda control. Procedural matters constituted fully 42 percent of all Senate roll-call votes during the period studied.[3] Outcomes of these votes affect more than policy. Control of the floor is a political commodity in its own right, and it is used not just to influence the ideological direction of public policy but also to convey partisan political messages. Each party wants to focus debate on issues that cast it in a favorable light. Each party regularly seeks to make political points by offering bills and amendments designed to cause political pain for their opponents. The outcomes of procedural votes also establish which party is effective at getting its proposals considered on the floor, a matter of pure political muscle that has political importance separate from policy outcomes. Analysis presented in chapter 6 reveals that procedural votes tend to break on party lines, *regardless of their ideological or policy content.* All types of policy issues become substantially more partisan when they are framed as procedural matters, rather than as substantive votes. Indeed, procedural votes on nonideological issues are equally partisan on average as substantive votes on ideological issues.

If ideological proximity were the most important bond between partisans as they cast votes in Congress, then the procedural posture of an issue should not have such an enormous impact on the level of party conflict. The extent of partisan disagreement, for example, should not be drastically affected by whether or not an issue comes up as a straightforward vote on policy or on a motion to table. Like presidential leadership, however, the procedural framing of an issue is an important political factor affecting the level of party conflict on both ideological and nonideological issues (and thus is listed in the two columns of table 8.1). Also as with presidential leadership, the effect of procedural framing on party conflict is greatest on issues that do not normally divide liberals from conservatives. In fact, policy issues that are typically not at all controversial when they occur as substantive votes on the merits become highly partisan when they are handled as procedural matters. The mean difference between the parties on substantive votes that do not involve conventional ideological issues is 21.7, but when those same types of issues occur as procedural votes, mean party difference more than doubles, to 51.[4]

Party conflict is intensified by each of these political factors because members' individual political interests so frequently dovetail with the collective interests of their parties. Collective action for political purposes often costs individual legislators little and may even benefit them, both with constituents and in their internal institutional careers. Criticizing an opposition party president and his policies or denouncing the opposing party for corruption and incompetence often has little, if any, downside. Legislators do not necessarily pay any price for supporting their own party's president, cooperating to shore up their own party's reputation for competence and integrity, or working with their party on procedural matters. Although collective action for partisan political gain is not always easy and there are competing considerations for particular members in certain cases, there is no reason to assume that it always, usually, or even frequently comes at a personal or political cost for individual legislators. Legislators are not firms, and collective action in a legislature is not closely analogous to collective action in the marketplace.

Given their powerful common interests and linked electoral fates, partisans willingly collaborate much of the time. Party politics involves a great deal of internal negotiation, consensus-building, and consultation about the party agenda itself. "The practice of prior consultation in order to agree upon a united front is an old one, usually described by the word 'caucus.' The caucus is the core of party politics" (Schattschneider 1942, 40). Legislative agendas and the topics on which votes will eventually be taken are not a given. Parties work together to develop a common approach to presidential initiatives, to scandals and reputational issues, and to procedural matters.

Even the extent to which the legislative agenda centers on issues that separate liberals from conservatives is, at least in part, a matter of collective choice. Both parties have incentives to steer the legislative agenda toward issues that help maintain internal party unity and differentiate them from their opposition. Chapter 7 examined how shifts in the legislative agenda from 1981 through 2004 fostered higher levels of party conflict. At the same time that parties strengthened both institutionally (in terms of the resources dedicated toward party leadership offices) and in the electorate (in terms of constituencies tilted toward one party or another) the legislative agenda shifted toward issues that better highlighted partisan differences. A substantial share of the rise in party conflict can be attributed to changes in the content of the legislative agenda rather than to changing preferences among individual senators.

Questions of Ultimate Ends

For some legislators, the ultimate motive for cooperating with their political parties on purely political matters may be their belief that their party is the best vehicle for advancing their ideological goals. Working on behalf of a political party is certainly one way to advance an ideological agenda in contemporary American politics. What helps the Republican party win elections and wield power tends also to benefit conservative causes in American politics. What helps the Democratic party tends to advance a liberal agenda. Ideological and partisan motives are unquestionably intertwined in legislative politics.

Nevertheless, one should not conflate ideology and partisanship. As discussed in chapter 3, political parties existed in the United States long before party politics was organized along its present-day left-right, liberal-conservative cleavages. Even setting contemporary ideology aside, political parties can be held together in the absence of a broad overarching policy agenda, but instead just as a means of securing and controlling government patronage. "For twenty years" before 1896, writes Sundquist (1983, 154), "the contests between Democrats and Republicans had been little more than sham battles that decided no consequential issues (except the tariff) but ordained mainly who would gain and allocate the spoils of office. The major parties had waged essentially empty campaigns. They appealed to wartime loyalties, they exposed each other's corruption and claimed moral superiority, and they magnified out of proportion the few real issues, like the tariff, that divided them."

Rather than viewing policy goals as the key political motivation, earlier psychological approaches to the study of politicians viewed them as primarily driven to seek power, rather than to achieve policy goals. According to Lasswell (1963, 39), political ambition itself is an "intense and ungratified craving for deference." A politician's desire for power then gets "rationalized in terms of public interest." According to this theory, public purposes are merely a politician's excuse for political involvement, not its root cause.

A much broader tradition in democratic theory posits that political parties themselves are nothing more than vehicles for winning political power. Under this account, ideologies are merely one of many tools that parties exploit for winning votes; they are not the goal of party organizing. "Politicians," writes Downs (1957, 28), "never seek office as a means of carrying out particular policies; their only goal is to reap the rewards of holding office per se." Or, as Schumpeter (1942, 283) contends, "all parties will of course, at any given time, provide themselves with a stock of principles or planks and these principles or planks may be as characteristic of the party that adopts them and as important for its success as the brands of goods a department store sells are characteristic of it and important for its success. But the department store cannot be defined in terms of its brands and a party cannot be defined in terms of its principles."

The ultimate motives of legislators simply cannot be discerned using any of the tools available to political science. Given that we do not know what comes first—ideological goals or power-seeking—this study has remained agnostic on the point. In all likelihood, most legislators are probably driven by a complex mixture of motives, with one goal being more important for some politicians than for others. Nevertheless, it is valuable both theoretically and empirically to distinguish as far as is possible between power-seeking and policy goals as bases for partisan cooperation and conflict, as this study has done. Certainly, it is not appropriate to simply collapse one motive into the other.

Implications for Party Theory

By highlighting the collective political interests that unite parties in opposition to one another, this study suggests some limitations of methodological individualism as an approach to the study of party politics. Since the "economic turn" in the study of Congress (Mayhew 1974), it has become the norm to theorize about party politics beginning with the individual legislator first. Accepting members' policy preferences as given, parties are thought to be capable of unified action when the individual members who make up the party are ideologically homogeneous. By the same token, parties are constrained when individual party members are ideologically heterogeneous (Cooper and Brady 1981; Rohde 1991; Sinclair 1995).

While not denying the importance of ideology for political elites (Converse 1964; Kritzer 1978), this study emphasizes that partisans can cooperate on the basis of their shared interests in winning office and wielding power. Votes do not break along party lines only because individual members have preexisting ideological preferences that range along a continuum with Republicans clustered on the right and Democrats on the left. Instead, party structure can derive from members' explicitly political calculations about their collective interests as fellow partisans.

Voting decisions regularly involve situations where one alternative is perceived to be more politically advantageous for a party and its members. Members' choices thus need to be understood in political context, not merely in relation to their policy views. Members' decisions and behavior are not a purely individual phenomenon. Instead, collective interests can figure into individual members' political calculations and give rise to partisan divisions.

More generally, it is possible that much of what scholars and analysts today think of as "liberalism" and "conservatism" is, at least in part, a product of social construction within political parties. Parties of the past were organized just as effectively on other grounds aside from what is today understood as "left" versus "right." As discussed in chapter 3, mid-nineteenth-century American political parties blended together issue positions that would today be regarded as simultaneously "liberal" and "conservative," even though their voting behavior in Congress was no less partisan than today. Ideologies themselves may be forged within and through conflicts between political parties and leaders.[5]

Our current way of thinking of "ideology" as a fixed characteristic of individuals—gauged using factorial methods similar to those used to measure other unobserved characteristics of individuals, such as IQ—is a recent intellectual development. As examined in chapter 2, early political science scholarship did not view ideology as an attribute of individual legislators; instead, "party principles" were hammered out through group deliberation, interest aggregation, and coalition building—the caucus. It is not clear that early scholarship was inferior to contemporary work in this respect. In any case, collective interests and caucus activity need to be returned to a more central place in party theory.

Implications for Party Polarization

One of the central themes of this study is that party differentiation—the tendency of one party to oppose the other in roll-call voting—is not necessarily equivalent to party polarization on an ideological continuum. Ideological proximity on a left-right continuum is only one potential source of party "glue." Parties can compete as teams in pursuit of their political interests as well as diverge on an ideological continuum. Party voting is therefore overdetermined, with multiple, simultaneous causes.

The only way to determine whether ideological polarization has occurred is to look at the substantive issues on which the parties are differentiating themselves. Patterns in roll-call behavior alone are fundamentally ambiguous in the absence of attention to the nature of the issues at stake. If the parties are waging intense battles over scandals, investigations, ethics disputes, and other good-government matters, they are not "polarizing" on an ideological continuum. If the parties cooperate better on procedural and substantive matters regardless of the underlying issue content at stake, then the parties have become more *organized* as competing teams but not necessarily more ideologically homogeneous. Internal party consensus on ideological issues may well have spill-over effects by facilitating better coordination on issues not related to left-right cleavages. Legislative parties may well benefit from "increasing returns on cohesiveness" (Roberts and Smith 2003, 316) in ideological terms. But unless "ideology" is to be redefined to mean *anything* on which the parties disagree, then it is important to maintain conceptual distinctions.

Bringing "Bickering" Back In

The role of political science is often to call into question conventional wisdom widely accepted outside the academy. By contrast, the analysis advanced here actually lends support for some widely held stereotypes about Congress that have received less respect among political scientists than they deserve. The public perceives party conflict in Congress as "bickering," as excessive quarrelling driven by members' power and electoral interests. Political scientists have instead tended to interpret congressional party conflict as evidence of members' principled differences on the proper role and scope of government. Influenced by a scholarly tradition that celebrated political parties, scholars tend to welcome clear partisan distinctions in Congress as a way to provide greater political accountability and coherence in government policymaking.

By emphasizing the raw political interests that can also foster party conflict in Congress, this study might be viewed as returning to an older "antiparty" school of thought, as reflected in James Madison's early writings. If partisanship has roots in members' political interests, then political parties actually exacerbate and institutionalize conflict, rather than merely represent and give voice to preexisting policy disagreements in the broader political environment. In their quest to win elections and wield power, partisans impeach one another's motives, question one another's ethics and competence, engage in reflexive partisanship, and—when it is politically useful to do so—exploit and deepen divisions rather than seeking common ground. At its worst, this political logic can devolve into the sort of cynicism expressed by one anonymous congressman in an interview with political scientist Randall Ripley (1967, 145): "In the minority, you are just looking for reasons to oppose what the majority supports."

Without embracing the idea that all or even most party conflict in Congress is manufactured for political gain, political parties are not immune to a basic failing of institutions everywhere, their tendency to redirect energies away from their larger external purposes toward institutional maintenance. An early critic of political parties, Moisei Ostrogorski (1964, originally published in 1902) explained the problem: "As soon as a party, were it created for the noblest object, perpetuates itself, it tends inevitably towards power, and as soon as it makes that its end, its master passion is to maintain itself against all opposition, with no scruple as to means" (355). Taking greater cognizance of the political interests that drive the two parties apart need not devolve into Ostrogorski's antipartyism. But it can contribute to greater realism and deeper understanding of party politics in Congress.

Coding the Presidential Agenda Status of Roll-Call Votes

On January 26, 1982, President Ronald Reagan gave the following State of the Union address before a joint session of Congress. This address has been highlighted and annotated with a description of how each agenda item was handled to code Senate roll-call votes. Immediately following is the list of agenda items in the 1982 State of the Union address used for coding purposes.

* * *

Mr. Speaker, Mr. President, distinguished Members of the Congress, honored guests, and fellow citizens:

Today marks my first State of the Union address to you, a constitutional duty as old as our Republic itself.

President Washington began this tradition in 1790 after reminding the Nation that the destiny of self-government and the "preservation of the sacred fire of liberty" is "finally staked on the experiment entrusted to the hands of the American people." For our friends in the press, who place a high premium on accuracy, let me say: I did not actually hear George Washington say that. But it is a matter of historic record.

But from this podium, Winston Churchill asked the free world to stand together against the onslaught of aggression. Franklin Delano Roosevelt spoke of a day of infamy and summoned a nation to arms. Douglas

MacArthur made an unforgettable farewell to a country he loved and served so well. Dwight Eisenhower reminded us that peace was purchased only at the price of strength. And John F. Kennedy spoke of the burden and glory that is freedom.

When I visited this Chamber last year as a newcomer to Washington, critical of past policies which I believed had failed, I proposed a new spirit of partnership between this Congress and this administration and between Washington and our State and local governments. In forging this new partnership for America, we could achieve the oldest hopes of our Republic—prosperity for our nation, peace for the world, and the blessings of individual liberty for our children and, someday, for all of humanity.

It's my duty to report to you tonight on the progress that we have made in our relations with other nations, on the foundation we've carefully laid for our economic recovery, and finally, on a bold and spirited initiative that I believe can change the face of American government and make it again the servant of the people.

Seldom have the stakes been higher for America. What we do and say here will make all the difference to autoworkers in Detroit, lumberjacks in the Northwest, steelworkers in Steubenville who are in the unemployment lines; to black teenagers in Newark and Chicago; to hard-pressed farmers and small businessmen; and to millions of everyday Americans who harbor the simple wish of a safe and financially secure future for their children. To understand the state of the Union, we must look not only at where we are and where we're going but where we've been. The situation at this time last year was truly ominous.

The last decade has seen a series of recessions. There was a recession in 1970, in 1974, and again in the spring of 1980. Each time, unemployment increased and inflation soon turned up again. We coined the word "stagflation" to describe this.

Government's response to these recessions was to pump up the money supply and increase spending. In the last 6 months of 1980, as an example, the money supply increased at the fastest rate in postwar history—13 percent. Inflation remained in double digits, and government spending increased at an annual rate of 17 percent. Interest rates reached a staggering 21 [and] 1/2 percent. There were 8 million unemployed.

Late in 1981 we sank into the present recession, largely because continued high interest rates hurt the auto industry and construction. And there was a drop in productivity, and the already high unemployment increased.

This time, however, things are different. We have an economic program in place, completely different from the artificial quick fixes of the past. It calls for a reduction of the rate of increase in government spending, and already that rate has been cut nearly in half. But reduced spending alone isn't enough. We've just implemented the first and smallest phase of a 3-year tax-rate reduction designed to stimulate the economy and create jobs. *Already interest rates are down to 15 [and] 3/4 percent, but they must still go lower.*[1] Inflation is down from 12.4 percent to 8.9, and for the month of December it was running at an annualized rate of 5.2 percent. If we had not acted as we did, things would be far worse for all Americans than they are today. Inflation, taxes, and interest rates would all be higher.

A year ago, Americans' faith in their governmental process was steadily declining. Six out of 10 Americans were saying they were pessimistic about their future. A new kind of defeatism was heard. Some said our domestic problems were uncontrollable, that we had to learn to live with this seemingly endless cycle of high inflation and high unemployment.

There were also pessimistic predictions about the relationship between our administration and this Congress. It was said we could never work together. Well, those predictions were wrong. The record is clear, and I believe that history will remember this as an era of American renewal, remember this administration as an administration of change, and remember this Congress as a Congress of destiny.

Together, we not only cut the increase in government spending nearly in half, we brought about the largest tax reductions and the most sweeping changes in our tax structure since the beginning of this century. And because we indexed future taxes to the rate of inflation, we took away government's built-in profit on inflation and its hidden incentive to grow larger at the expense of American workers.

Together, after 50 years of taking power away from the hands of the people in their States and local communities, we have started returning power and resources to them.

Together, we have cut the growth of new Federal regulations nearly in half. In 1981 there were 23,000 fewer pages in the Federal Register, which lists new regulations, than there were in 1980. By deregulating oil we've

---

1. Although this is the responsibility of the Federal Reserve, any vote on a sense of the Senate resolution expressing approval or disapproval of interest rate reductions was marked as a presidential agenda item. See Senate vote number 447.

come closer to achieving energy independence and helped bring down the cost of gasoline and heating fuel.

Together, we have created an effective Federal strike force to combat waste and fraud in government. In just 6 months it has saved the taxpayers more than $2 billion, and it's only getting started.

Together we've begun to mobilize the private sector, not to duplicate wasteful and discredited government programs, but to bring thousands of Americans into a volunteer effort to help solve many of America's social problems.

Together we've begun to restore that margin of military safety that ensures peace. Our country's uniform is being worn once again with pride.

Together we have made a New Beginning, but we have only begun.

No one pretends that the way ahead will be easy. In my Inaugural Address last year, I warned that the "ills we suffer have come upon us over several decades. They will not go away in days, weeks, or months, but they will go away . . . because we as Americans have the capacity now, as we've had it in the past, to do whatever needs to be done to preserve this last and greatest bastion of freedom."

The economy will face difficult moments in the months ahead. But the program for economic recovery that is in place will pull the economy out of its slump and put us on the road to prosperity and stable growth by the latter half of this year. And that is why I can report to you tonight that in the near future the state of the Union and the economy will be better—much better—if we summon the strength to continue on the course that we've charted.

And so, the question: If the fundamentals are in place, what now? Well, two things. First, we must understand what's happening at the moment to the economy. Our current problems are not the product of the recovery program that's only just now getting underway, as some would have you believe; they are the inheritance of decades of tax and tax and spend and spend.

Second, because our economic problems are deeply rooted and will not respond to quick political fixes, we must stick to our carefully integrated plan for recovery. That plan is based on four commonsense fundamentals: *continued reduction of the growth in Federal spending;*[2] *preserving the*

2. Given this presidential statement, the spending bills that are challenged as involving excessive federal spending are coded as involving a presidential agenda item. As discussed in chap. 3, I examine the debate in the *Congressional Record* to determine whether appropriations bills are controversial. Excessive spending was an issue with the urgent supplemental appropriations bill that President Reagan vetoed. (See vote number 199.) But appropriations

*individual and business tax reductions that will stimulate saving and invest-
ment;*[3] *removing unnecessary Federal regulations to spark productivity;*[4]
and maintaining a healthy dollar and a stable monetary policy, the latter a
responsibility of the Federal Reserve System.

The only alternative being offered to this economic program is a return
to the policies that gave us a trillion-dollar debt, runaway inflation, runaway interest rates and unemployment. The doubters would have us turn
back the clock with tax increases that would offset the personal tax-rate reductions already passed by this Congress. Raise present taxes to cut future
deficits, they tell us. Well, I don't believe we should buy that argument.

There are too many imponderables for anyone to predict deficits or
surpluses several years ahead with any degree of accuracy. The budget
in place, when I took office, had been projected as balanced. It turned
out to have one of the biggest deficits in history. Another example of the
imponderables that can make deficit projections highly questionable—a
change of only one percentage point in unemployment can alter a deficit
up or down by some $25 billion.

As it now stands, our forecast, which we're required by law to make,
will show major deficits starting at less than a hundred billion dollars and
declining, but still too high. More important, we're making progress with
the three keys to reducing deficits: economic growth, lower interest rates,
and spending control. The policies we have in place will reduce the deficit
steadily, surely, and in time, completely.

Higher taxes would not mean lower deficits. If they did, how would
we explain that tax revenues more than doubled just since 1976; yet in
that same 6-year period we ran the largest series of deficits in our history. In 1980 tax revenues increased by $54 billion, and in 1980 we had
one of our alltime biggest deficits. Raising taxes won't balance the budget; it will encourage more government spending and less private investment. Raising taxes will slow economic growth, reduce production, and
destroy future jobs, making it more difficult for those without jobs to find
them and more likely that those who now have jobs could lose them. So,

---

that pass without senators raising objections over spending (as measured by the content of
debate) were not defined as involving a presidential agenda item.

3. Any vote that would roll back the Reagan tax cuts passed the previous year is counted as
a presidential agenda item. For example, see Senate vote 132 that would eliminate the third-
year tax cut to be phased in under the Reagan plan.

4. A major regulatory reform package designed to reduce regulatory burdens was considered in the 97th Congress, 2d session. See, for example, Senate vote number 59.

I will not ask you to try to balance the budget on the backs of the American taxpayers.

I will seek no tax increases this year,[5] and I have no intention of retreating from our basic program of tax relief. I promise to bring the American people—to bring their tax rates down and to keep them down, to provide them incentives to rebuild our economy, to save, to invest in America's future. I will stand by my word. Tonight I'm urging the American people: Seize these new opportunities to produce, to save, to invest, and together we'll make this economy a mighty engine of freedom, hope, and prosperity again.

Now, the budget deficit this year will exceed our earlier expectations. The recession did that. It lowered revenues and increased costs. To some extent, we're also victims of our own success. We've brought inflation down faster than we thought we could, and in doing this, we've deprived government of those hidden revenues that occur when inflation pushes people into higher income tax brackets. And the continued high interest rates last year cost the government about $5 billion more than anticipated.

We must cut out more nonessential government spending and rout out more waste, and *we will continue our efforts to reduce the number of employees in the Federal work force by 75,000.*[6]

The budget plan I submit to you on February 8th will realize major savings by *dismantling the Departments of Energy and Education and by eliminating ineffective subsidies for business.*[7] We'll continue to *redirect our resources to our two highest budget priorities—a strong national defense to keep America free and at peace*[8] and a reliable safety net of social programs for those who have contributed and those who are in need.

Contrary to some of the wild charges you may have heard, this administration has not and will not turn its back on America's elderly or America's poor. Under the new budget, funding for social insurance programs will be more than double the amount spent only 6 years ago. But it would be foolish to pretend that these or any programs cannot be made more efficient and economical.

---

5. Votes on measures to increase taxes were included as presidential agenda issues. See, for example, the debate over increasing the gas tax by 5 cents a gallon (Senate vote number 401).

6. There were no votes explicitly on reducing the number of employees in the Federal workforce.

7. No votes occurred on these requests.

8. Any votes to cut funding for defense were included. See, for example, roll-call vote 439 proposing across-the-board defense cuts.

The entitlement programs that make up our safety net for the truly needy have worthy goals and many deserving recipients. *We will protect them. But there's only one way to see to it that these programs really help those whom they were designed to help. And that is to bring their spiraling costs under control.*[9]

Today we face the absurd situation of a Federal budget with three-quarters of its expenditures routinely referred to as "uncontrollable." And a large part of this goes to entitlement programs.

Committee after committee of this Congress has heard witness after witness describe many of these programs as poorly administered and rife with waste and fraud. Virtually every American who shops in a local supermarket is aware of the *daily abuses that take place in the food stamp program*,[10] which has grown by 16,000 percent in the last 15 years. Another example is Medicare and Medicaid—programs with worthy goals but whose costs have increased from 11.2 billion to almost 60 billion, more than 5 times as much, in just 10 years.

Waste and fraud are serious problems. Back in 1980 Federal investigators testified before one of your committees that "corruption has permeated virtually every area of the Medicare and Medicaid health care industry." One official said many of the people who are cheating the system were "very confident that nothing was going to happen to them." Well, something is going to happen. Not only the taxpayers are defrauded; the people with real dependency on these programs are deprived of what they need, because available resources are going not to the needy, but to the greedy.

The time has come to control the uncontrollable. In August we made a start. I signed a bill to reduce the growth of these programs by $44 billion over the next 3 years while at the same time preserving essential services for the truly needy. *Shortly you will receive from me a message on further reforms we intend to install*[11]—some new, but others long recommended by your own congressional committees. I ask you to help make these savings for the American taxpayer.

9. This is a reference to the administration's major Medicare/Medicaid proposal that created cost savings in the program through increased fees and co-pays. See, for example, votes 234–36.

10. There were no Senate roll-call votes dealing with the food stamp program in 1982.

11. This is further discussion of the Medicare/Medicaid initiative that the president proposed and the Senate considered.

The savings we propose in entitlement programs will total some \$63 billion over 4 years and will, without affecting social security, go a long way toward bringing Federal spending under control.

But don't be fooled by those who proclaim that spending cuts will deprive the elderly, the needy, and the helpless. *The Federal Government will still subsidize 95 million meals every day. That's one out of seven of all the meals served in America. Head Start, senior nutrition programs, and child welfare programs will not be cut from the levels we proposed last year.*[12] More than *one-half billion dollars has been proposed for minority business assistance.*[13] And research at the National Institute of Health will be increased by over \$100 million. While meeting all these needs, *we intend to plug unwarranted tax loopholes and strengthen the law which requires all large corporations to pay a minimum tax.*[14]

I am confident the economic program we've put into operation will protect the needy while it triggers a recovery that will benefit all Americans. It will stimulate the economy, result in increased savings and provide capital for expansion, mortgages for homebuilding, and jobs for the unemployed.

Now that the essentials of that program are in place, our next major undertaking must be a program—just as bold, just as innovative—to make government again accountable to the people, *to make our system of federalism work again.*[15]

Our citizens feel they've lost control of even the most basic decisions made about the essential services of government, such as schools, welfare, roads, and even garbage collection. And they're right. A maze of interlocking jurisdictions and levels of government confronts average citizens in trying to solve even the simplest of problems. They don't know where to turn for answers, who to hold accountable, who to praise, who to blame, who to vote for or against. The main reason for this is the overpowering growth of Federal grants-in-aid programs during the past few decades.

In 1960 the Federal Government had 132 categorical grant programs, costing \$7 billion. When I took office, there were approximately 500, costing

12. There were no votes on measures proposing cuts or increases in any of these programs in 1982.

13. There were no votes on these proposals to provide more (or less) money for minority business assistance or the NIH.

14. Corporate tax reform was not considered in the 97th Congress, 2d session.

15. The Senate did not take votes on any of Reagan's "new federalism" initiatives referenced here or discussed below in the address.

nearly a hundred billion dollars—13 programs for energy, 36 for pollution control, 66 for social services, 90 for education. And here in the Congress, it takes at least 166 committees just to try to keep track of them.

You know and I know that neither the President nor the Congress can properly oversee this jungle of grants-in-aid; indeed, the growth of these grants has led to the distortion in the vital functions of government. As one Democratic Governor put it recently: The National Government should be worrying about "arms control, not potholes."

The growth in these Federal programs has—in the words of one intergovernmental commission—made the Federal Government "more pervasive, more intrusive, more unmanageable, more ineffective and costly, and above all, more [un]accountable." Let's solve this problem with a single, bold stroke: the return of some $47 billion in Federal programs to State and local government, together with the means to finance them and a transition period of nearly 10 years to avoid unnecessary disruption.

I will shortly send this Congress a message describing this program. I want to emphasize, however, that its full details will have been worked out only after close consultation with congressional, State, and local officials.

Starting in fiscal 1984, the Federal Government will assume full responsibility for the cost of the rapidly growing Medicaid program to go along with its existing responsibility for Medicare. As part of a financially equal swap, the States will simultaneously take full responsibility for Aid to Families with Dependent Children and food stamps.[16] This will make welfare less costly and more responsive to genuine need, because it'll be designed and administered closer to the grassroots and the people it serves.

In 1984 the Federal Government will apply the full proceeds from certain excise taxes to a grassroots trust fund that will belong in fair shares to the 50 States. The total amount flowing into this fund will be $28 billion a year.[17] Over the next 4 years the States can use this money in either of two ways. If they want to continue receiving Federal grants in such areas as transportation, education, and social services, they can use their trust fund money to pay for the grants. Or to the extent they choose to forgo the Federal grant programs, they can use their trust fund money on their own for those

16. The Senate did not take votes on proposals to transfer grant program authority to the states.

17. The Senate did not take votes on the creation of a new revenue-sharing style trust fund in the 97th Congress, 2d session.

or other purposes. There will be a mandatory pass-through of part of these funds to local governments.

By 1988 the States will be in complete control of over 40 Federal grant programs. The trust fund will start to phase out, eventually to disappear, and the excise taxes will be turned over to the States. They can then preserve, lower, or raise taxes on their own and fund and manage these programs as they see fit.

In a single stroke we will be accomplishing a realignment that will end cumbersome administration and spiraling costs at the Federal level while we ensure these programs will be more responsive to both the people they're meant to help and the people who pay for them.

Hand in hand with this program to strengthen the discretion and flexibility of State and local governments, we're proposing legislation for an experimental effort to improve and develop our depressed urban areas in the 1980's and '90's. *This legislation will permit States and localities to apply to the Federal Government for designation as urban enterprise zones.*[18] A broad range of special economic incentives in the zones will help attract new business, new jobs, new opportunity to America's inner cities and rural towns. Some will say our mission is to save free enterprise. Well, I say we must free enterprise so that together we can save America.

Some will also say our States and local communities are not up to the challenge of a new and creative partnership. Well, that might have been true 20 years ago before reforms like reapportionment and *the Voting Rights Act, the 10-year extension of which I strongly support.*[19] It's no longer true today. This administration has faith in State and local governments and the constitutional balance envisioned by the Founding Fathers. We also believe in the integrity, decency, and sound, good sense of grass-roots Americans.

Our faith in the American people is reflected in another major endeavor. Our private sector initiatives task force is seeking out successful community models of school, church, business, union, foundation, and civic programs that help community needs. Such groups are almost invariably far more efficient than government in running social programs.

18. The Senate did not take any votes on urban enterprise zones in the 97th Congress, 2d session.

19. The Voting Rights Act reauthorization was considered and passed by the Senate in 1982, and a good number of roll-call votes occurred on the measure. See roll-call votes 172–90.

We're not asking them to replace discarded and often discredited government programs dollar for dollar, service for service. *We just want to help them perform the good works they choose and help others to profit by their example.*[20] Three hundred and eighty-five thousand corporations and private organizations are already working on social programs ranging from drug rehabilitation to job training, and thousands more Americans have written us asking how they can help. The volunteer spirit is still alive and well in America.

Our nation's long journey towards civil rights for all our citizens—once a source of discord, now a source of pride—must continue with no backsliding or slowing down. We must and shall see that those basic laws that guarantee equal rights are preserved and, when necessary, strengthened.

Our concern for equal rights for women is firm and unshakable. *We launched a new Task Force on Legal Equity for Women and a Fifty States Project that will examine State laws for discriminatory language.*[21] And for the first time in our history, a woman sits on the highest court in the land.

So, too, the problem of crime—one as real and deadly serious as any in America today. *It demands that we seek transformation of our legal system, which overly protects the rights of criminals while it leaves society and the innocent victims of crime without justice.*[22]

We look forward to the *enactment of a responsible clean air act to increase jobs while continuing to improve the quality of our air.*[23] We're encouraged by the bipartisan initiative of the House and are hopeful of further progress as the Senate continues its deliberations.

So far, I've concentrated largely, now, on domestic matters. To view the state of the Union in perspective, we must not ignore the rest of the world. There isn't time tonight for a lengthy treatment of social—or foreign policy, I should say, a subject I intend to address in detail in the near future. A few words, however, are in order on the progress we've made over the past year, reestablishing respect for our nation around the globe and some of the challenges and goals that we will approach in the year ahead.

20. This proposal did not receive major consideration, but there was an amendment to the continuing appropriations package (vote number 432) that would allow FEMA funds to be spent by religious charities to reach the homeless.

21. These task forces did not receive legislative consideration by the Senate.

22. The Senate considered and passed a legal reform measure stiffening criminal penalties. See roll-call votes 381–83.

23. Clean Air legislation did not receive consideration in the Senate in 1982.

At Ottawa and Cancun, I met with leaders of the major industrial powers and developing nations. Now, some of those I met with were a little surprised that I didn't apologize for America's wealth. Instead, I spoke of the strength of the free marketplace system and how that system could help them realize their aspirations for economic development and political freedom. I believe lasting friendships were made, and the foundation was laid for future cooperation.

In the *vital region of the Caribbean Basin, we're developing a program of aid, trade, and investment incentives to promote self-sustaining growth and a better, more secure life for our neighbors to the south.*[24] Toward those who would export terrorism and subversion in the Caribbean and elsewhere, especially Cuba and Libya, we will act with firmness.

Our foreign policy is a policy of strength, fairness, and balance. By restoring America's military credibility, by pursuing peace at the negotiating table wherever both sides are willing to sit down in good faith, and by regaining the respect of America's allies and adversaries alike, we have strengthened our country's position as a force for peace and progress in the world.

When action is called for, we're taking it. *Our sanctions against the military dictatorship that has attempted to crush human rights in Poland*[25]—and against the Soviet regime behind that military dictatorship—clearly demonstrated to the world that America will not conduct "business as usual" with the forces of oppression. If the events in Poland continue to deteriorate, further measures will follow.

Now, let me also note that private American groups have taken the lead in *making January 30th a day of solidarity with the people of Poland.*[26] So, too, the European Parliament has called for March 21st to be an *international day of support for Afghanistan.*[27] Well, I urge all peace-loving peoples to join together on those days, to raise their voices, to speak and pray for freedom.

Meanwhile, we're working for reduction of arms and military activities, as I announced in my address to the Nation last November 18th. *We have proposed to the Soviet Union a far-reaching agenda for mutual reduction of military forces and have already initiated negotiations with them in Geneva*

24. The Caribbean Basin initiative was the subject of several amendments to the supplemental appropriations bill. See, for example, roll-call votes 302–4.

25. Votes were taken on the oppression in Poland and sanctions against the regime. See, for example, roll-call votes 41 and 162.

26. The "Polish solidarity day" was approved by Senate roll-call vote 395.

27. The "Afghanistan day" measure passed on Senate roll-call vote 43.

on intermediate-range nuclear forces. In those talks it is essential that we negotiate from a position of strength.[28] There must be a real incentive for the Soviets to take these talks seriously. This requires that we rebuild our defenses.

In the last decade, while we sought the moderation of Soviet power through a process of restraint and accommodation, the Soviets engaged in an unrelenting buildup of their military forces. The protection of our national security has required that *we undertake a substantial program to enhance our military forces.*[29]

We have not neglected to strengthen our traditional alliances in Europe and Asia, or to develop key relationships with our partners in the Middle East and other countries. Building a more peaceful world requires a sound strategy and the national resolve to back it up. When radical forces threaten our friends, when economic misfortune creates conditions of instability, when strategically vital parts of the world fall under the shadow of Soviet power, our response can make the difference between peaceful change or disorder and violence. That's why we've *laid such stress not only on our own defense but on our vital foreign assistance program.*[30] Your recent passage of the Foreign Assistance Act sent a signal to the world that America will not shrink from making the investments necessary for both peace and security. Our foreign policy must be rooted in realism, not naivete or self-delusion.

A recognition of what the Soviet empire is about is the starting point. Winston Churchill, in negotiating with the Soviets, observed that they respect only strength and resolve in their dealings with other nations. That's why we've moved to reconstruct our national defenses. We intend to keep the peace. We will also keep our freedom.

We have made pledges of a new frankness in our public statements and worldwide broadcasts. In the face of a climate of falsehood and misinformation, we've promised the world a season of truth—the truth of our great civilized ideas: individual liberty, representative government, the rule of law under God. We've never needed walls or minefields or barbed

28. There were Sense of the Senate resolutions concerning these negotiations. See, for example, roll-call votes 98 and 102.

29. Any votes to reduce defense spending were coded as involving a presidential agenda item. There were no votes taken on increasing defense spending levels.

30. Any votes on cuts to the foreign aid program were coded as involving an issue on which the president was asserting leadership. See, for example, roll-call vote 128.

wire to keep our people in. Nor do we declare martial law to keep our people from voting for the kind of government they want.

Yes, we have our problems; yes, we're in a time of recession. And it's true, there's no quick fix, as I said, to instantly end the tragic pain of unemployment. But we will end it. The process has already begun, and we'll see its effect as the year goes on.

We speak with pride and admiration of that little band of Americans who overcame insuperable odds to set this nation on course 200 years ago. But our glory didn't end with them. Americans ever since have emulated their deeds.

We don't have to turn to our history books for heroes. They're all around us. One who sits among you here tonight epitomized that heroism at the end of the longest imprisonment ever inflicted on men of our Armed Forces. Who will ever forget that night when we waited for television to bring us the scene of that first plane landing at Clark Field in the Philippines, bringing our POW's home? The plane door opened and Jeremiah Denton came slowly down the ramp. He caught sight of our flag, saluted it, said, "God bless America," and then thanked us for bringing him home.

Just 2 weeks ago, in the midst of a terrible tragedy on the Potomac, we saw again the spirit of American heroism at its finest—the heroism of dedicated rescue workers saving crash victims from icy waters. And we saw the heroism of one of our young government employees, Lenny Skutnik, who, when he saw a woman lose her grip on the helicopter line, dived into the water and dragged her to safety.

And then there are countless, quiet, everyday heroes of American life—parents who sacrifice long and hard so their children will know a better life than they've known; church and civic volunteers who help to feed, clothe, nurse, and teach the needy; millions who've made our nation and our nation's destiny so very special—unsung heroes who may not have realized their own dreams themselves but then who reinvest those dreams in their children. Don't let anyone tell you that America's best days are behind her, that the American spirit has been vanquished. We've seen it triumph too often in our lives to stop believing in it now.

A hundred and twenty years ago, the greatest of all our Presidents delivered his second State of the Union message in this Chamber. "We cannot escape history," Abraham Lincoln warned. "We of this Congress and this administration will be remembered in spite of ourselves." The "trial through which we pass will light us down, in honor or dishonor, to the latest [last] generation."

Well, that President and that Congress did not fail the American people. Together they weathered the storm and preserved the Union. Let it be said of us that we, too, did not fail; that we, too, worked together to bring America through difficult times. Let us so conduct ourselves that two centuries from now, another Congress and another President, meeting in this Chamber as we are meeting, will speak of us with pride, saying that we met the test and preserved for them in their day the sacred flame of liberty—this last, best hope of man on Earth.

God bless you, and thank you.

Action Items in the 1982 State of the Union Address

- Reduce interest rates further
- Continue with tax reductions begun last year; no new taxes
- Remove federal regulations to spark productivity
- Reduce numbers of federal workers
- Dismantle the Departments of Energy and Education
- Eliminate ineffective subsidies for business
- Redirect resources toward defense
- Make entitlement programs more economical and efficient (Medicare and Medicaid, not Social Security)
- Stop Food Stamp abuses, as well as waste and fraud in Medicare and Medicaid
- Maintain Head Start, senior nutrition, or child welfare spending below levels proposed last year
- Provide funds for minority business assistance
- Increase spending for NIH
- Plug unwarranted tax loopholes and strengthen the law that requires all large corporations to pay a minimum tax
- Undertake a Federalism initiative: return some $47 billion in Federal programs to state and local governments; make the Federal government responsible for the cost of Medicaid; make States responsible for AFDC
- Apply proceeds from excise taxes to a trust fund that will be shared with the 50 states
- Create urban enterprise zones
- Extend the Voting Rights Act
- Build private sector initiatives task force
- Create task force on legal equity for women
- Transform the legal system, which overly protects rights of criminals

- Enact a responsible Clean Air Act
- Impose sanctions against the military dictatorship in Poland
- Join an international day of support for Afghanistan
- Enhance U.S. military forces
- Negotiate with Soviet Union on arms reductions
- Support foreign assistance program, including a program for the Caribbean Basin

Does Party Polarization on an Issue Topic Increase the Likelihood That Presidents Will Include the Issue on Their Agenda?

	Logit coefficient	Robust standard error
Party polarization on the topic (lag)	.01	.01
Fixed effects for presidents		
Reagan	-.71*	.34
Bush	.70	.49
Fixed effects for major topics		
Civil rights	1.43***	.05
Health	.96***	.03
Agriculture	-.29*	.14
Labor, Employment	2.21***	.05
Environment	.18*	.09
Energy	-.74***	.08
Transportation	-1.85***	.12
Law, Crime	2.37***	.12
Social Welfare	1.51***	.05
Banking	-.07	.08
Defense	2.30***	.06
Space, Science	.78***	.12
Foreign Trade	2.47***	.20
International Affairs	2.48***	.20
Public Lands	-1.44***	.06

APPENDIX B (*continued*)

	Logit coefficient	Robust standard error
Constant	.37	.52
n	317	
Pseudo log likelihood	-132.54	
LR χ^2 (18)	95.24***	
Pseudo R^2	.26	

Note: Dependent variable is a *Topic Mentioned*, a dummy variable indicating whether each major topic (using the Policy Agendas Project classification scheme) was mentioned in the State of the Union address each year between 1982 and 1999. Entries are logit coefficients estimated with robust standard errors with clusters for issue type. Coefficients could not be estimated for the categories of Macroeconomics, Education, and Government Operations because these topics always appeared in State of the Union addresses. Data on topics mentioned and not mentioned drawn from the State of the Union Address Data Set available at policyagendas.org.
*$p < .05$; **$p < .01$; ***$p < .001$.

Estimates of Multinomial Logit Model of Partisan Voting Patterns on Senate Roll-Call Votes, 1981–2004 ($n = 8596$)

	Party line vote vs. not party vote	Unanimous party vote vs. not party vote	Party line vote vs. unanimous party vote
Issue Type			
Good-government issues	1.07***	2.23***	1.16***
	(.10)	(.22)	(.21)
Economic issues	1.32***	1.19***	−.14
	(.06)	(.19)	(.19)
Social issues	.92***	−.91	−1.83**
	(.09)	(.72)	(.72)
Hawk vs. dove issues	1.89***	1.56**	−.33
	(.14)	(.55)	(.53)
Type of Vote			
Procedural	1.08***	1.23***	.14
	(.06)	(.18)	(.18)
Passage	−.96***	−.50	.46
	(.08)	(.28)	(.27)
Routine Matters			
Appropriations	.12	−.33	−.45*
	(.06)	(.23)	(.22)
Nominations	−.79***	.33	1.12***
	(.13)	(.33)	(.34)
Purely symbolic	−.48***	.21	.68***
	(.10)	(.28)	(.28)

APPENDIX C *(continued)*

	Party line vote vs. not party vote	Unanimous party vote vs. not party vote	Party line vote vs. unanimous party vote
Congress			
98th Congress	−.30* (.11)	−.18 (.77)	.12 (.77)
99th Congress	−.02 (.11)	−.23 (.77)	−.21 (.77)
100th Congress	−.30** (.11)	.22 (.65)	.52 (.65)
101st Congress	−.09 (.11)	−.57 (.87)	−.48 (.87)
102d Congress	.19 (.12)	−.27 (.87)	−.45 (.87)
103d Congress	.55*** (.11)	1.91*** (.56)	1.36* (.56)
104th Congress	.74*** (.11)	2.22*** (.54)	1.47** (.54)
105th Congress	.36*** (.12)	1.53* (.59)	1.18* (.59)
106th Congress	.39** (.12)	2.86*** (.53)	2.47*** (.53)
107th Congress	−.17 (.12)	2.47*** (.53)	2.64*** (.53)
108th Congress	.88*** (.12)	2.12*** (.57)	1.24* (.57)
Constant	−.97*** (.08)	−5.57*** (.52)	−4.71*** (.52)
Summary Statistics			
Pseudo R^2	.18		
χ^2 (df=40)	2409.45		

Note: Entries are multinomial logit coefficients (standard errors in parentheses).
*$p<.05$; **$p<.01$; ***$p<.001$.

Notes

Chapter One

1. *Congressional Record*, September 10, 2003, S11263.

2. Transcript, "The Democratic Debate in Cleveland," *New York Times*, February 26, 2008.

3. Hillary Clinton had been rated by the magazine as the 16th most liberal senator for 2007.

4. Obama's claim was accurate. There were only two of 99 rated roll-call votes on which he and his opponent had taken opposing positions (*National Journal* 2008). There were a number of votes on which one or both candidates had failed to cast votes, but of those on which both candidates voted there were only two votes that registered them in opposition to one another.

5. Roll-call vote number 18, 110th Congress, 1st session.

6. Roll-call vote number 189, 110th Congress, 1st session.

7. Disagreements between the candidates were on what types of workers would qualify for guest worker status and how the program would be administered.

8. Even in the case of broad public interests, a number of scholars have contended that Olson overstates the obstacles to collective action; see, e.g., Frolich and Oppenheimer 1970; Marsh 1976; Moe 1980, 1981.

9. Olson (1965, 44) writes, "In a group in which no one member got such a large benefit from the collective good that he had an interest in providing it even if he had to pay all the cost, but in which the individual was still so important in terms of the whole group that his contribution or lack of contribution to the group objective had a noticeable effect on the costs or benefits or others in the group, the result is indeterminate."

10. See Table 5–1 in *Vital Statistics on Congress*, 2001–2002 (Ornstein, Mann, and Michael Malbin 2002, 126).

11. There is a long tradition of literature finding only weak effects of whipping; see, e.g., Clapp 1963; Matthews 1960, 133; Norpoth 1976.

12. The combinations are as follows: Republican president and Republican Senate (the 97th, 98th, 99th, part of the 107th, and the 108th congresses), Republican president and Democratic Senate (the 100th, 101st, 102d, and part of the 107th), Democratic president and Democratic Senate (the 103d), and Democratic president and Republican Senate (the 104th, 105th, 106th).

Chapter Two

1. Representative Tom DeLay (R-Tex.) Announces His Intent to Resign from Congress. Houston, Texas. Federal News Service, April 4, 2006, retrieved using *LexisNexis Academic*, accessed September 17, 2007.

2. Smith (2007, 206) provides an extensive critique of the legislative politics literature arguing that a "clearer focus on parties' multiple collective interests would enrich our theory of legislative parties."

3. Searching all the articles on Congress archived in the JSTOR database for the use of "ideology" (in any of its variants), Kammerer (1951, 1134) was the first scholar to make use of "ideology" to describe congressional politics. She writes: "Perhaps symbolic of the ideological cleavage within the [House Education and Labor] committee was the physical separation of minority from majority staff during both Congresses." The term appears in two previous articles, but the first article only used the term to refer to the content of constituent letters (Wyant and Herzog 1941, 601) and the second usage appears only in a footnoted quotation from a newspaper article (Berdahl 1949, 508).

4. "Mr. Hoar on Imperialism," *New York Times*, January 10, 1899 (ProQuest Historical Newspapers), p. 5.

5. "A Long and Anxious Day: The Senate Fight Wound Up with a Twelve-Hour Session, Tariff Bill Passes Senate," *New York Times,* July 4, 1894 (ProQuest Historical Newspapers), p. 1.

6. Full-text searches in ProQuest Historical Newspapers database of the *New York Times (*1857-*current file)* were conducted looking for any article about Congress that employed any variant of the word "ideology" (ideolog). Articles about Congress were identified as those with a Washington dateline with "House," "Senate," or "Congress" in the headline. No *New York Times* report on Congress had employed any variant of the word "ideology" prior to 1938. Each of first six articles using the term in 1938 and early 1939 were references to totalitarian ideologies overseas.

7. Full-text searches of all the political science journals archived in JSTOR were conducted to identify use of any variant of the word "ideology" (ideolog). Articles on the U.S. Congress were identified as those with "House," "Senate," or "Congress" in the title, excluding any articles about any legislature not the U.S. Congress.

8. Delbert Clark, "Business Index Climbs as Causes Are Disputed: Some Credit Tax Revision and Revolt of Congress," *New York Times*, July 23, 1939 (ProQuest Historical Newspapers), p. E6.

9. Special to the *New York Times*, "Shake-Up in the House," *New York Times*, December 6, 1903 (ProQuest Historical Newspapers), p. 13.

10. Special to the *New York Times*, "Senate Regulars Claim 45 Votes," *New York Times*, May 6, 1919 (ProQuest Historical Newspapers), p. 3.

11. This article was identified through full-text searching of all the political science journals archived in JSTOR as described in footnote 3 above.

12. Compiled by the author from full-text Boolean searches in the JSTOR database. The searches encompassed the longest-standing scholarly journals publishing articles on American politics: the *American Political Science Review, Journal of Politics, American Journal of Political Science* (and its predecessor, *Midwest Journal of Political Science*), and *Political Science Quarterly.*

13. Data compiled by the author from the results of Boolean searches in the ProQuest Historical Newspapers database of the *New York Times (1857-current file)*. Articles about Congress using ideology were identified as those containing any variant of the word "ideology," "conservative" or "liberal."

14. Even since 1990, at the peak level of its usage, "ideology" per se is mentioned in only 4–5 percent of news articles on Congress, while about 20 percent of articles make reference to liberals and/or conservatives.

15. Regressing the change in the percentage of scholarly articles on Congress using ideology on the change in the percentage of *New York Times* articles using ideology yields a positive but not statistically significant coefficient.

16. Regressing the change in the percentage of *New York Times* articles on Congress using ideology on the change in the percentage of scholarly articles on Congress using ideology yields a positive, but not statistically significant coefficient.

17. The Pearson Correlation of the change in the percentage of *New York Times* articles on Congress using ideology with the change in the percentage of scholarly articles on Congress using ideology is only .30, and it is not statistically significant.

18. Articles dealing with party loyalty were identified with full text searches in the JSTOR database for "party w/2 loyalty." Articles discussing party organization were identified with full text searches for "party w/3 organization or partisan organization." Articles on party leaders were identified with full text searches for "party leader or majority leader or minority leader or speaker." Articles on partisanship were identified with searches for "partisan" excluding articles that mention "ideology." Searches were confined to the same set of journals used in the preceding analyses, *APSR, AJPS, JOP,* and *PSQ.*

19. At that time, the *New Republic* self-consciously envisioned itself as a movement publication for liberalism, broadly speaking. See "The Record of the House" and "The Record of the Senate," *New Republic*, May 8, 1944, 647–56.

20. Incidentally, the first major journal article in political science that used an advocacy organization's scorecard to measure the liberalism and conservatism of individual members of Congress was Huntingon 1950.

Chapter Three

1. Quoted in Mike Allen, "DeLay's Week to Reassert Command," *Washington Post*, July 30, 2005, A10.

2. Some of the most reliable New Dealers in the 74th Congress were Senators James F. Byrnes (S.C.), John H. Bankhead (Ala.), and Theodore G. Bilbo (Miss.), also among the hardest line segregationists (Morgan 1985). All three of these senators receive DW-NOMINATE scores placing them among the top 15 most liberal senators in the 74th Congress.

3. Before WWII votes on the minimum wage could not be predicted accurately using first dimension D-NOMINATE scores. Even using the second dimension (which tends to reflect North-South divisions) votes on the minimum wage issue still "mapped poorly onto the space" during this period (Poole and Rosenthal 1997, 112).

4. *Congressional Record*, August 2, 2001, S8635.

5. See Senate roll-call vote number 265, 107th Congress, 1st session.

6. At the time, the *New Republic* explicitly styled itself as an organ of the liberal movement in American politics. Note, for example, the exhortations to political action in an editorial article "The Truth about the PAC" (August 21, 1944). In that article, the magazine also spells out its ideological commitments: "This 'ideology' is neither a mystery nor a closely guarded secret. . . . It rests upon the belief that we can and must find a way to utilize the vast spiritual resources of this nation that every American who is reasonably industrious and prudent may enjoy at least the minimum elements of a good life—that is, adequate housing, food, clothing, medical care, education, recreation and an opportunity for advancement. . . . [We also cannot] permit democracy to be betrayed here at home by social or economic barriers to be erected against anyone by reason of his race, religion, or national origin" (210–11).

7. See Senate roll-call vote 262, 109th Congress, 1st session.

8. See Senate roll-call vote 229 in the 109th Congress, 1st session, and Senate roll-call vote 6 in the 109th Congress, 2d session.

9. When Senators Hillary Clinton (D-N.Y.) and John Ensign (R-Nev.) offered an amendment to distribute homeland security grants to state and local governments, it was tabled on a party-line vote, with 79 percent of Republicans voting in favor of setting aside the measure, and 63 percent of Democrats to continue consideration of the measure. See Senate roll-call vote 183, 108th Congress, 2d session.

10. Using NOMINATE scores to track party polarization, the difference between the median Republican and Democrat in Congress ranged from .7 to .9

between 1827 and 1889 (Poole and Rosenthal 1997, 83–84); by comparison, between 1990 and 2002 the difference between the median Republican and Democrat in Congress ranged from .7 to .8 (Jacobson 2004, 5).

11. The Democratic Policy Committee *Record Vote* series serves as an excellent finding tool for use in conjunction with the *Congressional Record*. These publications note the dates and times when debate on votes occurs, and they cross-reference other closely related votes, enabling me to identify and locate the relevant deliberations in the Record.

12. For example, the debate in the *Congressional Record* indicates that Interior Secretary Gale Norton's nomination was controversial because of Democratic fears that she would not adequately enforce environmental laws. (See the debate surrounding Senate roll-call vote number 6 in the 107th Congress, 1st session.) This nomination is thus coded as involving an *economic issue* (in the subcategory "regulation of private economic activity"). President Clinton's nomination of David M. Satcher for Surgeon General was controversial because of Republican concerns regarding his views on partial birth abortion. (See the debate surrounding Senate roll-call vote number 9 in the 105th Congress, 2d session.) This nomination is thus coded as involving a *social issue*.

13. For example, the debate in the *Congressional Record* reveals that the urgent supplemental appropriations legislation in 1982 was controversial because of overall spending levels. (See the debate surrounding Senate roll-call votes numbers 199 and 214 in the 97th Congress, 2d session). It is thus coded as an *economic issue* (in the "government's share of the economy" category). Most appropriations bills pass without any senator raising concerns about overall spending levels during the debate in the *Congressional Record*. When no senator offers objections to spending levels or to a policy rider involving an ideological issue, an appropriations bill is not coded in any of the ideological categories.

14. For example, the U.S.-Singapore Free Trade Agreement was controversial because some senators saw it as weakening protections for displaced U.S. workers. (See the debate surrounding Senate roll-call vote number 318 in the 108th Congress, 1st session.) This vote is coded as an economic policy issue (in the "regulations of private economic activity" category).

15. The author is responsible for coding all the data, eliminating concerns about intercoder reliability.

16. A party vote is defined as one on which at least a majority of senators of one major party voted in opposition to at least a majority of the other major party.

17. Differences in the issue content of party and nonparty votes are statistically significant: for economic issues, $t = 27.1$ $(p < .001)$; for hawk vs. dove, $t = 10.4$ $(p < .001)$; for social issues, $t = 4.5$ $(p < .001)$; for the proportion of votes involving issues that did not fall into any ideological issue category, $t = 27.1$ $(p < .001)$. Votes involving multilateralism/unilateralism issues were not more common among party votes than among nonparty votes.

18. This proportion of party conflict occurring on ideological issues is calculated by summing the party differences (defined as the absolute difference between the percentage of Republicans voting yea and the percentage of Democrats voting yea) on all votes involving ideological issues and dividing that by the sum of party differences on all roll-call votes.

19. On this score, it is also worth noting that the multilateralism/unilateralism issue is not always seen as an ideological matter in American politics. This is one area of disagreement among scholars. Definitions of liberalism and conservatism often do not mention liberals being more favorable toward multilateral institutions than conservatives are. Because some do see these issues as having ideological content, I included them in the study. Clearly, however, Republicans and Democrats do not have positions that are as well defined and differentiated in this area as on the other types of issues in the study.

20. In calculating this probability, I assume a Senate made up of 50 Republicans and 50 Democrats. The probability of a majority of members of a party voting together is calculated as a binomial experiment (Ott and Longnecker 2001, 146). Given a .65 probability of a yea vote, the likelihood of 26 or more Republicans voting yea is .98. Given a .35 probability of a nay vote, the probability of 26 or more Democrats voting nay is .01. The probability of the two conditions holding simultaneously is .01 (Ott and Longnecker 2001, 133). If one assumes purely random voting (a probability of voting yea of .5), the same procedure yields a .20 probability of a party vote.

Chapter Four

1. Karl Rove, "Interview with Karl Rove," interview by Chris Wallace, *Fox News Sunday*, Fox News Network, August 19, 2007.

2. First, votes are grouped by government function—e.g., social welfare, environment, health, etc.—using a topical classification scheme developed by Frank Baumgartner, Bryan Jones, and John Wilkerson (2002). Second, the ideological content dataset introduced in chapter 3 is used to isolate for separate analysis Senate voting decisions on highly divisive, ideological issues.

3. See Senate roll-call votes 20 and 34 in the 103d Congress, 2d session.

4. See Senate roll-call votes 99, 171, 172, 173, 174, 176 and 183 in the 107th Congress, 1st session.

5. See, for example, Senate roll-call votes 295, 198, 354 in the 97th Congress, 1st session and roll-call votes 115, 330, and 370 in the 98th Congress, 1st session.

6. See, for example, Senate roll-call votes 568, 569 in the 104th Congress, 1st session and roll-call votes 2 and 24 in the 104th Congress, 2d session.

7. See Senate roll-call votes 197 and 202 in the 107th Congress, 1st session and roll-call votes 57 and 213 in the 108th Congress, 2d session.

8. See, for example, the following Senate roll-call votes: number 464 in the 104th Congress, 1st session; number 37 in the 104th Congress, 2d session; and number 286 in the 106th Congress, 1st session.

9. As in chap. 3, party polarization is measured using the average Rice Index of party difference across votes. For each vote this index is the absolute difference between the percentage of Democrats voting yea and the percentage of Republicans voting yea.

10. The codebook and dataset are available on the Policy Agendas website at policyagendas.org.

11. The table shows the party difference scores in the Congress following the address in order to evaluate the counter hypothesis that presidents anticipate party polarizing issues and direct their agenda toward those issues. The findings are not different if I instead show the level of party polarization on issues in the immediately preceding Congress, on the alternative theory that presidents react to congressional party conflict on issues by including those issues in their agendas. In neither case is there any evidence that presidents actively prefer partisan issues in constructing their agenda.

12. As a stricter test of the counter hypothesis, I also estimated a cross-sectional time-series logit model to test whether presidents steer their agendas toward issues that are party polarizing. The dependent variable was *Topic Mentioned$_t$*, a dummy variable reflecting whether or not a major topic type (using the Policy Agendas classification scheme) was mentioned in the State of the Union address each year between 1982 and 1999. The key independent variable was the level of party polarization on that issue in the preceding Congress. The model includes fixed effects for individual presidents (in order to capture any preference for particular issues that particular presidents exhibit during their time in office) and for each category of issue (to control for the fact that some types of issues are more likely to appear in a president's address than others). Logit coefficients were estimated with robust standard errors with clustering for issue type. The results provide no evidence that higher levels of party polarization on an issue type increase the likelihood that presidents will include it in their agenda. The coefficient on the party polarization variable is small (.01) and statistically insignificant ($p = .30$). Complete findings are displayed in Appendix B.

13. Important distributive programs in the environment category include waste-water treatment grants, Superfund, and land and water conservation programs.

14. Predicted party polarization increases from 55.6 to 65.9 when redistributive issues are mentioned in the State of the Union address. The difference between these two estimates is statistically significant ($p < .001$). Predicted values calculated with CLARIFY: Software for Interpreting and Presenting Statistical Results. Version 2.1 (Tomz, Wittenberg, and King 2001).

15. Predicted party polarization increases from 60.2 to 64.7 when economic issues are mentioned in the State of the Union address. The difference is statistically significant ($p < .001$).

16. Predicted party polarization increases from 52.9 to 58.4 when hawk vs. dove issues are mentioned in the State of the Union address. The difference is statistically significant ($p < .01$).

17. Predicted party polarization increases from 30.8 to 41.3 when redistributive issues are mentioned in the State of the Union address. The difference is statistically significant ($p < .001$).

18. Party cohesion is calculated for each vote in three steps so as to adjust for votes that exhibit high cohesion merely because the issue is uncontroversial. (1) Cohesion of the president's party is calculated as the absolute difference between the percentage of the president's party voting yea and the percentage of the president's party voting nay. (2) The level of overall chamber cohesion is calculated as the absolute difference between the percentage of senators voting yea and the percentage voting nay. (3) Overall chamber cohesion (calculated in step 2) is subtracted from overall party cohesion (calculated in step 1). These three steps yield a negative score when a vote divides the president's party more deeply than it divides the chamber as a whole, and it yields a positive score when the president's party is more unified on a vote than the chamber as a whole. When 100% of senators vote on the same side of an issue, the final score will be zero, because the president's party is no more or less unified than the chamber as a whole.

19. Multiple regression analysis along the lines shown in table 4.4 was conducted to ensure that the results are not the product of spurious correlation. The bivariate findings in table 4.6 are confirmed by the multivariate results in 37 of the 38 regression equations. The only exception is that the positive coefficient for presidential leadership fails to meet standards of statistical significance in the model for opposition party cohesion in votes on labor, employment, and immigration.

20. The very low level of attention to presidential agenda items in the second session of the 108th Congress probably results more from an unusual State of the Union address in 2004. That address was largely focused on claiming credit for past successes, especially in foreign policy, providing little forward agenda guidance to Congress.

21. The regression equation results are as follows: *Presidential agenda items as a percent of roll-call votes (by year)* = $14.43 + .635(time)$. $F = 5.02$ ($p < .05$). $R^2 = .19$.

22. See figure 7.6 for a visual display of quarterly variation within Congresses.

23. With the inclusion of the lagged dependent variable, Breusch-Godfrey Lagrange-Multiplier tests fail to reject the null hypothesis of no remaining first-, second-, or higher-order autoregressive errors.

24. An augmented Dickey-Fuller test strongly rejects the presence of a unit root.

25. At one standard deviation below the mean of *presidential agenda items (%)*, party polarization is estimated at 37.1; at one standard deviation above the mean, party polarization is estimated at 43.6. The standard error of the difference is 6.18 ($p < .001$).

26. Two alternative models were estimated to determine if divided government would have an effect. In one model a control was added for whether the majority

party in the Senate was the party in control of the presidency; in a second model a control was added for whether the majority party in either House or Senate held the White House. The first coefficient took a negative sign, the second took a positive sign, and neither reached statistical significance. Other coefficients were not affected.

Chapter Five

1. A vast scholarly literature has established that parties presiding over economic growth enjoy significant electoral advantages over those that govern during economic trouble. See, for example, Kinder and Kiewiet 1981, Owens and Olson 1980, and Tufte 1975.

2. For example, proposals to protect whistleblowers who report executive agency abuses can be disputed both because there may be alternative ways to address the problem (means) or because one believes that problems are simply not widespread or serious enough to require the policy (facts). The goal of stopping government mismanagement is neither liberal nor conservative.

3. The party difference index score for each roll-call vote is calculated as the absolute difference between the percentage of Republicans voting yea and the percentage of Democrats voting yea.

4. *Procedural votes* are motions that would table or recommit a bill or amendment, motions determining whether a bill or amendment can be considered under Budget Act rules, and all votes involving rules of procedure or control of the floor, such as motions to proceed, cloture, appeals of the ruling of the chair.

5. *Purely symbolic votes* are resolutions that merely express Senate or congressional sentiment on a particular subject. To be classified in this category, the resolution cannot require any actions from the executive branch or have any other policy content.

6. Beyond this, the fixed effects coefficients provide no additional information— they merely capture variation unique to particular Congresses that is otherwise unaccounted for—but their large positive coefficients indicate clearly that the causes of partisanship go beyond the types of votes before the Senate.

7. Ordered logit or probit is not appropriate given the nonlinear distribution of party polarization evident in figure 5.2.

8. *Congressional Record*, May 8 1990, S5794.

9. *Congressional Record*, May 7, 1992, S6306.

10. *Congressional Record*, March 8, 1989, S2295.

11. If a nomination becomes controversial because of a nominee's views or previous actions on ideological matters, the dispute is not, by definitions of this study, a good-government case.

12. Battles over nominations are often fought out on both grounds of ideology and good government simultaneously. The fight over the nomination of Justice

Clarence Thomas, for example, raised both questions of character (sexual harassment) and ideology (views on constitutional interpretation). If both are raised in the debate the nomination is not regarded as a purely good-government matter for purposes of this study.

13. Reports of the U.S. Senate Armed Services Committee on the Nomination of J. Tower to be Secretary of Defense, CQ Electronic Library, CQ Public Affairs Collection, 1990 [retrieved March 24, 2007]. Available from http://library.cqpress.com/cqpac/hsdc89–0001181388.

14. U.S. Senate Committee on Armed Services, *Consideration of the Honorable John G. Tower to Be Secretary of Defense*, 101st Cong., 1st sess., 1989, Exec. Rept. 101–1.

15. *Congressional Record*, March 8, 1989, S 2295.

16. Ibid.

17. Senate roll-call vote 153, 103d Cong., 2d sess.

18. Senate roll-call vote 154, 103d Cong., 2d sess.

19. U.S. Senate Committee on Banking, Housing, and Urban Affairs, *Madison Guaranty S&L and the Whitewater Development Corporation, Washington DC Phase*, 103d Cong., 2d. sess., 1995, S. Rept. 103–433.

20. U.S. Senate Committee to Investigate Whitewater Development Corporation and Related Matters, *Investigation of Whitewater Development Corporation and Related Matters, Final Report*, 104th Cong., 2d sess. 1996, S. Rept. 104–280.

21. Senate roll-call votes 17 and 18, 106th Cong., 1st sess.

22. Senate roll-call vote 281, 108th Cong., 1st sess.

23. Senate roll-call vote 279, 108th Cong., 1st sess.

24. Senate roll-call vote 283, 108th Cong., 1st sess.

25. Senate roll-call vote 284, 108th Cong., 1st sess.

26. Senate roll-call vote 138, 108th Cong., 2d sess.

27. *Congressional Record*, July 16, 2003, S 9448-S9480.

28. Senate roll-call vote 5, 105th Cong., 1st sess.

29. Senate roll-call vote 110, 106th Cong., 1st sess.

30. See roll-call vote 47 in the 101st Congress, 1st session: 89 percent of Democrats voted in favor of putting the S&L bailout on budget, while 98 percent of Republicans voted against it.

31. See, for example, roll-call vote 90 in the 100th Congress, 2d session.

32. *Congressional Record*, July 31, 1995, S10973.

33. See, for example, Republicans disputing whether funds for the International Monetary Fund and Bosnian peacekeepers really constitute emergency spending (*Congressional Record*, March 24, 1998, S 2463) and Democrats disputing the inclusion of Iraq reconstruction projects in an emergency defense supplemental (*Congressional Record*, September 29, 2003, S 12106).

34. See also roll-call vote 212 in the 100th Congress, 1st session.

35. *Congressional Record*, May 3, 1989, S4675.

36. Ibid., S4676.

37. Quoted in Rubin 1995, 3597.

38. *Congressional Record*, November 16, 1995, S17113–4.

39. *Congressional Record*, November 18, 1995, S 17441

40. *Congressional Record*, May 3, 1989, S4675.

41. *Congressional Record*, May 7, 1992, S6315.

42. Votes on public financing of campaigns are not, for purposes of this study, regarded as ideologically neutral, good-government causes. Good-government causes in the area of campaign finance include: disclosure requirements for candidates and parties; rules about coordination between national parties, state parties, and individual candidates; and limits on where or when candidates can raise campaign funds.

43. Roll-call votes 77, 78, 80–87, and 90 in the 101st Cong., 2d sess. and roll-call votes 195, 196, and 198–201 in the 103d Cong., 1st sess.

44. *Congressional Record*, July 20, 1993, S8759, S8766.

45. *Congressional Record*, May 8, 1990, S5804.

46. *Congressional Record*, May 7, 1992, S6307.

47. Ibid., S6315.

48. *Congressional Record*, March 17, 1993, S2990.

49. Senate roll-call vote 36, 103d Cong., 1st sess.

50. *Congressional Record*, February 26, 2002, S1172.

51. *Congressional Record*, March 1, 2002, S1385.

52. For a sustained critique of the literature on congressional parties along these lines, see Smith 2007.

Chapter Six

1. Motions are made for attendance, for cloture on debate, to table a question, to recommit a bill to committee, to proceed to consider a measure, to waive the Budget Act, to appeal the ruling of the chair, to adjourn, among others.

2. These motions are made when an amendment violates a provision of the Budget Act (such as the spending limits for a committee agreed to in the Budget Resolution) and would otherwise be subject to a point of order; adopting a waiver requires 60 votes.

3. "Substantive votes" are those not occurring on motions: adoption of amendments, passage of legislation, confirmation of nominees, and the like.

4. Smith (1989, 28–48), for example, contends that the introduction of recorded voting in the House amending process weakened the influence of committee and party leaders because the visibility of recorded votes enhanced the pressures on members to vote in ways that their constituents could support.

5. *Congressional Record*, September 23, 1975, 29814; quoted in Oleszek (2007, 234).

6. *Congressional Record*, February 25, 1985, S2029.

7. The difference in ideological content between substantive and procedural votes is statistically significant ($t = 11.4$, $p < .001$).

8. One major reason that procedural votes occur more frequently on economic issues is simply the need for senators to adopt a motion to waive the Budget Act in order to propose amendments that would increase spending beyond the budget agreement; otherwise such amendments would be subject to a budget point of order.

9. Analysis of variance confirms that it is useful to subdivide procedural votes in this way. For both ideological and nonideological issues, party votes occur at different rates across each of the three types of vote: substantive, procedural, and parliamentary. For differences across ideological issues, $F = 78.6$ ($p < .001$), and for differences across nonideological issues, $F = 560.1$ ($p < .001$).

10. Party votes took place on fully 68 percent of all procedural votes on nonideological issues and on fully 59 percent of all parliamentary votes on nonideological issues. By comparison, party votes occurred on 29 percent of all substantive votes on nonideological issues.

11. The small number of multilateralism vs. unilateralism votes is probably a factor here. In this issue category, there were only 20 parliamentary votes, 41 procedural votes, and 62 substantive votes over the entire 1981–2004 time frame.

12. Analysis of variance reveals that the higher levels of partisanship on procedural and parliamentary votes are statistically significant ($p < .001$) for every category of vote.

13. *Congressional Record*, June 23, 1987, S8438.

14. *Congressional Record*, September 30, 1988, S13866.

15. *Congressioanl Record*, March 24, 1993, S3623.

16. *Congressional Record*, January 5, 1995, S474.

17. *Congressional Record*, May 3, 1999, S4525.

18. *Congressional Record*, June 19, 1998, S6695.

19. *Congressional Record*, October 13, 1989, S13350.

20. Senate Majority Leader Robert Dole (R-Kans.), *Congressional Record*, January 24, 1995.

21. Senate Majority Leader George Mitchell (D-Maine), *Congressional Record*, March 24, 1993.

22. *Congressional Record*, February 24, 1995, S3102, quoted in Den Hartog and Monroe 2006.

23. *Congressional Record*, March 8, 1990, S2430, emphasis added.

24. *Congressional Record*, October 11, 2001, S10547.

25. *Congressional Record*, December 8, 1987, S17798.

26. Balanced-budget Constitutional Amendment, 1997 legislative chronology, 1998, CQ Electronic Library, CQ Public Affairs Collection [retrieved December 3, 2007]. Available from http://library.cqpress.com/cqpac/cqa197-0000181039.

27. *Congressional Record*, February 10, 1997, S1164.

28. An amendment offered by Sen. Robert Torricelli (D-N.J.) to waive the requirements of the Balanced Budget Amendment in a time of war received a direct vote; see Senate roll-call vote 16, 105th Congress, 1st session.

29. *Congressional Record*, February 24, 1997, S1468.

30. *Congressional Record*, June 27, 1988, S8615.

31. Ibid.

32. See Senate roll-call votes 2–11, 13, and 14 in the 104th Congress, 1st session.

33. Based on a systematic study of the use of the motion to table, Den Hartog and Monroe (2006, 18) similarly report that "the majority party uses [tabling] motions to kill amendments offered by minority party senators far more often than it uses them to kill majority offered amendments."

34. See Senate roll-call votes 197–202.

35. If the vote occurred on a motion of any kind, it is classed as "procedural" for purposes of the analysis in this section.

36. These proportions were calculated by summing the party differences across each different type of vote and then setting that over the total sum of party differences across all votes in each Congress.

Chapter Seven

1. "Nondecisions" is not an entirely apt term. Legislative strategies developed through party consultation often do involve decisions. The term emphasizes, however, that these decisions are often made informally or tacitly. Not everything is brought to a vote, and party members often do not bother to raise issues that have no hope of gaining party or leadership support. I employ the term in reference to the earlier literature on agenda setting.

2. Regressing economic issue content on the size of the deficit or surplus as a percentage of GDP yields a coefficient of 1.45 ($p < .01$) and an R^2 of .26.

3. Precisely the same pattern appears when the unemployment rate is correlated with the percentage of the roll-call agenda devoted to economic issues. Regressing the economic content of the roll-call agenda on the unemployment rate yields a coefficient of 2.08 ($p < .05$). Periods of higher unemployment do not result in more ideological controversy over economic issues in the Senate.

4. Regressing economic issue content on changes in GDP yields a statistically insignificant coefficient of $-.58$ ($p = .43$).

5. These results do not change if the effect of economic indicators is lagged to take into account a possible delay between economic conditions and the content of the agenda.

6. Regressing the percent of the Senate roll-call agenda devoted to social issues on the culture war events measure yields a statistically insignificant coefficient of .264 ($p = .75$).

7. There is also no pattern when a lag of the culture war measure is employed instead.

8. Regressing the percent of the Senate roll-call agenda devoted to hawk v. dove issues on the number of named military operations in the previous year also yields a statistically insignificant coefficient of 1.26 ($p = 726$).

9. Between 1981 and 1989, hawk vs. dove votes comprised 7.5 percent of the Senate roll-call agenda on average; between 1990 and 2004, they comprised 2.3 percent of the Senate roll-call agenda.

10. An augmented Dickey-Fuller test strongly rejects the presence of a unit root in the dependent variable and in all the agenda content variables included in the model.

11. The lag corrects for first-order autoregressive errors. With its inclusion, Breusch-Godfrey Lagrange-Multiplier tests fail to reject the null hypothesis of no remaining first- or higher-order autoregressive errors. Durbin's alternative test for autocorrelation corroborates the results of the Breusch-Godfrey Lagrange-Multiplier tests.

12. A partial F test confirms that the improvement in the model gained from adding the agenda block of variables is statistically significant.

13. This approach to goodness of fit analysis is adapted from Carmines and Stimson (1989, 171–74).

14. All else being equal, when economic issues were at their minimum, party polarization is estimated at 32 percentage points (standard error = 2.1); at their maximum, party polarization is estimated at 52 percentage points (standard error = 2.9).

15. Unlike the other variables in the model, the results of an augmented Dickey-Fuller test for *leadership funds* indicate that it is not possible to reject the presence of a unit root.

16. Differencing the variable makes the time series for *leadership funds* stationary. When the *first difference of leadership funds* is included in the model, however, it does not yield a statistically significant result.

17. Including a year counter in the model (either in addition to or instead of *leadership funds*) has no effect on any of the agenda content variables.

18. The standard error of the estimated difference of 6.3 percentage points is 1.5, and the 95 percent confidence interval ranges from 3.5 to 9.3.

19. There is no reason why membership turnover per se should necessarily increase party polarization, and it did not have this effect in other periods of congressional history (Patterson and Caldeira 1988, 126).

Chapter Eight

1. See roll-call vote number 296, 98th Congress, 1st session.
2. See roll-call vote number 166, 107th Congress, 2d session.

3. Motions are made for attendance, for cloture on debate, to table a question, to recommit a bill to committee, to proceed to consider a measure, to waive the Budget Act, to appeal the ruling of the chair, to adjourn, among others.

4. These are average Rice Index of Party Difference scores.

5. Mannheim (1936, 238) envisions a dialogic process by which ideologies evolve within social group settings and conflicts, especially through political parties.

References

Abramowitz, Alan I., Brad Alexander, and Matthew Gunning. 2006. Incumbency, Redistricting, and the Decline of Competition in US House Elections. *Journal of Politics* 68 (1): 75–88.

Abramowitz, Alan I., and Kyle L. Saunders. 1998. Ideological Realignment in the U.S. Electorate. *Journal of Politics* 60 (3): 634–52.

———. 2008. Is Polarization a Myth? *Journal of Politics* 70 (2): 542–55.

Adler, E. Scott, and John S. Lapinski. 2006. The Substance of Representation: Studying Policy Content and Legislative Behavior. In *The Macropolitics of Congress*, edited by E. Scott Adler and John S. Lapinski. Princeton, NJ: Princeton University Press.

Aldrich, John H. 1995. *Why Parties? The Origin and Transformation of Party Politics in America*. Chicago: University of Chicago Press.

Aldrich, John H., and David W. Rohde. 2000. The Consequences of Party Organization in the House: The Role of the Majority and the Minority Parties in Conditional Party Government. In *Polarized Politics: Congress and the President in a Partisan Era*, edited by Jon R. Bond and Richard Fleisher. Washington, DC: CQ Press.

Alston, Chuck. 1993. Democrats Flex New Muscle with Trio of Election Bills. *CQ Weekly Online*, March 19, 643–45.

Altman, O. R. 1936. Second Session of the Seventy-fourth Congress, January 3, 1936, to June 20, 1936. *American Political Science Review* 30 (6): 1086–1107.

American Political Science Association, Committee on Political Parties. 1950. Toward a More Responsible Two-Party System: A Report of the Committee on Political Parties. *American Political Science Review* 44 (September): 1–14.

Ansolabehere, Stephen, and James M. Snyder, Jr. 1998. Valence Politics and Equilibrium in Spatial Election Models. *Public Choice* 103: 327–36.

Ansolabehere, Stephen, James M. Snyder, Jr., and Charles Stewart, III. 2001a. The Effects of Party and Preferences on Congressional Roll-Call Voting. *Legislative Studies Quarterly* 26 (November): 533–72.

———. 2001b. Candidate Positioning in U.S. House Elections. *American Journal of Political Science* 45 (1): 136–59.

Arnold, R. Douglas. 1990. *The Logic of Congressional Action*. New Haven: Yale University Press.

Bach, Stanley, and Steven S. Smith. 1988. *Managing Uncertainty in the House of Representatives: Adaptation and Innovation in Special Rules*. Washington, DC: Brookings Institution.

Bachrach, Peter, and Morton Baratz. 1962. The Two Faces of Power. American Political Science Review 56 (4): 947–52.

———. 1963. Decisions and Nondecisions: An Analytical Framework. American Political Science Review 57 (3): 632–42.

Baker, Peter. 2007. An Unlikely Partnership Left Behind. *Washington Post*, November 5, A1.

Baker, Ross K. 2001. *House and Senate*. New York: W. W. Norton & Co.

Baron, David P., and John A. Ferejohn. 1989. Bargaining in Legislatures. *American Political Science Review* 83 (4): 1181–1206.

Baumgartner, Frank R., and Bryan D. Jones. 1993. *Agendas and Instability in American Politics*. Chicago: University of Chicago Press.

Baumgartner, Frank R., Bryan D. Jones, and John D. Wilkerson. 2002. Studying Policy Dynamics. In *Policy Dynamics*, edited by Frank R. Baumgartner and Bryan D. Jones. Chicago: University of Chicago Press.

Bensel, Richard F. 2004. Roundtable on Congress and History. Presented at the American Political Science Association Annual Meeting, Chicago, IL, September 3.

Berdahl, Clarence A. 1949. Some Notes on Party Membership in Congress, II. *American Political Science Review* 43 (3): 492–508.

Bernstein, Robert A., Gerald C. Wright, Jr., and Michael B. Berkman. 1988. Do U.S. Senators Moderate Strategically? *American Political Science Review* 82 (1): 237–45.

Binder, Sarah A., Eric D. Lawrence, and Forrest Maltzman. 1999. Uncovering the Hidden Effect of Party. *Journal of Politics* 61 (3): 815–31.

Binkley, Wilfred. 1949. The President and Congress. *Journal of Politics* 11 (1): 65–79.

Black, Duncan. 1948. On the Rationale of Group Decision-Making. *Journal of Political Economy* 56 (1): 23–34.

———. 1958. *The Theory of Committees and Elections*. London: Cambridge University Press.

Bond, Jon R., and Richard Fleisher. 1992. *The President in the Legislative Arena*. Chicago: University of Chicago Press.

Brady, David W., and Charles S. Bullock, III. 1980. Is There a Conservative Coalition in the House? *Journal of Politics* 42 (2): 549–59.

Brady, David W., Joseph Cooper, and Patricia A. Hurley. 1979. The Decline of Party in the U.S. House of Representatives, 1887–1968. *Legislative Studies Quarterly* 4 (3): 381–407.

Brady, David W., and Hahrie Han. 2004. An Extended Historical View of Congressional Party Polarization. Paper presented at Princeton University.

Brady, David W., and Craig Volden. 1998. *Revolving Gridlock*. Boulder: Westview Press.

Brewer, Mark D. 2005. The Rise of Partisanship and the Expansion of Partisan Conflict within the American Electorate. *Political Research Quarterly* 58 (2): 219–29.

Brewer, Mark D., Mack D. Mariana, and Jeffrey M. Stonecash. 2002. Northern Democrats and Party Polarization in the U.S. House. *Legislative Studies Quarterly* 27: 423–44.

Brimhall, Dean R., and Arthur S. Otis. 1948. Consistency of Voting by Our Congressmen. *Journal of Applied Psychology* 32 (1): 1–14.

Broder, David S. 2007. Three Words for the Next President. *Washington Post*, November 22, A37.

Brownstein, Ronald. 2007. *The Second Civil War: How Extreme Partisanship Has Paralyzed Washington and Polarized America*. New York: Penguin Press.

Burden, Barry C. 2001. The Polarizing Effects of Congressional Primaries. In *Congressional Primaries and the Politics of Representation*, edited by P. Galderisi, M. Ezra and M. Lyons. Lanham, MD: Rowman & Littlefield.

———. 2007. *Personal Roots of Representation*. Princeton: Princeton University Press.

Burden, Barry C., Gregory A. Caldeira, and Tim Groseclose. 2000. Measuring the Ideologies of U.S. Senators: The Song Remains the Same. *Legislative Studies Quarterly* 25 (2): 237–58.

Calvert, Randall L., Mathew D. McCubbins, and Barry R. Weingast. 1989. A Theory of Political Control and Agency Discretion. *American Journal of Political Science* 33 (3): 588–611.

Cameron, Charles M. 2000. *Veto Bargaining: Presidents and the Politics of Negative Power*. Cambridge: Cambridge University Press.

Cameron, Charles M., Albert D. Cover, and Jeffrey Segal. 1990. Senate Voting on Supreme Court Nominees: A Neoinstitutional Model. *American Political Science Review* 84 (2): 525–34.

Canes-Wrone, Brandice. 2001. The President's Legislative Influence from Public Appeals. *American Journal of Political Science* 45 (2): 313–29.

Canes-Wrone, Brandice, David W. Brady, and John F. Cogan. 2002. Out of Step, Out of Office: Electoral Accountability and House Members' Voting. *American Political Science Review* 96 (1): 127–40.

Cannon, Carl M. 2006. Administration: A New Era of Partisan War. *National Journal*, March 16.

Carmines, Edward G., and James A. Stimson. 1989. *Issue Evolution: Race and the Transformation of American Politics*. Princeton, NJ: Princeton University Press.

Chait, Jonathan. 2007. Captives of the Supply Side. *New York Times*, October 9, A31.

Clapp, Charles L. 1963. *The Congressman: His Work as He Sees It*. Washington, DC: Brookings Institution.

Clausen, Aage R. 1967. Measurement Identity in the Longitudinal Analysis of Legislative Voting. *American Political Science Review* 61 (4): 1020–35.

———. 1973. *How Congressmen Decide: A Policy Focus*. New York: St. Martin's Press.

Clinton, Joshua D. 2006. Representation in Congress: Constituents and Roll Calls in the 106th House. *Journal of Politics* 68 (2): 397–409.

Clinton, Joshua, Simon Jackman, and Douglas Rivers. 2004. The Statistical Analysis of Roll Call Data. *American Political Science Review* 98 (2): 355–70.

Cohen, Jeffrey E., and David C. Nice. 1983. Changing Party Loyalty of State Delegations to the U.S. House of Representatives, 1953–1976. *Western Political Quarterly* 36 (2): 312–25.

Cohen, Richard E. 2004. Maverick Conservatives. *National Journal*, February 28.

Collie, Melissa P. 1988. The Rise of Coalition Politics: Voting in the U.S. House, 1933–1980. *Legislative Studies Quarterly* 13 (3): 321–42.

Collier, Kenneth, and Terry Sullivan. 1995. New Evidence Undercutting the Linkage of Approval with Presidential Support and Influence. *Journal of Politics* 57: 197–209.

Converse, Philip. 1964. The Nature of Belief Systems in Mass Publics. In *Ideology and Discontent*, edited by David E. Apter. New York: Free Press of Glencoe.

Cooper, Joseph, and David W. Brady. 1981. Institutional Context and Leadership Style. *American Political Science Review* 75 (2): 411–25.

Cooper, Joseph, and Garry Young. 2002. Party and Preference in Congressional Decision Making: Roll Call Voting in the House of Representatives, 1889–1999. In *Party, Process, and Political Change in Congress*, edited by David Brady and Mathew McCubbins. Stanford: Stanford University Press.

Cox, Gary W., and Mathew D. McCubbins. 1991. On the Decline of Party Voting in Congress. *Legislative Studies Quarterly* 16 (4): 547–70.

———. 1993. *Legislative Leviathan: Party Government in the House*. Berkeley: University of California Press.

———. 2005. *Setting the Agenda: Responsible Party Government in the U.S. House of Representatives*. New York: Cambridge University Press.

Cox, Gary W., and Keith T. Poole. 2002. On Measuring Partisanship in Roll-Call Voting: The U.S. House of Representatives, 1877–1999. *American Journal of Political Science* 46 (3): 477–89.

Dempsey, Paul. 1962. Liberalism-Conservatism and Party Loyalty in the U.S. Senate. *Journal of Social Psychology* 56 (April): 159–70.

Den Hartog, Chris, and Nathan W. Monroe. 2006. Home Field Advantage: An Asymmetric-Costs Theory of Legislative Agenda Influence in the U.S. Senate. Paper presented at the Conference on Party Effects in the Senate, Duke University, April 6–9.

———. 2008. The Value of Majority Status: The Effects of Jeffords's Switch on Asset Prices of Republican and Democratic Firms. *Legislative Studies Quarterly* 33 (1): 63–84.

Dewar, Helen, and Eric Pianin. 2004. Congress Is Losing Leaders and Unifiers. *Washington Post*, November 21, A12.

Dionne, E. J., Jr. 1991. *Why Americans Hate Politics*. New York: Simon & Schuster.

Downs, Anthony. 1957. *An Economic Theory of Democracy*. New York: Harper & Row.

Dwyer, Paul E. 2005. *Congressional Research Service Report for Congress, RL32819, Legislative Branch: FY2006 Appropriations*. Washington, DC: Congressional Research Service.

Edwards, George C., III. 1990. *At the Margins: Presidential Leadership of Congress*. New Haven: Yale University Press.

———. 2003. *On Deaf Ears: The Limits of the Bully Pulpit*. New Haven: Yale University Press.

Edwards, George C., III, and B. Dan Wood. 1999. Who Influences Whom? The President, Congress, and the Media. *American Political Science Review* 93: 327–44.

Eilperin, Juliet. 2006. *Fight Club Politics: How Partisanship Is Poisoning the House of Representatives*. Lanham: Rowman & Littlefield.

Enelow, James M., and Melvin J. Hinich. 1982. Nonspatial Candidate Characteristics and Electoral Competition. *Journal of Politics* 44 (1): 115–30.

———. 1984. *The Spatial Theory of Voting: An Introduction*. Cambridge: Cambridge University Press.

Erikson, Robert S. 1990. Roll Calls, Reputations, and Representation in the U.S. Senate. *Legislative Studies Quarterly* 15 (4): 623–42.

Erikson, Robert S., Michael B. MacKuen, and James A. Stimson. 2002. *The Macro Polity*. New York: Cambridge University Press.

Evans, C. Lawrence. 2001. Committees, Leaders, and Message Politics. In *Congress Reconsidered*, edited by Lawrence C. Dodd and Bruce I. Oppenheimer. Washington, DC: CQ Press.

Farris, Charles D. 1958. A Method of Determining Ideological Groupings in the Congress. *Journal of Politics* 20 (2): 308–38.

Fenno, Richard F., Jr. 1973. *Congressmen in Committees*. Boston: Little, Brown.

———. 1978. *Home Style: House Members in Their Districts*. Boston: Little, Brown.

Fessler, Pamela. 1989. CBO Keeps Its Profile Low. *CQ Weekly Online*, October 19, 2761–64.

Fiorina, Morris P., Paul E. Peterson, and D. Stephen Voss. 2005. *America's New Democracy*. New York: Longman Publishing Group.

Fleisher, Richard, and Jon R. Bond. 2004. The Shrinking Middle in the U.S. Congress. *British Journal of Political Science* 34: 429–51.

Fowler, James. 2005. Dynamic Responsiveness in the U.S. Senate. *American Journal of Political Science* 49 (2): 299–312.

Fowler, Linda L. 1982. How Interest Groups Select Issues for Rating Voting Records of Members of the U.S. Congress. *Legislative Studies Quarterly* 7 (3): 401–13.

Friel, Brian. 2008. Vote Ratings—Rating Their Records. *National Journal*, February 2.

Frolich, Norman, and Joe A. Oppenheimer. 1970. I Get By with a Little Help from My Friends. *World Politics* 23 (1): 104–20.

Gage, N. L., and Ben Shimberg. 1949. Measuring Senatorial "Progressivism." *Journal of Abnormal and Social Psychology* 44 (January): 112–17.

Gerring, John. 1998a. Ideology: A Definitional Analysis. *Political Research Quarterly* 50 (4): 957–94.

———. 1998b. *Party Ideologies in America, 1828–1996*. New York: Cambridge University Press.

Goldwater, Barry M. 1960. *The Conscience of a Conservative*. Shepherdsville, KY: Victor Publishing Co.

Groseclose, Tim. 2001. A Model of Candidate Location When One Candidate Has a Valence Advantage. *American Journal of Political Science* 45 (4): 862–86.

Hamilton, Alexander, John Jay, and James Madison. 1987. *The Federalist Papers*. Edited by Isaac Kramnick. New York: Penguin.

Harris, Chester W. 1948. A Factor Analysis of Selected Senate Roll Calls, 80th Congress. *Educational and Psychological Measurement* 8 (Winter): 583–91.

Hartz, Louis. 1955. *The Liberal Tradition in America*. New York: Harcourt, Brace & World.

Haynes, George H. 1938. *The Senate of the United States: Its History and Practice*. Boston: Houghton Mifflin.

Heberlig, Eric, Marc Hetherington, and Bruce Larson. 2006. The Price of Leadership: Campaign Money and the Polarization of Congressional Parties. *Journal of Politics* 68 (4): 992–1005.

Heckman, James J., and James M. Snyder. 1997. Linear Probability Models of the Demand for Attributes with an Empirical Application to Estimating the Preferences of Legislators. *RAND Journal of Economics* 28 (Special Issue in Honor of Richard E. Quandt): S142–89.

Herring, E. Pendleton. 1935. First Session of the Seventy-fourth Congress, January 3, 1935 to August 26, 1935. *American Political Science Review* 29 (6): 985–1005.

Herring, E. Pendleton. 1933. Second Session of the Seventy-second Congress, December 5, 1932, to March 4, 1933. *American Political Science Review* 27 (3): 404–22.

Herron, Michael C. 1999. Artificial Extremism in Interest Group Ratings and the Preferences versus Party Debate. *Legislative Studies Quarterly* 24 (4): 525–42.

Hibbing, John, and Elizabeth Theiss-Morse. 1995. *Congress As Public Enemy*. Cambridge: Cambridge University Press.

———. 2002. *Stealth Democracy*. Cambridge: Cambridge University Press.

Hill, Kim Quaile, Stephen Hanna, and Sahar Shafqat. 1997. The Liberal-Conservative Ideology of U.S. Senators: A New Measure. *American Journal of Political Science* 41 (4): 1395–1413.

Hofstadter, Richard. 1948. *The American Political Tradition*. New York: Vintage Books.

Hood, M. V., III, Quentin Kidd, and Irwin L. Morris. 1999. Of Byrd(s) and Bumpers: Using Democratic Senators to Analyze Political Change in the South, 1960–1995. *American Journal of Political Science* 43: 465–87.

Horowitz, Juliana Menasce. 2006. The Culture Wars and the Agenda of the U.S. Congress. Ph.D. diss., Department of Government and Politics, University of Maryland.

Hotelling, Harold. 1929. Stability in Competition. *Economic Journal* 39 (153): 41–57.

Howell, William G., and Jon C. Pevehouse. 2007. When Congress Stops Wars. *Foreign Affairs* 86 (5): 95–108.

Huber, John D., and Charles R. Shipan. 2000. The Costs of Control: Legislators, Agencies, and Transaction Costs. *Legislative Studies Quarterly* 25 (1): 25–52.

Huntington, Samuel P. 1950. A Revised Theory of American Party Politics. *American Political Science Review* 44 (3): 669–77.

Hurley, Patricia A., and Rick K. Wilson. 1989. Partisan Voting Patterns in the U.S. Senate, 1877–1986. *Legislative Studies Quarterly* 14 (2): 225–50.

Inglehart, John K. 2004. The New Medicare Prescription-Drug Benefit—A Pure Power Play. *New England Journal of Medicine* 350 (8): 826–33.

Jackson, John E., and John W. Kingdon. 1992. Ideology, Interest Group Scores, and Legislative Votes. *American Journal of Political Science* 36 (3): 805–23.

Jacobson, Gary C. 2000. Party Polarization in National Politics: The Electoral Connection. In *Polarized Politics: Congress and the President in a Partisan Era*, edited by Jon R. Bond and Richard Fleisher. Washington, DC: CQ Press.

———. 2004. Explaining the Ideological Polarization of the Congressional Parties since the 1970s. Paper presented at the Annual Meeting of the Midwest Political Science Association, Chicago, IL, April 15–18.

———. 2009. *The Politics of Congressional Elections*. 7th ed. New York: Pearson Longman.

Jacobson, Gary C., and Michael A. Dimock. 1994. Checking Out: The Effects of Bank Overdrafts on the 1992 House Elections. *American Journal of Political Science* 38 (3): 601–24.

Janda, Kenneth, Jeffrey M. Berry, and Jerry Goldman. 2008. *The Challenge of Democracy*. 9th ed. Boston: Houghton Mifflin.

Jenkins, Jeffery A. 1999. Examining the Bonding Effects of Party: A Comparative Analysis of Roll-Call Voting in the U.S. and Confederate Houses. *American Journal of Political Science* 43 (4): 1144–65.

———. 2000. Examining the Robustness of Ideological Voting: Evidence from the Confederate House of Representatives. *American Journal of Political Science* 44 (4): 811–22.

Jennings, M. Kent. 1992. Ideological Thinking among Mass Publics and Political Elites. *Public Opinion Quarterly* 56 (4): 419–41.

Johnston, David, and Tim Weiner. 1996. Seizing the Crime Issue, Clinton Blurs Party Lines. *New York Times*, August 1, A1.

Kalt, Joseph P., and Mark Zupan. 1984. Capture and Ideology in the Economic Theory of Politics. *American Economic Review* 74 (3): 279–300.

———. 1990. The Apparent Ideological Behavior of Legislators: Testing for Principal-Agent Slack in Political Institutions. *Journal of Law and Economics* 33 (1): 103–31.

Kammerer, Gladys M. 1951. The Record of Congress in Committee Staffing. *American Political Science Review* 45 (4): 1126–36.

Kane, Paul. 2008. "NRCC Treasurer Under Scrutiny Was Thought of as 'Gold Standard,'" *Washington Posts*, March 13, A1.

Katznelson, Ira, and John S. Lapinski. 2006. The Substance of Representation: Studying Policy Content and Legislative Behavior. In *The Macropolitics of Congress*, edited by John S. Lapinski and E. Scott Adler. Princeton: Princeton University Press.

Kernell, Samuel. 1997. *Going Public: New Strategies of Presidential Leadership*. Washington, DC: CQ Press.

Kiewiet, D. Roderick, and Mathew D. McCubbins. 1991. *The Logic of Delegation: Congressional Parties and the Appropriations Process*. Chicago: University of Chicago Press.

Kinder, Donald R., and D. Roderick Kiewiet. 1981. Sociotropic Politics: The American Case. *British Journal of Political Science* 11: 129–61.

King, Gary, Michael Tomz, and Jason Wittenberg. 2000. Making the Most of Statistical Analyses: Improving Interpretation and Presentation. *American Journal of Political Science* 44 (2): 347–61.

Kingdon, John W. 1981. *Congressmen's Voting Decisions*. New York: Harper & Row.

———. 1995. *Agendas, Alternatives, and Public Policies.* 2d ed. New York: HarperCollins.

Kirkpatrick, David D. 2008. Question of Timing on Bush's Push on Earmarks. *New York Times,* January 29, A18.

Knight, Kathleen. 2006. Transformations of the Concept of Ideology in the Twentieth Century. *American Political Science Review* 100 (4): 619–26.

Krauthammer, Charles. 1988. The Democrats Move Left; It's Not Just Jackson. *Washington Post,* April 8, A21.

Krehbiel, Keith. 1991. *Information and Legislative Organization.* Ann Arbor: University of Michigan Press.

———. 1993. "Where's the Party." *British Journal of Political Science* 23: 235–66.

———. 1994. Deference, Extremism, and Interest Group Ratings. *Legislative Studies Quarterly* 19 (1): 61–77.

———. 1998. *Pivotal Politics: A Theory of U.S. Lawmaking.* Chicago: University of Chicago Press.

———. 2000. Party Discipline and Measures of Partisanship. *American Journal of Political Science* 44 (2): 212–27.

Kritzer, Herbert M. 1978. Ideology and American Political Elites. *Public Opinion Quarterly* 42 (4): 484–502.

Krugman, Paul. 2002. America the Polarized. *New York Times,* January 4, 21.

Kuhn, Thomas S. 1996. *The Structure of Scientific Revolutions.* 3d ed. Chicago: University of Chicago Press.

Lasswell, Harold C. 1963. *Power and Personality.* New York: Viking.

Layman, Geoffrey C., and Thomas M. Carsey. 2002. Party Polarization and "Conflict Extension" in the American Electorate. *American Journal of Political Science* 46 (4): 786–802.

Leake, James Miller. 1917. Four Years of Congress. *American Political Science Review* 11 (2): 252–83.

Lee, Frances E. 2000. Senate Representation and Coalition Building in Distributive Politics. *American Political Science Review* 94 (1): 59–72.

———. 2005. Interests, Constituencies, and Policy Making. In *The Legislative Branch,* edited by Paul J. Quirk and Sarah A. Binder. New York: Oxford University Press.

———. 2008. Agreeing to Disagree: Agenda Content and Senate Partisanship, 1981–2004. *Legislative Studies Quarterly* 32 (2): 199–222.

Lowell, A. Lawrence. 1902. The Influence of Party upon Legislation in England and America. In *Annual Report of the American Historical Association for 1901.* Washington, DC: Government Printing Office.

Lowi, Theodore J. 1964. American Business, Public Policy, Case-Studies, and Political Theory. *World Politics* 16 (July): 667–715.

Lowry, William R., and Charles R. Shipan. 2002. Party Differentiation in Congress. *Legislative Studies Quarterly* 27: 33–60.

MacKay, Scott. 2008. Chafee's New Book Is Tough on Pro-War Democrats, Republicans, President Bush. *Providence Journal,* January 27.

MacRae, Duncan, Jr. 1952. The Relation between Roll-Call Votes and Constituencies in the Massachusetts House of Representatives. *American Political Science Review* 46 (4): 1046–55.

————. 1954. Some Underlying Variables in Legislative Roll Call Votes. *Public Opinion Quarterly* 18 (2): 191–96.

————. 1958. *Dimensions of Congressional Voting*. Berkeley: University of California Press.

————. 1970. *Issues and Parties in Legislative Voting: Methods of Statistical Analysis*. Berkeley: University of California Press.

Maltzman, Forrest. 1997. *Competing Principals: Committees, Parties, and the Organization of Congress*. Ann Arbor: University of Michigan Press.

Mann, Thomas E., and Norman J. Ornstein. 2006. *The Broken Branch: How Congress Is Failing America and How to Get It Back on Track*. New York: Oxford University Press.

Mannheim, Karl. 1936. *Ideology and Utopia: An Introduction to the Sociology of Knowledge*. New York: Harcourt, Brace & Co.

Marsh, David. 1976. On Joining Interest Groups: An Empirical Consideration of the Work of Mancur Olson Jr. *British Journal of Political Science* 6 (3): 257–71.

Marshall, Bryan W., Brandon C. Prins, and David W. Rohde. 1999. Fighting Fire with Water: Partisan Procedural Strategies and the Senate Appropriations Committee. *Congress and the Presidency* 26 (2): 114–32.

Marx, Karl, and Friedrich Engels. 1998. *The German Ideology*. New York: Prometheus Books.

Matthews, Donald R. 1960. *U.S. Senators and Their World*. Chapel Hill: University of North Carolina Press.

Matthews, Donald R., and James A. Stimson. 1975. *Yeas and Nays: Normal Decisionmaking in the U.S. House of Representatives*. New York: John Wiley & Sons.

Mayhew, David R. 1974. *Congress: The Electoral Connection*. New Haven: Yale University Press.

————. 1991. *Divided We Govern: Party Control, Lawmaking, and Investigations*. New Haven: Yale University Press.

————. 2006. Lawmaking and History. In *The Macropolitics of Congress*, edited by E. Scott Adler and John S. Lapinski. Princeton: Princeton University Press.

McCarty, Nolan, Keith T. Poole, and Howard Rosenthal. 2001. The Hunt for Party Discipline in Congress. *American Political Science Review* 95 (3): 673–87.

————. 2006. *Polarized America: The Dance of Ideology and Unequal Riches*. Cambridge: MIT Press.

McGann, Anthony J., William Koetzle, and Bernard Grofman. 2002. How an Ideologically Concentrated Minority Can Trump a Dispersed Majority: Nonmedian Voter Results for Plurality, Run-off, and Sequential Elimination Elections. *American Journal of Political Science* 46 (1): 134–47.

Miller, Gary, and Norman Schofield. 2003. Activists and Partisan Realignment in the United States. *American Political Science Review* 97: 245–60.

Miller, Warren E., and Donald E. Stokes. 1963. Constituency Influence in Congress. *American Political Science Review* 57 (1): 45–56.

Milligan, Susan. 2004. Back-room Dealing a Capitol Trend: GOP Flexing Its Majority Power. *Boston Globe*, October 3.

Minar, David W. 1961. Ideology and Political Behavior. *Midwest Journal of Political Science* 5 (4): 317–31.

Moe, Terry M. 1980. *The Organization of Interests: Incentives and the Internal Dynamics of Political Interest Groups*. Chicago: University of Chicago Press.

———. 1981. Toward a Broader View of Interest Groups. *Journal of Politics* 43 (2): 531–43.

Mondak, Jeffrey. 1993. Public Opinion and Heuristic Processing of Source Cues. *Political Behavior* 15 (2): 167–92.

Moon, Woojin. 2004. Party Activists, Campaign Resources, and Candidate Position Taking: Theory, Tests and Applications. *British Journal of Political Science* 34: 611–13.

Morgan, Chester M. 1985. *Redneck Liberal: Theodore G. Bilbo and the New Deal*. Baton Rouge: Louisiana State University Press.

Murphy, James T. 1974. Political Parties and the Pork Barrel: Party Conflict and Cooperation in House Public Works Committee Decision Making. *American Political Science Review* 68: 169–74.

National Journal Staff. 2007. How the Vote Ratings Are Calculated. *National Journal*, March 2.

———. 2008. 2007 Vote Ratings—Key Votes Used to Calculate the Ratings. *National Journal*, March 2.

Neustadt, Richard E. 1990. *Presidential Power and the Modern Presidents*. New York: Free Press.

Nokken, Timothy P. 2000. Dynamics of Congressional Loyalty: Party Defection and Roll-Call Behavior, 1947–97. *Legislative Studies Quarterly* 25 (3): 417–44.

Norpoth, Helmut. 1976. Explaining Party Cohesion in Congress: The Case of Shared Policy Attitudes. *American Political Science Review* 70 (4): 1156–71.

Oleszek, Walter J. 2007. *Congressional Procedures and the Policy Process*. 7th ed. Washington, D.C.: CQ Press.

Olson, Mancur. 1965. *The Logic of Collective Action*. Cambridge: Harvard University Press.

Oppenheimer, Bruce I. 2005. Deep Red and Blue Congressional Districts: The Causes and Consequences of Declining Party Competition. In *Congress Reconsidered*, edited by Lawrence D. Dodd and Bruce I. Oppenheimer. Washington, DC: CQ Press.

Ornstein, Norman J., Thomas E. Mann, and Michael Malbin. 1996. *Vital Statistics on Congress: 1995–1996*. Washington, DC: American Enterprise Institute for Public Policy Research.

———. 2002. *Vital Statistics on Congress, 2001–2002*. Washington, DC: AEI Press.

Ostrogorski, Moisei. 1964. *Democracy and the Organization of Political Parties*. Volume II: *The United States*. Translated by Frederick Clarke. New York: Anchor Books.

Ott, R. Lyman, and Michael Longnecker. 2001. *An Introduction to Statistical Methods and Data Analysis*. Pacific Grove: Thomson Learning.

Owens, John R., and Edward C. Olson. 1980. Economic Fluctuations and Congressional Elections. *American Journal of Political Science* 24 (3): 469–93.

Patterson, Samuel C., and Gregory A. Caldeira. 1988. Party Voting in the United States Congress. *British Journal of Political Science* 18: 111–31.

Patterson, Thomas E. 1994. *Out of Order*. New York: Vintage Books.

———. 2008. *The American Democracy*. 8th ed. New York: McGraw-Hill.

Peters, John G., and Susan Welch. 1980. The Effects of Charges of Corruption on Voting Behavior in Congressional Elections. *American Political Science Review* 74 (3): 697–708.

Poole, Keith T. 1981. Dimensions of Interest Group Evaluation of the U.S. Senate, 1969–1978. *American Journal of Political Science* 25 (1): 49–67.

———. 1988. Recent Developments in Analytical Models of Voting in the U.S. Congress. *Legislative Studies Quarterly* 13 (1): 117–33.

———. 1998. Changing Minds? Not in Congress. GSIA Working Paper #1997–22: Carnegie-Mellon University.

Poole, Keith T., and Howard Rosenthal. 1997. *Congress: A Political-Economic History of Roll Call Voting*. New York: Oxford University Press.

Riker, William H. 1990. Political Science and Rational Choice. In *Perspectives on Positive Political Economy*, edited by James E. Alt and Kenneth A. Shepsle. New York: Cambridge University Press.

Ripley, Randall B. 1967. *Party Leaders in the House of Representatives*. Washington, DC: Brookings Institution.

Roach, Hannah Grace. 1925. Sectionalism in Congress. *American Political Science Review* 19 (3): 500–526.

Roberts, Jason M. 2007. The Statistical Analysis of Roll-Call Data: A Cautionary Tale. *Legislative Studies Quarterly* 32 (3): 341–60.

Roberts, Jason M., and Steven S. Smith. 2003. Procedural Contexts, Party Strategy, and Conditional Party Voting in the U.S. House of Representatives. *American Journal of Political Science* 47 (2): 305–17.

Rogers, Lindsay. 1922. American Government and Politics: The First (Special) Session of the Sixty-Seventh Congress, April 11, 1921–November 23, 1921. *American Political Science Review* 16 (1): 41–52.

Rohde, David W. 1991. *Parties and Leaders in the Postreform House*. Chicago: University of Chicago Press.

———. 1992. Electoral Forces, Political Agendas and Partisanship in Congress. In *The Postreform Congress*, edited by Roger H. Davidson. New York: St. Martin's Press.

Rubin, Alissa J. 1995. Reality of Tough Job Ahead Dampens Joy over Deal. *CQ Weekly Report*, November 22, 3597–98.

Rudalevige, Andrew. 2005. The Executive Branch and the Legislative Process. In *Institutions of American Democracy: The Executive Branch*, edited by Joel D. Aberbach and Mark A. Peterson. New York: Oxford University Press.

Sammon, Richard. 1993a. Voting Registration: House OKs "Motor Voter" for Final Senate Vote. *CQ Weekly Online*, May 7, 1144.

———. 1993b. Voting Registration: Senate Approves Moter Voter with Concessions to the GOP. *CQ Weekly Online*, March 19, 664.

Samuelson, Robert J. 2004. How Polarization Sells. *Washington Post*, June 30, A21.

Sartori, Giovanni. 1969. Politics, Ideology, and Belief Systems. *American Political Science Review* 63 (2): 398–411.

Schattschneider, E. E. 1942. *Party Government*. New York: Farrar & Rinehart.

———. 1975. *The Semisovereign People: A Realist's View of Democracy in America*. Fort Worth, TX: Harcourt, Brace, Jovanovich College Publishers.

Schatz, Joseph J. 2005. Bush's Long View Called Too Rosy. *CQ Weekly Report*, February 14, 372.

Schickler, Eric. 2000. Institutional Change in the House of Representatives, 1867–1998: A Test of Partisan and Ideological Power Balance Models. *American Political Science Review* 94 (2): 269–88.

Schneider, Jerome. 1979. *Ideological Coalitions in Congress*. Westport, CT: Greenwood Press.

Schor, Elana. 2007. Leahy Gets OK to Subpoena Rove; Sampson Hesitates on Testimony. *The Hill*, March 22.

Schumpeter, Joseph A. 1942. *Capitalism, Socialism, and Democracy*. New York: Harper & Brothers Publishers.

Shapiro, Catherine R., David W. Brady, Richard A. Brody, and John A. Ferejohn. 1990. Linking Constituency Opinion and Senate Voting Scores: A Hybrid Explanation. *Legislative Studies Quarterly* 15 (4): 599–622.

Shapiro, Michael J. 1968. The House and the Federal Role: A Computer Simulation of Roll-Call Voting. *American Political Science Review* 62 (2): 494–517.

Sinclair, Barbara. 1982. *Congressional Realignment, 1925–1978*. Austin: University of Texas Press.

———. 1989. *The Transformation of the U.S. Senate*. Baltimore: Johns Hopkins University Press.

———. 1995. *Legislators, Leaders, and Lawmaking*. Baltimore: Johns Hopkins University Press.

———. 2000. *Unorthodox Lawmaking: New Legislative Processes in the U.S. Congress*. 2d ed. Washington, DC: CQ Press.

———. 2002. Do Parties Matter? In *Party, Process, and Political Change in Congress*, edited by David Brady and Mathew McCubbins. Stanford: Stanford University Press.

———. 2005. Parties and Leadership in the House. In *Institutions of American Democracy: The Legislative Branch*, edited by Paul J. Quirk and Sarah A. Binder. New York: Oxford University Press.

———. 2006. *Party Wars: Polarization and the Politics of National Policy Making*. Norman: University of Oklahoma Press.

Skowronek, Stephen. 1993. *The Politics Presidents Make: Leadership from John Adams to George Bush*. Cambridge, MA: Belknap Press.

Smith, Steven S. 1989. *Call to Order: Floor Politics in the House and Senate*. Washington, D.C.: Brookings Institution.

———. 2005. Parties and Leadership in the Senate. In *Institutions of American Democracy: The Legislative Branch*, edited by Paul J. Quirk and Sarah A. Binder. New York: Oxford University Press.

———. 2007. *Party Influence in Congress*. New York: Cambridge University Press.

Snyder, James M., Jr. 1992. Artificial Extremism in Interest Group Ratings. *Legislative Studies Quarterly* 17 (4): 525–42.

Snyder, James M., Jr., and Tim Groseclose. 2000. Estimating Party Influence in Congressional Roll-Call Voting. *American Journal of Political Science* 44 (2): 187–205.

Starr, Kenneth. 1998. *The Starr Report: The Findings of Independent Counsel Kenneth W. Starr on President Clinton and the Lewinsky Affair with Annotations by the Washington Post*. Washington, DC: Replica Books.

Stein, Robert M., and Kenneth N. Bickers. 1995. *Perpetuating the Pork Barrel: Policy Subsystems and American Democracy*. New York: Cambridge University Press.

Stimson, James A. 1975. Belief Systems: Constraint, Complexity, and the 1972 Election. *American Journal of Political Science* 19 (3): 393–417.

———. 2004. *Tides of Consent: How Public Opinion Shapes American Politics*. New York: Cambridge University Press.

Stokes, Donald E. 1963. Spatial Models of Party Competition. *American Political Science Review* 57 (2): 368–77.

———. 1992. Valence Politics. In *Electoral Politics*, edited by Dennis Kavanagh. New York: Oxford University Press.

Sundquist, James L. 1981. *The Decline and Resurgence of Congress*. Washington, DC: Brookings Institution.

———. 1983. *Dynamics of the Party System: Alignment and Realignment of Political Parties in the United States*. Washington, D.C.: Brookings Institution.

———. 1988. Needed: A Political Theory for the New Era of Coalition Government in the United States. *Political Science Quarterly* 103 (4): 613–35.

Theriault, Sean M. 2006. Procedural Polarization in the U.S. Congress. Paper presented at the Annual Meeting of the Midwest Political Science Association, Chicago, IL.

———. 2008. *Party Polarization in Congress*. New York: Cambridge University Press.

Thomas, Martin. 1985. Election Proximity and Senatorial Roll Call Voting. *American Journal of Political Science* 29 (1): 96–111.

Tomz, Michael, Jason Wittenberg, Gary King. 2001. CLARIFY: Software for Interpreting and Presenting Statistical Results 2.0. Harvard University, Cambridge, MA.

Truman, David. 1959. *The Congressional Party: A Case Study*. New York: John Wiley & Sons.

Tufte, Edward R. 1975. Determinants of the Outcomes of Midterm Congressional Elections. *American Political Science Review* 69 (3): 812–26.

Turner, Julius. 1951. *Party and Constituency: Pressures on Congress*. Baltimore: Johns Hopkins University Press.

U.S. Senate, Committee on Armed Services. 1989. Consideration of the Honorable John G. Tower To Be Secretary of Defense: 101st Cong., 1st sess.

U.S. Senate, Committee on Banking, Housing and Urban Affairs. 1995. Madison Guaranty S&L and the Whitewater Development Corporation, Washington DC Phase: 103d Cong., 2d sess.

U.S. Senate, Committee to Investigate Whitewater Development Corporation and Related Matters. 1996. Investigation of Whitewater Development Corporation and Related Matters, Final Report: 104th Cong., 2d sess.

Uslaner, Eric M. 1999. *The Movers and the Shirkers: Representatives and Ideologues in the Senate*. Ann Arbor: University of Michigan Press.

Van Houweling, Robert P. 2003. Legislators' Personal Policy Preferences and Partisan Legislative Organization, Ph.D. diss., Department of Government, Harvard University.

Weingast, Barry R. 1979. A Rational Choice Perspective on Congressional Norms. *American Journal of Political Science* 23 (2): 245–62.

Welch, Susan, and Eric H. Carlson. 1973. The Impact of Party on Voting Behavior in a Nonpartisan Legislature. *American Political Science Review* 67 (3): 854–67.

Welch, Susan, and John Hibbing. 1997. The Effects of Charges of Corruption on Voting Behavior in Congressional Elections, 1982–1990. *Journal of Politics* 59 (1): 226–39.

Whittington, Keith E. and Daniel P. Carpenter. 2003. Executive Power in American Institutional Development. *Perspectives on Politics* 1 (3): 495–513.

Wilcox, Clyde, and Aage Clausen. 1991. The Dimensionality of Roll-Call Voting Reconsidered. *Legislative Studies Quarterly* 16 (3): 393–406.

Wilson, James Q., and John J. DiIulio, Jr. 2006. *American Government.* Boston: Houghton Mifflin.

Witt, Howard. 2008. Immigration Issue Rerouted as National Interest Wanes. *Chicago Tribune*, March 23.

Woodward, C. Vann. 1951. Progressivism—For Whites Only. In *Origins of the New South.* Baton Rouge: Louisiana State University Press.

Wright, Gerald C., Jr. 1978. Candidates Policy Positions and Voting in U.S. Congressional Elections. *Legislative Studies Quarterly* 3 (3): 445–64.

Wright, Gerald C., and Brian F. Schaffner. 2002. The Influence of Party: Evidence from the State Legislatures. *American Political Science Review* 96 (2): 367–79.

Wyant, Rowena, and Herta Herzog. 1941. Voting Via the Senate Mailbag–Part II. *Public Opinion Quarterly* 5 (4): 590–624.

Zaller, John R. 1992. *The Nature and Origins of Mass Opinion.* New York: Cambridge University Press.

Index